2/10 IMCPL 1.00 (2004)

Quick, Delicious, and Nutritious —

Fabulous Healthy Meals for Folks Over 50

D1173415

Publisher's Note

The editors of FC&A have taken careful measures to ensure the accuracy and usefulness of the information in this book. While every attempt was made to assure accuracy, some information may have changed since printing.

This book is intended for general information only. It does not constitute medical advice or practice. We cannot guarantee the safety or effectiveness of any treatment or advice mentioned.

The publisher and editors disclaim all liability (including any injuries, damages, or losses) resulting from the use of the information in this book.

Love means living the way God commanded us to live. As you have heard from the beginning, his command is this: Live a life of love.

2 John 1:6

Quick, Delicious, and Nutritious — Fabulous Healthy Meals for Folks Over 50 and all material contained therein copyright © 2004 by Frank W. Cawood and Associates, Inc. All rights reserved. Printed in the United States of America.

This book or any portion thereof may not be reproduced or distributed in any form or by any means without written permission of the publisher. For information, or to order copies, contact:

FC&A Publishing
103 Clover Green
Peachtree City, GA 30269

Produced by the staff of FC&A

Distributed to the trade by National Book Network

Table of contents

Table of contents

Asparagus spears vinaigrette

Nutritional facts per serving: 286 calories; 9.1g carbohydrates; 0mg cholesterol; 27.3g total fat; 3.6g fiber; 4.1g protein; 96.9mg sodium

Fill a shallow 12" frying pan half full with salted water and bring to a boil. Reduce heat, add the asparagus, and simmer until the spears are crisp-tender, 3 to 5 minutes. While the asparagus cooks, fill the sink with very cold water. Plunge the asparagus into the cold water to stop the cooking, and then drain. The asparagus can be refrigerated at this point for 2 to 3 days. Bring it to room temperature before serving.

1	pound asparagus, ends trimmed and peeled
1/4	cup fresh lemon juice
1	tblsp Dijon mustard
1/2	cup olive oil
	Salt
	Freshly ground black pepper

In a small mixing bowl, whisk together lemon juice and Dijon mustard until smooth. In a slow steady stream, whisk in the oil until thick and emulsified. Season to taste with salt and pepper. Stir in the chopped herbs. The vinaigrette can be made ahead and refrigerated for 5 days. Just before serving, toss the asparagus with the vinaigrette, and serve at room temperature.

4 servings

Nutrition **Note**

Raw vegetables are a super source of fiber, but you can get high fiber from cooked vegetables if you know the right ones to eat. These hearty choices will load you up with lots of fiber even after they've been cooked — asparagus, broccoli, spinach, string beans, potatoes, turnips, peas, corn, brussels sprouts, cauliflower, squash, and rhubarb. Just remember, if you're adding more fiber to your diet, be sure to drink extra water, too.

Garlic and herb baked olives

Nutritional facts per serving: 206 calories; 3.1g carbohydrates; 0mg cholesterol; 22.1g total fat; 1.9g fiber; 0.7g protein; 889.6mg sodium

Preheat oven to 325 degrees.

Place olives in a 9" pie pan. Arrange herbs between olives. Pour olive oil over all. Bake for 30 minutes, stirring occasionally. Cool and serve.

About 8 servings

1	pound brine-cured black olives, drained
4	large garlic cloves, minced
3	3" sprigs fresh rosemary
2	2" sprigs fresh thyme
1/2	tsp hot pepper flakes (optional)
1/2	cup extra virgin olive oil

Nutrition **Note** It's been valued for thousands of years for its healing powers as well as its flavor. And now, modern science gives garlic a resounding stamp of approval. Not only can it act as a powerful antibiotic in your body, killing a variety of bacteria and viruses, but specific compounds in garlic keep your arteries soft and flexible, and thin your blood so it doesn't clump. All this means a lower risk of heart attack or stroke. Buy firm bulbs of garlic with white, papery skin, and store them in a cool, dry place. Then add at least one crushed clove to your daily menu.

Yummy hummus

Nutritional facts per serving: 133 calories; 20.6g carbohydrates; 5mg cholesterol; 3.2g total fat; 4.1g fiber; 6.3g protein; 191.7mg sodium

Puree beans, garlic, oil, and lemon juice in food processor. Remove and set aside. Process chickpeas in food processor until crumbly. Add chickpeas and remaining ingredients to bean mixture. Mix well. Cover and refrigerate at least 1 hour. Flavor improves the longer it stands. Serve with pita bread or fresh vegetables. Makes about 3 cups of dip.

10 servings

1   14-ounce can cannellini
     beans, drained

2   garlic cloves, crushed

1   tblsp olive oil

4   tblsp fresh lemon juice

1   14-ounce can chickpeas,
     drained

2   ounces crumbled feta cheese

2   tblsp finely chopped parsley

     Freshly ground black pepper

Nutrition **Note**

It protects your heart, lowers your cholesterol, fights cancer, and much more. Researchers have taken a good look at this miracle mineral and given it two thumbs up. Although it's the least common major mineral in your body, magnesium helps guard against almost a dozen health conditions. To stay fighting fit, get a hearty dose of it every day from foods like beans, avocados, nuts, whole grains, dark leafy greens, and seafood.

Fresh blue crab spread

Nutritional facts per serving: 274 calories; 11.7g carbohydrates; 95.2mg cholesterol; 20.4g total fat; 0.7g fiber; 12.4g protein; 701.2mg sodium

Whip cream cheese until fluffy. Fold in celery and green onions. Shape on a platter like a pie shell — round with an indented center.

Mix the lemon juice, Worcestershire, horseradish, and ketchup. Spread in the center of the cream cheese shell. Top with crabmeat. Garnish with lemon wedges, and serve.

For a lighter version of this dish, use low-fat cream cheese.

4 servings

1/2 pound cream cheese, room temperature

1 rib celery, finely chopped

1 green onion, finely chopped

1 tblsp fresh lemon juice

1 tblsp Worcestershire sauce

1 tblsp prepared horseradish

1/2 cup ketchup

1/2 pound fresh lump blue crab, gently picked over to remove any shell and cartilage

1 lemon, cut into wedges (optional)

This party spread is easy on the calories, easy to prepare, and packs a solid punch of protein. Because it also has plenty of flavor, you can serve it with good, whole-grain crackers or toasted whole-wheat pita instead of the bland white wheat crackers often used for spreads. Fresh blue crab spread is at its best when you use lump crabmeat, but the less-expensive backfin will also work. You may make this spread up to 6 hours ahead. To store it for a few hours, just cover with plastic wrap, and refrigerate.

Healthy herbed ranch-style dip

Nutritional facts per serving: 21 calories; 0.3g carbohydrates; 6.3mg cholesterol; 2g total fat; 0g fiber; 0.5g protein; 18.4mg sodium

---

Process the cream cheese in a food processor, using the buttermilk to thin it to the desired consistency. Add garlic, tarragon, basil, thyme, and pepper, and mix well. Add the parsley and chives. Add salt to taste. Cover and refrigerate. Serve chilled.

For even less fat, substitute low-fat cream cheese and nonfat buttermilk.

4 servings

8	ounces cream cheese
3/4	cup low-fat buttermilk, or enough to thin cheese
1	garlic clove, finely chopped
1	tsp dried tarragon
1/2	tsp dried basil
1/4	tsp dried thyme
1/4	tsp black pepper
1	tsp finely chopped fresh parsley
1	tblsp finely chopped fresh chives
	Salt

Nutrition **Note**

The cream cheese and buttermilk in this dip give you a calcium boost. Every little bit helps because calcium not only forges strong teeth and bones — it also helps you keep them that way. What's more, your need for calcium goes up as you pass 50, so extra calcium from low-fat dairy products is a wise choice.

And here's a bonus tip. Some calcium-rich foods also zap bad breath. Buttermilk and yogurt both bring you friendly lactobacillus — active cultures of bacteria that make it tough for odor-causing bacteria to grow. Sweeten your breath with these creamy treats, and building your bones may be twice as nice.

Superb shrimp and feta spread

Nutritional facts per serving: 136 calories; 2.3g carbohydrates; 45.1mg cholesterol; 11.6g total fat; 0.2g fiber; 6g protein; 220.8mg sodium

Heat olive oil, add green onions, and cook until soft. Chop shrimp, add to pan, and cook, stirring, until they turn pink, 2 to 3 minutes. Remove to a bowl, and let cool to room temperature. Add remaining ingredients, including salt and black pepper to taste, and chill.

Stuff in celery, or serve with crackers.

4 servings

2	tblsp olive oil
1/4	cup chopped green onions
1/2	pound medium shrimp, peeled and deveined
2	tblsp low-fat mayonnaise
2	ounces low-fat feta cheese, crumbled
1/2	tsp each dill weed and basil
1/2	tsp Dijon mustard
1/2	tsp Worcestershire sauce
1 1/2	tsp fresh lemon juice
	Salt
	Black pepper

Nutrition Note

If you can't tolerate milk and other dairy products, calcium may not be the only nutrient you're short on. You may also be running low on vitamin D — and that could be bad for your bones. Vitamin D helps your body absorb calcium and phosphorus, two minerals essential for strong bones and teeth. However, your body can't use their bone-building abilities without some help from vitamin D. So you need this vitamin to help maintain strong bones and prevent osteoporosis. While other people drink fortified milk to avoid vitamin D deficiency, you can get your vitamin D from sources like shrimp, fortified cereals, sardines, and salmon.

Mediterranean caponata

Nutritional facts per serving: 183 calories; 15g carbohydrates; 0mg cholesterol; 14.1g total fat; 5.1g fiber; 2.5g protein; 24.9mg sodium

Heat olive oil in a large frying pan or skillet over medium-high heat. Add eggplant and cook, stirring often, until it's free of juices. Add garlic, onion, bell pepper, and celery, and sauté, stirring frequently, until the eggplant softens, about 4 to 5 minutes. Add tomatoes and their juice, oregano, basil, black pepper, and vinegar. Bring mixture to a simmer, and simmer uncovered for 15 minutes over low heat, stirring occasionally.

Serve, or cool to room temperature, cover, and refrigerate overnight.

4 servings

4	tblsp olive oil
1	medium purple eggplant, unpeeled, chopped
1	garlic clove, chopped
1/2	cup chopped yellow onion
1/4	cup chopped green bell pepper
1/2	cup chopped celery
1	14-ounce can diced tomatoes with juice
1	tsp dried oregano
1/2	tsp dried basil
1/4	tsp freshly ground black pepper
2	tblsp red wine vinegar

Caponata can be used as a snack with toasted pita, an accompaniment to roasted meat or poultry, or a piquant addition to a green salad.

Bite-size marinated vegetables

Nutritional facts per serving: 192 calories; 13.4g carbohydrates; 0mg cholesterol; 15g total fat; 5.1g fiber; 4.5g protein; 80.2mg sodium

Drain artichokes and cut in half as needed to make bite-size. Separate onion into rings. Drain and pit olives, if necessary. Wipe mushrooms with damp cloth to clean them, and halve or quarter to make bite-size. Heat 1 tablespoon olive oil, and cook mushrooms until they just begin to soften. Combine all in a bowl.

Whisk together 1/4 cup olive oil, vinegar, pepper, and salt to taste. Pour over vegetables, cover, and refrigerate overnight. Drain and serve as is on lettuce, or add to other raw vegetables to serve with toothpicks for a party dish.

4 salad servings

1	14-ounce can artichoke hearts (not marinated)
1	small red onion, thinly sliced
1/2	cup black olives, preferably Kalamata-type
1/2	pound fresh mushrooms
1/4	cup plus 1 tblsp olive oil
1/4	cup red wine vinegar
1 1/2	tsp black pepper
	Salt

Nutrition **Note**

Ancient Romans used artichokes to treat indigestion, and that may work for you, too. An ingredient in artichoke leaves helps your liver form bile. If your liver doesn't produce enough bile, your food doesn't get broken down properly, and you get indigestion. If you feel sick to your stomach, overly full, and have stomach pain after eating a normal-sized meal, you may suffer from dyspepsia — another name for poor digestion. Several scientific studies showed dramatic improvements in people with dyspepsia after they were treated with artichoke extracts. But why wait for an extract? You can get help for your indigestion by eating a delicious artichoke with your dinner.

Oriental grilled chicken nuggets

Nutritional facts per serving: 199 calories; 1g carbohydrates; 75.3mg cholesterol; 13.4g total fat; 0.1g fiber; 18.1g protein; 1045.6mg sodium

Cut chicken off the bones into chunks. Rub with salt and pepper. In a bowl, combine soy sauce with melted butter, and dip the chunks in the mixture. Place them on skewers, and grill over charcoal while basting with the soy sauce-butter mixture. They will take up to 10 minutes to cook over a hot fire.

2   chicken breasts

Salt

Freshly ground black pepper

2   tblsp low-sodium soy sauce

2   tblsp butter, melted

For a change of pace, serve with Apricot honey-mustard sauce (see page 322).

4 servings

Nutrition **Note**   Chicken is heart-smart, but it may be head-smart, too. Some Japanese scientists found that a simple chicken extract can help you recover more quickly after mental stress. Eating fowl might also help you beat foul moods. After all, chicken gives you vitamin B6 — one of the nutrients your body uses to prevent memory loss and depression. Chicken also delivers other B vitamins that can help keep your brain, mood, and memory in better shape. So try this tasty dish. You might make both your head and your heart healthier.

Entertainer's chicken salad

Nutritional facts per serving: 351 calories; 4.5g carbohydrates; 184.2mg cholesterol; 20.1g total fat; 0.8g fiber; 35.7g protein; 385.1mg sodium

Take the meat off the chicken. Remove all skin, fat, and tendons. Chop meat fine. Sprinkle chicken with lemon pepper and black pepper and toss. Add mayonnaise and toss. Add capers if you're using them. Fold in eggs and celery. Season to taste with more lemon pepper, black pepper, or salt, if desired. Refrigerate for up to 1 day ahead of using.

Serve on a bed of lettuce for a lunch dish. For parties, serve the salad with crackers or tart shells. Add capers for extra zip.

4 salad servings

1	whole roasted chicken (3 1/2- 4 pounds)
1	tblsp lemon pepper
1	tsp black pepper
1/2	cup low-fat mayonnaise, or to taste
2	hard-boiled eggs, finely chopped
1	cup finely chopped celery
	Salt
	Capers

Nutrition **Note** When it comes to your eyes, the egg may come before the chicken in this dish. It turns out egg yolk is actually a top source of both lutein and zeaxanthin, two antioxidants that protect your eyes from diseases that could lead to vision loss. But that's not all. It turns out that eggs may not be as harmful to the arteries as experts once thought. So enjoy an occasional egg. Just remember to keep your consumption to three or four per week.

Chinese chicken wings

Nutritional facts per serving: 283 calories; 2.1g carbohydrates; 87.9mg cholesterol; 18.1g total fat; 0.2g fiber; 21.8g protein; 616.5mg sodium

---

Preheat oven to 250 degrees.

Lay out the drumettes in a single layer in a baking dish. Mix the wine and soy sauce, and pour it over them. Tuck garlic into liquid. (If you chop the garlic, it sticks to the drumettes.)

12   chicken drumettes (large piece only of wing)

1/2   cup light, dry white table wine

3/4   cup light soy sauce

2   garlic cloves, crushed

Bake for 2 hours, turning drumettes every 30 minutes. The liquid will evaporate, and the drumettes will turn a burnished golden brown. Serve warm or at room temperature.

4 servings

These are good with a sweet and sour dipping sauce. You can make an easy one by simmering apricot or plum jam with cider vinegar. Just be sure to use enough cider vinegar to get the right consistency for dipping. You can also add a little cayenne pepper or Chinese chili oil if you wish.

If the jar lid on the jam gives you fits, try this. Wrap a rubber band around the lid, or don a pair of latex dishwashing gloves. They will help you pop that top without the strain. Or try loosening the lid with a nutcracker. It comes in handy because it adjusts easily to the size of the jar.

Grilled marinated chicken drumettes

Nutritional facts per serving: 298 calories; 3.9g carbohydrates; 89.7mg cholesterol; 21.3g total fat; 0.9g fiber; 22.3g protein; 99.2mg sodium

Mix together the ginger, garlic, chili peppers, onions, parsley, lemon juice, and 1 tablespoon paprika in a food processor or blender. Heat the oil in a large pan. Add chicken wings, fleshy side down, and brown on both sides. Remove.

Add coriander, cumin, and the remaining paprika to the pan and cook 1 to 2 minutes. Add the lemon juice mixture. Boil, stirring occasionally, for 5 minutes. Add chicken broth and boil again.

Return chicken to the pan. Bring back to a boil, then lower the heat, cover, and simmer 20 minutes. Taste for seasoning, and add salt and pepper as desired. Remove chicken from its sauce, and set it aside to cool. You may refrigerate or freeze the chicken wings and sauce separately at this point.

When ready to serve, prepare the grill, or heat the broiler. Place a layer of chicken on the grill or on foil-lined baking sheets under the broiler. Brown in batches until crisp, about 5 minutes on each side. Remove and serve hot, without sauce.

1	slice fresh ginger (quarter-size), finely chopped
6	garlic cloves, finely chopped
3	fresh chili or hot peppers, finely chopped
2	onions, finely chopped
2	cups finely chopped fresh parsley
1/2	cup fresh lemon juice
2	tblsp paprika
1/4	cup vegetable oil
5	pounds chicken drumettes or chicken wings cut in two at the joints
1	tblsp ground coriander seeds
1	tblsp ground cumin seeds
3	cups low-sodium chicken broth
	Salt
	Freshly ground black pepper

20 servings

Butterflied leg of lamb

Nutritional facts per serving: 175 calories; 4.5g carbohydrates; 42.9mg cholesterol; 12.7g total fat; 0.1g fiber; 10.6g protein; 171.2mg sodium

Combine ketchup, water, Worcestershire sauce, vinegar, sugar, celery salt, and chili powder in a saucepan. Bring to a simmer over medium heat, but do not boil. Stir well, remove from heat, and let cool to room temperature. Add Tabasco to taste.

Lay the lamb out flat in a glass or plastic container and pour the cooled marinade over it. Cover and marinate overnight, turning at least once.

Place charcoal under half of the grill. Heat the grill to Medium-hot.

1	cup ketchup
1	cup water
1/4	cup Worcestershire sauce
1/4	cup cider vinegar
1/4	cup dark brown sugar
1	tsp celery salt
1	tsp chili powder
1	tsp Tabasco, or to taste
4	pound butterflied leg of lamb, all fat removed

This recipe is perfect for parties or other occasions where you want to serve lamb with cocktail bread or rolls. Ask the butcher to remove the bone and butterfly the leg of lamb so it will be easier for you to grill and slice.

Place the lamb over the coals and sear each side for 1 minute, then grill each side until nicely browned, about 5 minutes more per side. Move the lamb over to the half of the grill that doesn't have any charcoal under it, close the top, and let the lamb cook for 8 - 10 minutes per side for medium-rare. Remove from the grill, and let rest for 10 minutes before carving so the juices will settle.

Serve on bread of your choice.

30 servings

Tenderloin tidbits

Nutritional facts per serving: 153 calories; 1.5g carbohydrates; 42.2mg cholesterol; 8g total fat; 0g fiber; 14.4g protein; 55.2mg sodium

Combine wine, oil, garlic, shallots, Worcestershire sauce, peppercorns and rosemary, and bring to a boil. Simmer for 10 minutes. Let cool to room temperature.

Place tenderloin in a glass or plastic container, and pour the cooled marinade over it. Cover and refrigerate for 90 minutes. Let the tenderloin come to room temperature for 30 minutes before cooking.

2	cups red table wine
1/4	cup olive oil
2	large garlic cloves, smashed
2	shallots, thickly sliced
2	tblsp Worcestershire sauce
12	black peppercorns
1	tblsp chopped fresh rosemary
3	pound tenderloin (fat and membrane removed)

To grill, heat the grill to Medium-hot. Grill the tenderloin for 8 minutes on each side for rare. To roast, preheat the oven to 500 degrees. Place the tenderloin on a rack on a baking sheet, and roast for 5 minutes. Reduce heat to 425 degrees, and roast for about 15 minutes more for rare, or longer for your desired degree of doneness. Remove from grill or oven, and let rest for 10 minutes before carving so the juices will settle.

Serve on bread of your choice.

20 servings

Slip your open cookbook inside a large clear freezer bag to hold open your place and protect it from spills while you're cooking. The gallon-sized bag may be your wisest choice.

Lean-lover's grilled eye of round

Nutritional facts per serving: 127 calories; 3.2g carbohydrates; 36.7mg cholesterol; 5.7g total fat; 0.1g fiber; 15.1g protein; 143.7mg sodium

Whisk together oil, tomato juice, soy sauce, sugar, and pepper. Add garlic cloves. Place meat in a glass or plastic container, and pour the marinade over it. Cover and refrigerate overnight, turning occasionally. Take the container out of the refrigerator, and let meat come to room temperature for 30 minutes before cooking.

1/4   cup canola oil

1/4   cup tomato juice

1/4   cup low-sodium soy sauce

1/4   cup brown sugar

1/2   tsp black pepper

2   garlic cloves, mashed slightly

3   pound eye of round, fat and membrane removed

To grill, heat the grill to Medium-hot. Grill the meat for 10 minutes on each side for rare. To roast, preheat oven to 500 degrees. Put meat on a rack on a baking sheet, and roast for 5 minutes. Reduce heat to 425 degrees, and roast for about 15 minutes more for rare, or longer for your desired degree of doneness. Remove from grill or oven, and let rest for 10 minutes before carving so the juices will settle.

Serve on bread of your choice.

20 servings

An eye of round is a great meat to serve at parties. It has lots of flavor, and it's more economical than tenderloin. Eye of round is best when marinated, grilled or roasted to medium-rare, and sliced thinly. For super results, pierce the meat all over with a sharp-pronged carving fork or skewer, and then marinate it all night.

Fit-for-a-king crab cakes

Nutritional facts per serving: 321 calories; 22.1g carbohydrates; 194mg cholesterol; 12.9g total fat; 1.1g fiber; 27.3g protein; 968.9mg sodium

Preheat oven to 425 degrees. Cover a baking sheet with foil.

Heat oil in a frying pan over medium heat. Add green onions and peppers and cook, stirring frequently, until they begin to soften, 3 to 4 minutes.

Combine Worcestershire sauce, lemon juice, eggs, salt, and pepper in a large bowl, and mix well. Add the vegetables and crabmeat, and toss gently. Add the bread crumbs, and toss gently to combine.

Shape the crab mixture into 6 patties. Place them on the baking sheet, and bake until light brown and crispy, about 8 to 10 minutes.

6 servings

1	tblsp olive oil
1/2	cup finely chopped green onions
3	tblsp finely chopped green bell pepper
1	tblsp Worcestershire sauce
1	tsp fresh lemon juice
2	eggs, lightly beaten
1/2	tsp salt
1/8	tsp freshly ground black pepper
1	pound crabmeat
1/2	cup fresh toasted bread crumbs, finely crumbled

By baking the crab cakes instead of sautéing them in butter or oil, you achieve almost the same effect, but without using fat.

Decadent chili crab puff

Nutritional facts per serving: 449 calories; 23g carbohydrates; 260.4mg cholesterol; 26g total fat; 1.9g fiber; 31.1g protein; 829.2mg sodium

Preheat oven to 400 degrees. Grease a deep 1 1/2- to 2-quart baking dish.

Set aside 1/2 cup of the cheese for the top. Place 1/3 of the cheese on the bottom of the baking dish. Add 1/3 of the crab and 1/3 of the chilies. Repeat, making 3 layers of each. Whisk milk with eggs and flour, and slowly pour into the baking dish. Top with marinara sauce, and sprinkle with the reserved cheese. Bake, uncovered, for 1 hour, or until hot and set in center.

1	pound Monterey Jack cheese, grated
1	cup crabmeat
2	4-ounce cans diced green chilies
1 1/3	cups milk
4	eggs
1/2	cup flour
1	cup marinara tomato sauce

For a lower-fat version, use a reduced amount of low-fat cheese and low-fat or nonfat milk.

4 servings

Nutrition **Note**

As strange as it may sound, eating crab may make you feel less crabby. In one study, participants under physical and mental stress experienced a drop in zinc, iron, and selenium levels. If you are under stress, eat foods high in these minerals — like crabmeat, beans, yogurt, steak, clams, and oysters. And don't forget that poor eating habits during stressful times can weaken your immune system. This makes you more susceptible to illness and can magnify the effects of stress. By choosing nutritious foods, you'll give your body the ammunition it needs to fight off the damaging effects of stress — and that may be enough to help you feel better.

Broiled herbed oysters

Nutritional facts per serving: 81 calories; 5.7g carbohydrates; 28.8mg cholesterol; 4.2g total fat; 0.2g fiber; 4.7g protein; 151.8mg sodium

Preheat the grill or broiler.

Toss butter, garlic and oysters together. Thread oysters on small skewers, and place them on a hot grill or baking sheet 6" away from a hot broiler. Cook until oysters turn white and start to curl at the edges, about 5 to 8 minutes.

Season to taste with salt and pepper. Sprinkle with chopped herbs. Serve with Tabasco sauce and horseradish, as desired.

4 servings

1	tblsp butter, melted
3	garlic cloves, finely chopped
24	oysters, shucked
	Salt
	Freshly ground black pepper
1	tblsp chopped fresh parsley
1	tblsp chopped fresh thyme
	Tabasco sauce
	Horseradish

Nutrition **Note**   Handle oysters wisely so you won't need to worry about a deadly form of food poisoning. Raw oysters from the Gulf of Mexico can contain *Vibrio vulnificus* bacteria, which can cause diarrhea, serious illness, and even death. Cooking the oysters kills the bacteria. So only eat oysters that have been properly stored, cleaned, and fully cooked. And never take a chance on eating a raw oyster if any of these apply to you:

- Long-term steroid use is part of your treatment for asthma, arthritis, or another health condition.

- You have liver disease, diabetes, cancer, or immune disorders, including infection with HIV.

- You take antacids regularly.

- You drink two or more alcoholic drinks per day.

Pickled party shrimp

Nutritional facts per serving: 301 calories; 5.1g carbohydrates; 68.2mg cholesterol; 28.3g total fat; 1g fiber; 9.4g protein; 81.2mg sodium

Whisk together the oils, vinegar, and Worcestershire. Add salt to taste. Add capers, if using. Layer shrimp, lemon, and onion in a shallow dish. Pour the marinade over them. Refrigerate overnight. Drain and serve as is on lettuce, or add to other raw vegetables to serve with toothpicks for a party dish.

A couple of tablespoons of capers and their juice will give this an extra zip.

4 salad servings

1/4	cup olive oil
1/4	cup canola oil
1/3	cup cider vinegar
1	tsp Worcestershire sauce
	Salt
	Capers (optional)
1	pound medium shrimp, cooked, peeled, and deveined
1/2	lemon, thinly sliced
1	small white onion, thinly sliced

Nutrition **Note** Some people scamper away from scampi to ease their arthritis. That's because shrimp is one of the foods most often thought to aggravate arthritis. Others include milk, wheat products, certain meats, and nightshade vegetables like tomatoes, potatoes, eggplant, and bell peppers. If you suspect certain foods of making your arthritis worse, try eliminating them from your diet, one by one, until you see an improvement. Just remember that arthritis symptoms tend to come and go, and the relief you feel after eliminating a particular food could be a coincidence. Try eating the trouble-making food again to see if it causes symptoms.

Steamed shrimp in mouth-watering spices

Nutritional facts per serving: 147 calories; 15.2g carbohydrates; 136.5mg cholesterol; 3.5 g total fat; 3.7g fiber; 20g protein; 3979mg sodium

---

Fill a large pot with 2" or 3" of water. Add garlic, lemon, and pickling spice. Place a perforated pasta cooking insert, steamer basket, or small colander in the pot, but not touching the water. Cover tightly, and bring water to a simmer over medium-high heat.

Toss shrimp and lemon juice in a large bowl. Add the Old Bay seasoning, and toss to coat shrimp with spices.
Place the coated shrimp in the steamer. Cover and steam shrimp until they are pink and beginning to curl, 3 to 5 minutes. If the insert, basket, or colander is small, cook the shrimp in 2 batches.

Can be served with Quick homemade cocktail sauce (see page 323) or Spicy and creamy horseradish sauce (see page 324).

2 servings

3	garlic cloves, smashed
1	lemon, sliced
2	tblsp pickling spice
1	pound medium (26-30 count) shrimp, shells on
4	tblsp fresh lemon juice
4	tblsp Old Bay seasoning

Nutrition **Note**

Steaming shrimp instead of boiling them retains more of the nutrients and flavor. This can help prevent three deficiency threats that may be more likely than you think. Iron deficiency is the world's most common deficiency problem, and your odds of B12 and zinc deficiency go up as you grow older. Yet just 3 ounces of shrimp will supply you with nearly a third of your daily requirement for iron, more than half the vitamin B12 you need, and 10 percent of recommended zinc. And that's a pretty tasty defense against deficiency.

Succulent shrimp and scallop kebabs

Nutritional facts per serving: 125 calories; 7g carbohydrates; 28.1mg cholesterol; 7.5g total fat; 1.25g fiber; 8.9g protein; 81.6mg sodium

Set aside 16 skewers. If using long wooden skewers, soak them in water for 30 minutes first.

Whisk together olive oil, lemon juice, mustard, salt, and pepper. Toss with shrimp and scallops. Cover and refrigerate for 1 hour. Drain but reserve marinade. Assemble the skewers, placing a scallop, shrimp, mushroom, cherry tomato, and square of yellow pepper on each skewer.

Fire up a medium-hot grill, or preheat an oven on Broil. If broiling, cover two shallow pans with foil. Grill or broil the skewers for 3 to 4 minutes per side, basting once with the marinade when you turn them over. The shrimp should turn pink. Be careful not to overcook, or they will be tough. Serve hot or at room temperature.

8 servings

4	tblsp olive oil
2	tblsp fresh lemon juice
1/2	tsp Dijon mustard
1/4	tsp salt
1/8	tsp black pepper
16	medium shrimp, peeled and deveined
16	sea scallops
16	small mushrooms, wiped clean with a wet paper towel
16	cherry tomatoes
1	yellow pepper, cut into 1" cubes

If you need a shrimp deveiner, go to your sewing box. A small crochet hook makes a good substitute.

Peachy green tea

Nutritional facts per serving: 17 calories; 4.3g carbohydrates; 0mg cholesterol; 0.1g total fat; 1.2g fiber; 0.5g protein; 9.4mg sodium

Place tea bags and mint leaves in a large heatproof pitcher. Place sliced peaches in a saucepan, add the water, and bring to a boil. Remove from heat and pour the water and peaches over the tea bags. Steep for about 5 minutes, strain, cool, and serve over ice. Sweeten if desired.

6 servings

6	green tea bags
1/2	cup loosely packed fresh mint leaves
2	peaches, pitted and sliced
6	cups cold water

Nutrition **Note**

Tea, enjoyed around the world for centuries, can do wonders for your heart and arteries. Loaded with flavonoids, especially compounds called catechins, tea dilates arteries, easing the inflammation associated with atherosclerosis, thereby improving blood flow. It may also make your blood less sticky, lowering your chance of plaque buildup that can lead to heart attack and stroke. Store green tea in a dark, airtight container, and keep the container in a cool, dry place. Use it within a month or two to get the best health benefits. Because boiling water destroys some of the antioxidants in tea, you should steep it in water that is hot, but not boiling, for about three minutes.

Lemon blazer

Nutritional facts per serving: 116 calories; 30.9g carbohydrates; 0mg cholesterol; 0g total fat; 0.3g fiber; 0.2g protein; 17.2mg sodium

In a medium saucepan, combine water, lemon juice, and brown sugar. Place the cloves, allspice, and cinnamon sticks in a tea or spice ball (sometimes called a diffuser) and drop into the lemon mixture. You may have to break the cinnamon sticks in half to fit. Warm thoroughly over low heat. Keep warm for about 15 minutes then remove spice ball.

4 servings

3 1/4	cups water
3/4	cup lemon juice
1/2	cup firmly packed brown sugar
8	whole cloves
6	whole allspice
2	whole cinnamon sticks

Nutrition **Note** You could survive nearly a month without food, but only a few days without water. It carries the nutrients you eat to every cell in your body. It cushions joints, regulates body temperature, and lubricates your digestive tract. It soothes gout, arthritis, and heartburn. It can ward off kidney stones, gallstones, and urinary tract infections. It's a dieter's dream — with no fat, sugar, or calories.

But as a secret anti-aging agent, there's nothing to compare. Water keeps your lips and skin soft and smooth, and since your 15 billion brain cells are mostly water, drink plenty every day to keep from running dry.

Banana oat shake

Nutritional facts per serving: 194 calories; 32.5g carbohydrates; 6.5mg cholesterol; 2.9g total fat; 3.1g fiber; 10.8g protein; 100.8mg sodium

---

If making a breakfast shake, try coffee flavored yogurt. Otherwise, pick a flavor that suits you. Blend oats in blender until powdered. Add rest of ingredients and blend until smooth.

3 servings

3/4 cup uncooked rolled oats, old-fashioned or quick-cooking

1 cup low-fat milk

1 ripe banana, peeled and chunked

1 cup low-fat flavored yogurt

Nutrition **Note**

After a good night's sleep, your body and your brain feel refreshed and energetic. But if you're spending every night restless and awake, you might not have enough melatonin, a hormone that regulates your sleep cycle. To raise your melatonin levels naturally, try snacking on a banana an hour or so before bedtime.

Or perhaps you suffer at night from a dry cough that so often accompanies chronic heartburn or acid indigestion. Again, bananas are a great remedy. On top of that, this inexpensive, wholesome fruit has only about 100 calories and is full of potassium, folate, vitamins B6 and C, and fiber.

Kiwi cooler

Nutritional facts per serving: 291 calories; 59.2g carbohydrates; 11mg cholesterol; 3g total fat; 3.1g fiber; 9.8g protein; 126.3mg sodium

---

Combine all ingredients in blender and process until smooth and creamy.

1 serving

1	large kiwi, peeled and cubed
6	ounces low-fat lime yogurt
1/4	cup low-fat milk
2	tsp honey
1-3	ice cubes

Nutrition **Note**

If you're looking for a tasty way to protect yourself from heart attack and stroke, then kiwi should be on your grocery list. Ounce for ounce, the small fuzzy kiwifruit has more vitamin C than the mighty orange — in fact almost double. Vitamin C helps raise your levels of protective HDL cholesterol and prevents bad cholesterol from clogging your arteries. Kiwis are also loaded with potassium, an important nutrient in the battle against heart disease. Also known as Chinese Gooseberries, they originated in China but now are more commonly marketed from New Zealand.

Tropical smoothie

Nutritional facts per serving: 115 calories; 30g carbohydrates; 0mg cholesterol; 0.4g total fat; 2g fiber; 0.8g protein; 3.2mg sodium

---

Combine fruit, juice, and honey in blender. Blend until slushy and almost smooth. Add more honey if needed for taste. Pour mixture over cracked ice in a tall glass. Garnish each with a mint sprig and a pineapple cube.

5 servings

2	cups diced, peeled ripe papaya
2 1/2	cups diced pineapple
1/4	cup lime juice
1/4	cup honey
	Cracked ice

Nutrition **Note**

Get to know this tropical fruit — it's not hard to find and it's easy to love. Full of antioxidants and lycopene — a compound that gives certain foods their rich color, papayas protect against heart attack and prostate cancer. In addition, the folate in this sweet fruit works to maintain blood flow and to keep your nervous system in good working order.

Some researchers think not enough blood flowing to the inner ear can affect the electrical impulses from the ear to the brain. This could cause hearing loss. Although papayas won't reverse hearing damage you already have, they could help preserve your hearing. Eat a papaya for its vitamin E and you'll be fighting cataracts, as well. Sharp hearing and keen eyesight — not a bad combination from a delicious treat.

Strawberry sunrise

Nutritional facts per serving: 306 calories; 65.1g carbohydrates; 7.5mg cholesterol; 3.1g total fat; 2.8g fiber; 7.7g protein; 84.9mg sodium

Combine all ingredients in a blender and process until smooth.

2 servings

1 1/2   cups nonfat peach frozen yogurt

1   cup orange juice

1   banana, chopped

6   whole strawberries, fresh or frozen

Nutrition **Note**

If you have diabetes, there's a good chance you'll experience complications. You're 60 percent more likely to develop cataracts, and cholesterol problems are common, raising your risk for heart attack and stroke even more. In addition, wounds heal slowly in many diabetics.

Healthy food choices can keep these conditions at bay. Something as simple as a handful of strawberries can provide powerful protection — due to fiber, folate, potassium, and numerous antioxidants like vitamins C and E. Bring home a carton of fresh, juicy strawberries, or grow your own. They're delicious in salads, smoothies, desserts, or just as a snack.

Prune smoothie

Nutritional facts per serving: 139 calories; 29.7g carbohydrates; 3.6mg cholesterol; 0.8g total fat; 1.3g fiber; 3.8g protein; 55.9mg sodium

Combine all ingredients and blend with a whisk or hand mixer until fluffy.

1 serving

1/2   cup chilled prune juice

2   tblsp low-fat vanilla ice cream

2   tblsp nonfat evaporated milk

Dash salt (optional)

Nutrition **Note**   Fight Father Time with this humble dried fruit. Research shows prunes — more recently known as dried plums — may help protect you from diseases like Alzheimer's and Parkinson's.

This surprisingly tasty treat is full of fiber, potassium, and those all-important antioxidants that fight the effects of aging. For a healthy heart, strong bones, and a sharp memory, add diced prunes to salads, cereals, sandwiches, and baked goods. They'll keep in your pantry for months, or longer if you refrigerate them.

Moist and rich banana bread

Nutritional facts per serving: 153 calories; 34.6g carbohydrates; 53.1mg cholesterol; 1.4g total fat; 0.9g fiber; 1.9g protein; 318.5mg sodium

Preheat oven to 350 degrees. Grease 3 7" x 3" x 2" bread pans, and line with greased wax paper.

Mash bananas. Add brown sugar, granulated sugar, eggs, butter, and pecans, and blend well. Sift together flour, salt, and baking soda. Add dry ingredients to the banana mixture. Continue mixing until all ingredients are well blended. Pour batter into the prepared pans. Bake 15 minutes or until a knife inserted into the bread comes out clean.

30 servings

5-6	overripe bananas (about 2 1/2 cups mashed)
1	cup light brown sugar, packed
1	cup granulated sugar
4	eggs, slightly beaten
1/2	cup (1 stick) butter, softened
1	cup chopped pecans (optional)
2 1/2	cups all-purpose flour
1	tsp salt
2	tsp baking soda

Nutrition **Note**
Sweet, nutritious, and convenient, bananas may be the perfect alternative to packaged snack foods. These tropical treats are high in fiber; contain lots of vitamins C, B6, and folate; and give you potassium and magnesium. The nutrients found in bananas help fight cancer, heart disease, and a long list of other ills. Bananas even help you think clearly as you age. Maybe that explains why the Latin name for bananas means "fruit of the wise." As if all that weren't enough, bananas make a great on-the-go snack. Their sturdy skin provides a natural disposable wrapper, so they're easy to pack and carry anywhere. For a delicious, convenient snack with health appeal, peel a banana.

Fruity whole-wheat banana nut bread

Nutritional facts per serving: 170 calories; 38.5g carbohydrates; 0mg cholesterol; 2.1g total fat; 3g fiber; 2.9g protein; 54.8mg sodium

Preheat oven to 350 degrees. Spray nonstick cooking spray in a loaf pan.

Mix all ingredients until well blended. Pour into pan and bake for 1 hour.

12 servings

1 1/2	cups whole-wheat flour
1/2	tsp baking soda
1/2	tsp cinnamon
1/4	cup unsweetened applesauce
3/4	cup honey
3	ripe bananas, sliced
1/4	cup golden raisins
1/4	cup chopped walnuts

Nutrition **Note**

Fruits, vegetables, and grains may be your most important weapons in the war on cancer. Whether it's due to their antioxidants, their fiber, or some combination of nutrients, the National Cancer Institute says to eat more every day. Since colorectal cancer is the second leading cancer killer in the U.S., and the third most common cancer, keeping your digestive system healthy should be priority one. Whole-wheat breads are full of fiber, which adds bulk to your stool and hurries it through your large intestine. This limits the time cancer-causing agents spend in your body. Experiment with whole-wheat flour substitutions in your favorite baked recipes for extra cancer-fighting punch.

Mellow carrot and squash nut bread

Nutritional facts per serving: 375 calories; 40.6g carbohydrates; 85.1mg cholesterol; 21.5g total fat; 3.7g fiber; 7.1g protein; 383.9mg sodium

Preheat oven to 350 degrees. Grease and flour 2 7" x 3" x 2" loaf pans. Also, cut a piece of wax paper to fit the bottom of each pan, and grease and flour the paper.

Mix together the squash, carrots, pecans, sugar, and orange peel. Combine the butter, yogurt, and eggs separately. Sift together the flour, coriander, and nutmeg. Stir the egg mixture into the flour and mix well. Fold in the squash and carrot mixture, and stir until just combined. Pour batter into the prepared pans, and bake 35 to 40 minutes until golden and a toothpick inserted in the center comes out clean. Cool for 10 minutes on a rack, and then remove the breads from the pans and cool on a rack.

2 loaves

2	yellow squash, grated
2	carrots, peeled and grated
3/4	cup chopped pecans
1/2	cup sugar
2	tblsp grated orange peel (no white attached)
1	stick melted butter
1/2	cup low-fat plain yogurt
2	eggs, beaten
1 3/4	cups self-rising flour
1/2	tsp ground coriander
	Pinch freshly grated nutmeg

Nutrition **Note**

"Lose 15 pounds the first week," the ad claims. Diets that promise fast and major weight loss are too good to be true. Be wary of diets that try to sell a product based on testimonials instead of research — or exclude whole categories of food. Instead, plan to lose one to two pounds a week on any diet. Eat 300 to 500 fewer calories every day, and exercise regularly, and you could win weight loss that lasts.

Whole-wheat cinnamon raisin bread

Nutritional facts per serving: 234 calories; 52.4g carbohydrates; 1.9mg cholesterol; 1.1g total fat; 4.2g fiber; 6.7g protein; 424mg sodium

---

In a large bowl, combine flours, baking soda, salt, cinnamon, and raisins. Stir in buttermilk and molasses, mixing well. Pour into a nonstick bread pan. Let stand for 1 hour.

When standing time is almost done, preheat oven to 325 degrees.

Bake for 1 hour or until wooden pick inserted in center comes out clean. Cool in pan for 10 minutes, then transfer to a wire rack to cool.

10 servings

2	cups whole-wheat flour
1	cup unbleached all-purpose flour
2	tsp baking soda
1/2	tsp salt
1	tblsp cinnamon
1	cup raisins
2	cups low-fat buttermilk
1/2	cup molasses

Keep bread as soft and fresh as the day you baked it. Pop a rib of celery into the storage bag, and say goodbye to stale bread.

Quick and easy gingerbread

Nutritional facts per serving: 332 calories; 52g carbohydrates; 20.8mg cholesterol; 13.2g total fat; 0.8g fiber; 2.8g protein; 354.8mg sodium

Preheat oven to 350 degrees. Grease and flour a 9" square baking pan.

In a large mixing bowl, combine sugar, oil (or oil and prune puree), and egg. Beat well and set aside. Combine flour and other dry ingredients in another bowl, stirring until well blended. Stir the molasses and water together. Alternate adding flour mixture and molasses mixture to the sugar, oil, and egg mixture. When everything is well blended, pour into the baking pan. Bake for about 1 hour.

9 servings

1/2	cup sugar
1/2	cup oil (or 1/4 cup oil plus 1/8 cup prune puree)
1	egg
2 1/2	cups flour
1 1/2	tsp baking soda
1	tsp cinnamon
1	tsp ginger
1/2	tsp cloves
1/2	tsp salt
1	cup molasses
1	cup hot water

The next time you bake, simply replace the cooking oil with a prune puree, and save 217 grams of fat. To make this heart-healthy fat substitute, puree about 1 1/3 cups of pitted prunes with 6 tablespoons of hot water. You'll end up with about a cup of prune puree totaling just 1 gram of fat. A cup of oil, on the other hand, weighs in at 218 grams of fat. You can store your puree in the refrigerator for up to one month. Then when you're ready to bake, use half the recommended butter or oil in your recipe, and replace the rest with half as much prune puree. If you make the prune puree substitution in this recipe, for each serving, you cut 47 calories and 6 grams of fat.

Divinely healthy orange-flaxseed muffins

Nutritional facts per serving: 205 calories; 28.5g carbohydrates; 21.3mg cholesterol; 10.6g total fat; 6.2g fiber; 5.7g protein; 159.8mg sodium

Preheat oven to 375 degrees. Lightly grease muffin pan, or use paper liners.

In a large mixing bowl, combine oat bran, flour, flaxseed, wheat bran, baking powder, and salt. Mix well. In a blender or food processor, combine oranges, brown sugar, buttermilk, oil, eggs, and baking soda. Blend well. Pour orange mixture into dry ingredients. Mix well. Stir in raisins. Fill muffin tins almost to the top. Bake for 18 to 20 minutes.

18 muffins

1 1/2	cups oat bran
1	cup unbleached all-purpose flour
1	cup flaxseed, whole or ground
1	cup wheat bran
1	tblsp baking powder
1/2	tsp salt
2	oranges, peeled, seeded, and sectioned
1/2	cup brown sugar
1	cup buttermilk
1/2	cup canola oil
2	eggs
1	tsp baking soda
1/2	cup golden raisins

Nutrition **Note**
This wonder food, once praised by Gandhi, lowers blood pressure and your risk for stroke, helps improve your cholesterol levels, fights arthritis, heart disease, and diabetes, and protects against cancers of the breast, prostate, and colon. What's more, flaxseed is a key ingredient for amazing bread that works like cholesterol-lowering drugs but without the side-effects. Plus, it tastes heavenly!

Sweet and nutty dried fruit muffins

Nutritional facts per serving: 379 calories; 87.7g carbohydrates; 23.6mg cholesterol; 4g total fat; 8.6g fiber; 5.5g protein; 131.1mg sodium

---

Preheat oven to 350 degrees. Grease muffin tins.

Beat eggs and sugar until light in color and thick. Sift together flour, baking powder, baking soda, and salt. Whisk together canola oil and orange juice. Stir dry ingredients into the egg-sugar mixture in thirds, alternating with the orange juice and beginning and ending with the dry ingredients. Fold in the chopped dried fruit, almonds, and orange peel.

2	eggs
1	cup packed dark brown sugar
2	cups all-purpose flour
1 1/2	tsp baking powder
1	tsp baking soda
	Pinch salt
1	tblsp canola oil
1	cup orange juice
3/4	cup chopped dried fruit, any combination
3/4	cup chopped almonds
2	tblsp finely chopped orange peel (no white attached)

Nutrition Note

Almonds, ounce for ounce, provide nearly as much protein as red meat. They are cholesterol free, low in saturated fat, and high in vitamin E, calcium, and fiber. Just remember that nuts are high in calories, so be sure you don't eat so many almonds that you gain weight.

Pour batter into the prepared muffin cups about 2/3 full. Bake 20 minutes or until a wooden skewer inserted near the center comes out clean. Cool briefly in the pan on a rack, then remove the muffins from the tins, and cool on a rack.

17 muffins

Honey-nut bran muffins

Nutritional facts per serving: 187 calories; 36g carbohydrates; 24mg cholesterol; 4.1g total fat; 2g fiber; 3.7g protein; 414.5mg sodium

Preheat oven to 400 degrees. Grease or line muffin tins.

Mix together buttermilk, honey, butter, eggs, and brown sugar. Separately, sift together the cake flour, baking soda, salt, and nutmeg. Stir in bran flakes.

Pour the liquids into the flour, and blend well. Stir in the dates and nuts without overmixing. Fill tins so that each muffin cup is 3/4 full. Bake in hot oven 20 to 25 minutes until golden brown.

18 muffins

3/4	cup buttermilk
1/4	cup honey
2	ounces butter
2	eggs
1	cup packed brown sugar
2	cups sifted cake flour
1	tblsp baking soda
1	tsp salt
1/4	tsp freshly grated nutmeg
3	cups bran flakes
1/4	cup chopped dates
1/4	cup chopped nuts

Nutrition **Note**

Here's a whole new reason to get sweet on honey. Natural and delicious, honey comes in all kinds of varieties — but if you want more antioxidants, buy the darkest-colored honey you can find. Dr. Nicki Engeseth, a professor of food science at the University of Illinois, tested the antioxidant properties of honey. Many varieties are full of nutritious plant chemicals called phenols and flavonoids. These are known cancer fighters that pack a lot of power. What's more, honey is a versatile and tasty treat that you can easily add to many foods and drinks.

Satisfying buckwheat oat-nut muffins

Nutritional facts per serving: 230 calories; 25.5g carbohydrates; 46.6mg cholesterol; 12.5g total fat; 2.3g fiber; 5.6g protein; 220.3mg sodium

Preheat oven to 400 degrees. Grease a 12-cup muffin pan.

Mix together the flours, rolled oats, nuts, baking powder, baking soda, and salt. Whisk together the buttermilk, melted butter, maple syrup, and eggs. Pour into dry ingredients, and stir until moistened but still lumpy. Spoon muffin cups to top edge. Bake 20 minutes until a toothpick comes out clean. Cool 5 minutes and remove.

12 muffins

1 1/2	cups all-purpose flour
2/3	cup buckwheat flour
1/4	cup rolled oats
1/3	cup chopped and toasted nuts
2	tsp baking powder
1/2	tsp baking soda
1	tsp salt
1	cup buttermilk
4	tblsp butter, melted
1/4	cup maple syrup
2	eggs, lightly beaten

Nutrition **Note**

Quercetin is a natural chemical in certain plants that may just prevent your next sneezing attack. To stop an allergic reaction, you have to keep your body from releasing histamine — the substance that causes sneezing, coughing, and wheezing. Quercetin acts like a commercial antihistamine, regulating the membranes in your body that release histamine. Delicious buckwheat is a good source of quercetin, but you can also get it from apples, onions, and citrus fruits. In addition to eating these healthy foods, try this to help soothe allergy-ridden sinuses. Dissolve a half teaspoon of salt in a cup of warm water. With a bulb syringe, flush your nose with the mixture. You may be surprised at how much this helps.

Spicy hot-pepper corn muffins

Nutritional facts per serving: 148 calories; 26.8g carbohydrates; 40.6mg cholesterol; 2.2g total fat; 1.5g fiber; 6.2g protein; 146.1mg sodium

Preheat oven to 400 degrees. Grease a 12-cup muffin pan.

Mix together flour, cornmeal, sugar, baking powder, salt, red pepper flakes, and jalapeños. Separately, whisk together buttermilk, olive oil, and eggs. Stir in the green chilies and creamed corn. Pour the liquid mixture into the dry ingredients, and mix until just blended. Ladle batter into the prepared muffin pan. Bake on the middle rack of the oven 20 to 25 minutes, or until golden brown. Remove from the oven, and cool briefly on a wire rack.

12 muffins

1 1/2	cups all-purpose flour
1	cup yellow cornmeal
2	tblsp sugar (optional)
2	tsp baking powder
1/2	tsp salt
1/4	tsp red pepper flakes
2	jalapeño peppers, chopped (optional)
3/4	cup buttermilk
1/4	cup olive oil
2	eggs
1	4-ounce can green chilies, chopped
1	8-ounce can creamed corn

Nutrition **Note** Curb colon cancer and cut high cholesterol by cramming more corn and farm-fresh vegetables into your diet.

According to a study, fruits and vegetables that supply the powerful plant nutrient lutein may help prevent colon cancer. Leading lutein sources include corn, spinach, tomatoes, broccoli, oranges, cabbage, and kale. In addition, corn fiber is a good cholesterol reducer. It lowered cholesterol 5 percent in one study. The researchers used 20 grams of corn fiber a day. While you'd be hard pressed to eat that much in a day, every little bit helps.

Country-style buttermilk cornbread

Nutritional facts per serving: 133 calories; 17.5g carbohydrates; 72mg cholesterol; 4.6g total fat; 0.8g fiber; 5.1g protein; 293.7mg sodium

Preheat oven to 425 degrees. Generously grease a 9" x 13" pan. Three minutes before you are ready to pour the batter in the pan, place the pan in the oven. (This makes the crust crisp.)

Mix dry ingredients together. In a separate bowl, whisk oil and milk into the eggs. Make a well in the dry ingredients, and pour in the liquid ingredients. Stir quickly until barely mixed. Pour into the hot pan. Bake for 20 minutes, or until a tester inserted into the center comes out clean.

1 1/2	cups all-purpose flour
1/2	cup white corn meal
2	tsp baking powder
1/2	tsp baking soda
1	tsp salt
2	tblsp canola oil
1 1/2	cups buttermilk
4	eggs, lightly beaten

12 servings

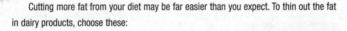

Cutting more fat from your diet may be far easier than you expect. To thin out the fat in dairy products, choose these:

- skim, 1/2-percent, or 1-percent milk, buttermilk, or yogurt

- part-skim cheese products

- low-fat or fat-free ice cream, frozen yogurt, and sour cream

When cruising the meat department, speed past the sausage, bacon, frankfurters, and lunch meats, especially bologna and salami. You can linger in the poultry section, but remember to remove that skin before cooking. Water-packed tuna and salmon are good low-fat fish choices. With all meats, think about slimming your serving size to 3 ounces.

Southwestern salsa-buttermilk cornbread

Nutritional facts per serving: 234 calories; 39.7g carbohydrates; 28.4mg cholesterol; 5.9g total fat; 3.2g fiber; 6.8g protein; 484.9mg sodium

Preheat oven to 425 degrees. Pour oil into a 10" ovenproof skillet, and place in the oven until very hot.

Mix together cornmeal, flour, baking powder, soda, and salt. Add egg, buttermilk, and the hot oil from the skillet, and combine thoroughly. Stir in salsa and pepper, and combine with a few quick strokes. Pour the mixture into the hot skillet, and bake 20 to 24 minutes, or until the cornbread is a nice golden brown. Remove from the oven, cool briefly on a rack, invert, and turn out of the pan. Cut into wedges to serve.

8 servings

2	tblsp canola oil
2	cups cornmeal
1	cup all-purpose flour
1	tblsp baking powder
1	tsp baking soda
1	tsp salt
1	egg
1 1/2	cups buttermilk
1	cup tomato salsa
1	tsp black pepper, or to taste

Nutrition **Note**
Cornmeal may seem like a small player on the nutrition team, but when it comes to folate — cornmeal scores big. Folate is a B vitamin that helps keep your wits sharp, defends against some kinds of cancer, and protects you from depression. It's also a heart protector. Folks over 50 need about 400 micrograms of folate daily. Fortunately, manufacturers "enrich" many grain products by adding back some of the nutrients lost during processing. Just one cup of enriched yellow cornmeal gives you at least 71 percent of the recommended dietary allowance (RDA) for iron, at least 80 percent of the RDAs for thiamin and folate, and at least 40 percent of the RDAs for riboflavin and niacin.

Feed-a-crowd whole-wheat refrigerator rolls

Nutritional facts per serving: 45 calories; 8.4g carbohydrates; 5.1mg cholesterol; 0.6g total fat; 0.6g fiber; 1.6g protein; 147.2mg sodium

1	cup whole-wheat flour
3	cups bread flour
1	package dry yeast
1	tsp salt
1	tblsp sugar
1 1/2	cups warm water (130 degrees)
1	tblsp butter, melted
1	egg, beaten

Grease one baking sheet or 1 1/2" muffin cups. Preheat oven to 425 when ready to bake.

Mix together whole-wheat flour and 1 cup bread flour with yeast, salt, and sugar. Add water, butter, and egg. Stir two minutes. Stir in rest of flour, 1/2 cup at a time, until dough holds together. Knead until soft and elastic, adding flour as needed. Let double in size in greased plastic bag. Punch down, store in refrigerator until ready to use, up to a week.

Pull off as many golf-ball-sized pieces of dough as you'll need. Let double on a greased baking dish or in muffin tins. Cover and let double, about 2 hours due to cold start. Bake 20 minutes.

48 rolls

Maybe your mom had time to wait for bread to rise, but you've got places to go. To speed things up, exchange a packet of regular, dry active yeast for a packet of fast-acting yeast. The fast-acting yeast will go right to work making those bubbles in the dough that cause it to rise.

Perfect popovers

Nutritional facts per serving: 72 calories; 10.5g carbohydrates; 18.5mg cholesterol; 2g total fat; 0.3g fiber; 2.7g protein; 17.4mg sodium

Preheat oven to 400 degrees.
Grease 12 heavy popover pans.

Mix flour with salt and sugar. Add oil, milk, and egg, and beat three minutes on medium-high speed in electric mixer until very smooth.

Fill cups half full with batter. Bake 40 minutes until dark brown. Turn off oven. Prick popovers with a skewer. Return to oven 10 minutes, door ajar.

1	cup bread flour
1/4	tsp salt
1	tblsp sugar
1	tblsp canola oil
1	cup milk at room temperature
1	large egg

12 servings

Nutrition **Note**

A celebration is coming up and — to make it extra special — you want to add something unique and exciting to your cooking. Why not give your dishes a healthy and nutty change with walnut oil? It has a pleasant flavor that's great for salad dressings, cooking, baking, and sautéing. And just like the nut, walnut oil has lots of omega-3 fatty acid — a healthy alternative to soybean or corn oil. Although some supermarkets and gourmet food stores carry it, it's a bit pricier than ordinary oils. But it may just be worth it for that special occasion.

Homemade loaf bread

Nutritional facts per serving: 110 calories; 20.1g carbohydrates; 14.4mg cholesterol; 1.3g total fat; 0.8g fiber; 4g protein; 148.3mg sodium

Preheat oven to 350 degrees. Grease 2 9" x 5" loaf pans.

Mix together yeast, 2 cups of flour, salt, and sugar. Stir in water, milk, and shortening. Add the remaining flour, 1/2 cup at a time, as needed. Knead in the food processor about 1 minute or with the dough hook of a mixer for 10 minutes until soft, smooth, and elastic. Move to an oiled plastic bag, and let rest for 20 minutes.

Remove and form the dough into 2 loaves. Place in the prepared pans. Let rise until double at room temperature.

Brush the top of the loaves with the egg glaze. Bake until a rich golden brown and a quick-read thermometer registers 200 degrees, about 35 to 40 minutes. Turn loaves onto a wire rack to cool.

2 loaves

1	package quick-rising yeast
3	cups bread flour
1	tsp salt
1	tblsp sugar
4	ounces warm water (130 degrees)
4	ounces milk
1	tblsp vegetable shortening
1	egg mixed with 1 tblsp water (optional)
	Pinch salt

Don't throw away those bread ends that are too dry for sandwiches. They're perfect for making sturdy French toast. Keep them in a plastic bag in the freezer until you have enough for breakfast.

Molasses-glazed dark bread

Nutritional facts per serving: 201 calories; 42.2g carbohydrates; 0.8mg cholesterol; 1.1g total fat; 3.1g fiber; 6.4g protein; 270.7mg sodium

Preheat oven to 375 degrees.

Dissolve yeast and molasses in water. Mix salt, buttermilk, rye flour, cereal, cocoa, and yeast mixture. Add 1 cup of the bread flour and mix. Add remaining flour, a half cup at a time. Knead until soft but lightly sticky. Let double in an oiled plastic bag, 1 1/2 hours. Punch down. Shape into a round. Let double again on greased baking sheet.

To make glaze, dissolve molasses in the water. Brush loaf with the glaze. Bake 45 to 50 minutes. Cool on a rack.

12 servings

2	packages active dry yeast
1/4	cup dark molasses
1/4	cup warm water (105 degrees)
1	tsp salt
1	cup buttermilk
1	cup light rye flour
1	cup wheat and barley cereal such as Grape-Nuts
2	tsp unsweetened cocoa powder
2-3	cups bread flour
1/2	tblsp molasses
1	tblsp hot water

Try these tips to make breads and biscuits even better.

- Coax a golden-yellow glow from your biscuits by tossing in a teaspoon of sugar with the dry ingredients. The sugar crystals caramelize on the crust to give the biscuits a lovely tan.

- Save the water you boil potatoes in, and use it to make yeast breads. It will keep the bread fresh longer.

- If you make your own bread, be bold. Experiment with different liquids in your recipes. To give your bread a wonderfully distinctive flavor, you can substitute milk, fruit juices, even meat or vegetable broth for water.

Black and white sesame bread sticks

Nutritional facts per serving: 48 calories; 6.9g carbohydrates; 13mg cholesterol; 1.6g total fat; 0.2g fiber; 1.3g protein; 58.1mg sodium

Preheat oven to 375 degrees. Grease 2 baking sheets.

Add yeast and salt to 2 cups of the bread flour in a food processor bowl. Quickly pour in the milk, then add water, honey, and butter, processing until dough is smooth, about two minutes. Cover the food processor bowl, and let sit for a half hour.

Punch dough down, and roll out on a floured surface until 1/4" thick and approximately a 10" x 14" rectangle. Cut into 10" x 1/2" strips. Roll each strip into sticks. Place on the baking sheet, 3/4" apart.

1	package quick-rising yeast
1/2	tsp salt
2-3	cups bread flour
1/2	cup warm milk (130 degrees)
1/4	cup water
1	tblsp honey
1	tblsp butter, softened
1	egg yolk, mixed with 2 tblsp water
1/4	tblsp white sesame seeds
1/4	tblsp black sesame seeds

Variation:
Sprinkle coarse salt on the sticks along with the sesame seeds before baking, or just salt alone.

Make an egg glaze by mixing the egg yolk and water. Brush sticks with the glaze, and sprinkle with the mixed sesame seeds. Place the sheets immediately into the oven and bake 12 to 15 minutes, until light golden brown. Remove from oven and cool on a rack. Freezes well.

28 servings

Lavash quick-bake flatbread

Nutritional facts per serving: 171 calories; 32.2g carbohydrates; 0.2mg cholesterol; 2.3g total fat; 3.5g fiber; 6.4g protein; 586mg sodium

Preheat oven to 400 degrees. Oil two baking sheets.

Mix 1 cup bread flour, 1 cup whole-wheat flour, yeast, and salt. Pour in water, and beat with a wooden spoon to mix. Add remaining cup of whole-wheat flour, and stir vigorously to blend. Add remaining white flour until the dough holds together.

Knead on a floured surface until soft and elastic, adding flour as needed to make a soft and elastic dough.

Put in an oiled plastic bag until doubled. Punch down and let rise for 30 minutes. Divide into 10 balls and let rest, covered, for 5 minutes.

Roll the first ball as flat and thin as possible, lifting and stretching over the back of your hands. Lay on the oiled pan. Proceed with another piece, brush both with milk, and sprinkle with seeds.

Bake 10 minutes or until pulled away from the baking sheet and dappled with brown. Meanwhile proceed with the remaining dough. Cool on racks.

10 10" servings

2	cups bread flour
2	cups whole-wheat flour
1	package yeast
1	tblsp salt
1 1/2	cups warm water (130 degrees)
1/4	cup milk
1/4	cup toasted sesame and/or poppy seeds

Nutrition **Note**

Many folks over 60 develop diverticulosis, a symptom-free colon condition that can become more serious and painful. To help prevent diverticulosis or keep it from getting worse, add extra fiber from whole grains, and drink extra water.

Oven-fresh oatmeal flatbread

Nutritional facts per serving: 96 calories; 9.5g carbohydrates; 21.9mg cholesterol; 5.2g total fat; 3g fiber; 2.8g protein; 158.6mg sodium

Preheat oven to 350 degrees.

Stir together honey, melted butter, and salt. Separately, add soda to the buttermilk. Combine flours, and add flours and buttermilk alternately to the honey mixture. Stir in the oats. Turn the dough onto a floured board, and knead until soft. Divide dough into 2 pieces, and cut off 1/3 cup-size pieces of dough. Shape the pieces of dough into round balls. Flatten down and roll paper-thin. Move to baking sheet, and bake 8 minutes or until dappled with brown. Slip on to rack to cool, and break into pieces.

1	tblsp honey
3/4	cup melted butter
1/2	tsp salt
1	tsp baking soda
1 1/2	cups buttermilk
2	cups white flour
1	cup whole-wheat flour
2	cups quick-cooking oats

10 8" servings

Nutrition **Note**

A steaming bowl of hearty oatmeal is a great start for a chilly morning, and it may help you manage diabetes, too. A high-fiber diet — starring soluble and cereal fibers like oats — has been recommended by experts as an effective way to deal with diabetes. According to a study in the famous *New England Journal of Medicine*, a diet with 25 grams of soluble fiber plus 25 more grams of insoluble fiber helped keep blood sugar, insulin, and cholesterol under control in folks with type 2 diabetes. It also showed that you can achieve this type of diet without fiber supplements or specially fiber-fortified foods.

Exotic naan flatbread

Nutritional facts per serving: 105 calories; 16.6g carbohydrates; 0.9mg cholesterol; 2.7g total fat; 0.6g fiber; 3.4g protein; 12.8mg sodium

Preheat oven to 450 degrees. Grease two baking sheets.

Reconstitute the dehydrated onions in the water. Mix 2 cups of the flour with yeast, salt, and sugar. Stir in milk, add oil, 3 tablespoons of the yogurt, and onions. Add the remaining flour, 1/4 cup at a time, stirring, until dough holds together. Knead on a floured board, adding flour as necessary, until dough is smooth and elastic. Let the dough double in size in an oiled plastic bag, about 1 hour. Roll the dough into 16 golf-ball-sized pieces. Cover and let rest 20 minutes.

Press and flatten each into a circle 1/16" thick and 6" to 8" in diameter. Move to the baking sheets, brush with one tablespoon yogurt, and bake 5 minutes until they begin to puff. Turn over and bake until firm to the touch, about 8 to 10 minutes. Slide under a broiler for a minute to turn the tops lightly golden brown.

18 servings

2	tblsp dehydrated onions
1	tblsp water
3	cups all-purpose flour
1	package dry yeast
1	tsp salt
1	tsp sugar
1 1/2	cups warm milk (130 degrees)
3	tblsp canola oil
4	tblsp plain yogurt

If you freeze bread for later use, put a paper towel into the bag or container. The towel will absorb moisture that can make bread soggy when it thaws.

Party thyme buttermilk biscuits

Nutritional facts per serving: 131 calories; 19.7g carbohydrates; 0.8mg cholesterol; 4.3g total fat; 0.7g fiber; 3.2g protein; 563.2mg sodium

---

Preheat oven to 500 degrees. Grease a baking sheet.

Sift 3 cups of the flour and the salt together into a bowl. Add the thyme. Cut in the shortening until the mixture resembles coarse meal. Add buttermilk, and mix until the dough holds together. It will be wet and sticky.

4	cups self-rising flour
2	tsp salt
2	tblsp finely chopped fresh thyme
6	tblsp shortening
1 3/4	cups buttermilk

Put the remaining cup of flour in another bowl. Flour your hands, and then pull off a piece of dough about the size of a golf ball. Roll the piece of dough lightly in the flour to coat on all sides. Roll it gently into a smooth ball in the palm of your hand to knead and shape it. Place the biscuits, barely touching each other, on the pan and flatten slightly. Bake 8 to 10 minutes on the top rack or until golden brown. Serve hot.

20 biscuits

Suddenly you realize you're out of fresh buttermilk. Don't worry. You can whip up a super substitute in just seconds. A single teaspoon of lemon juice will "sour" a cup of regular milk, giving it a tang similar to buttermilk. You can also try powdered buttermilk. Not only does it reconstitute with water, it also works especially well in baking recipes.

Golden glacé feta biscuits

Nutritional facts per serving: 96 calories; 16.5g carbohydrates; 21.9mg cholesterol; 1.5g total fat; 0.3g fiber; 3.6g protein; 32.4mg sodium

Preheat oven to 425 degrees.

Sift flour, salt, baking powder, and sugar into a bowl. Cut the butter in until mixture resembles coarse oatmeal. Add milk and cheese, and stir briefly to make a soft dough. Turn onto a floured board, and knead for another 30 seconds. Press the dough flat and fold in half, and repeat the action a half dozen times. Roll out 1/2" thick. Cut into 24 biscuits, move to an ungreased baking sheet, and brush with egg-water mixture. Bake until lightly golden brown, 12 to 14 minutes.

24 biscuits

2	cups all-purpose flour
1/2	tsp salt
3	tsp baking powder
1	tblsp sugar
6	tblsp butter
3/4	cup milk
3/4	cup feta cheese, crumbled
1	egg yolk beaten with 1 tblsp water

Have you ever heard anyone say, "It's the greatest thing since sliced bread," and wondered exactly how long sliced bread has been around? In 1928, a bread slicer was used for the first time in a commercial bakery in Chillicothe, Mo. While we've been able to slice bread ourselves for centuries, we've only been able to buy a pre-sliced loaf since 1928.

Hearty oat bran and whole-wheat biscuits

Nutritional facts per serving: 92 calories; 10.6g carbohydrates; 12.9mg cholesterol; 5g total fat; 1.1g fiber; 2.1g protein; 165.6mg sodium

Preheat oven to 425 degrees.

Mix the dry ingredients in a bowl. Cut in butter with a pastry cutter or two knives until it is the size of peas. Make a well in the center of the mixture and pour in the buttermilk. Gradually incorporate the dry ingredients. Turn out on a floured surface, and knead gently 2 or 3 times until the dough comes together. Cut with a 2" biscuit cutter. Bake on an ungreased baking sheet for 10 to 12 minutes, or until lightly golden brown.

1	cup whole-wheat flour
1	cup all-purpose flour
1/4	cup oat bran
2	tsp baking powder
1/2	tsp baking soda
1/2	tsp salt
1/2	cup butter, diced and chilled
1	cup buttermilk

20 biscuits

Nutrition **Note**

Famed as a Scottish favorite, oats can do you a few favors, too. Both oats and oat products have many health benefits, largely because of their soluble fiber called beta glucan. But that's not all they do. Oats also serve up a delicious boost of protein and a variety of key minerals like potassium, magnesium, phosphorous, manganese, copper, and zinc. Eating a healthy portion of oats each day can help you lower your cholesterol, manage diabetes, prevent cancer, and cure constipation. So take your cue from the Scots, and roll a few more oats into your meals. You'll be glad you did.

Two-cheese Sicilian pizza

Nutritional facts per serving: 461 calories; 54.1g carbohydrates; 18.5mg cholesterol; 18.6g total fat; 2.5g fiber; 18.7g protein; 1221.6mg sodium

Preheat oven to 475 degrees. Oil an 11" x 16" jelly roll pan.

Mix 2 cups of the flour with the yeast and salt. Beat in water and oil. Gradually beat in the remaining flour, 1/4 cup at a time, until a loose dough is formed. Knead by hand until soft and elastic, adding flour as necessary. Let double in size in an oiled plastic bag, about an hour.

Punch down dough, return to bag, and let rise about 45 minutes. Punch down dough. Remove dough from the bag, place in the oiled pan and flatten, pushing it up the sides. Cover and let rise 30 minutes.

Uncover the dough, and spread the tomato sauce over the dough. Bake on the lower shelf for 10 minutes. Remove from oven. Spread with cheese and any other optional garnishes. Sprinkle with olive oil and return to oven. Bake 20 minutes until sauce is bubbling and the edges are brown.

6 servings

3	cups bread flour
1	package dry yeast
2	tsp salt
1 1/2	cups warm water (130 degrees)
1	tblsp olive oil
1	cup tomato sauce
1 1/2	cups part-skim mozzarella cheese, grated
1/4	cup finely grated Parmesan cheese
1/4	cup olive oil

Rolling out dough leaves a sticky, floury mess. When it's time to clean up, sprinkle salt over the area, then wipe up with a sponge. Lumps and clumps will rinse right away.

French olive-anchovy pizza

Nutritional facts per serving: 364 calories; 15.8g carbohydrates; 59.5mg cholesterol; 27.1g total fat; 2g fiber; 14.9g protein; 791.1mg sodium

Preheat oven to 425 degrees.

Dissolve yeast in 1/2 cup of water. Stir together 2 cups of bread flour, remaining 1/2 cup of water, salt, olive oil, and dissolved yeast. Beat in the eggs, and add the remaining flour, 1/2 cup at a time, until a dough is formed. Turn out onto a floured board and knead, adding flour as needed, until soft and elastic.

Let rise in an oiled plastic bag until doubled, about 1 hour. Remove from bag, knock down, and divide into parts for 4 pizza pans. Roll dough thinly (3/16") and push to edges of the pans.

Meanwhile, cook onions over medium heat in the 1/2 cup of olive oil until soft. Turn up heat, and cook until deep brown but not burned. Spread onions over doughs, sprinkle with cheese, arrange anchovies in spokes, decorate with olive halves, sprinkle with salt, herbs, and Parmesan. Bake 20 minutes.

4 10" pizzas

2	packages dry yeast
1	cup warm water (130 degrees) divided
	Pinch sugar
2-3	cups bread flour
1	tsp salt
6	tblsp olive oil
2	eggs
2	pounds chopped onions
1/2	cup olive oil
1	cup shredded mozzarella cheese
14	anchovies
20	black olives, halved
1	tsp salt
1	tsp oregano
1	tsp basil
1	cup freshly grated Parmesan cheese

Eggs and cheese

Delightfully different cheese omelet

Nutritional facts per serving: 299 calories; 2.4g carbohydrates; 274.7mg cholesterol; 23.7g total fat; 0g fiber; 18.6g protein; 178.2mg sodium

Preheat the broiler.

Whisk eggs lightly with salt and pepper. Heat butter in a 9" omelet or nonstick pan over high heat until it stops foaming and begins to brown. Add eggs immediately. Stir briskly for 8 to 10 seconds until the eggs start to thicken. Then quickly pull the egg at the sides of the pan to the center, rolling and tipping the pan to pour uncooked egg to the sides. When half the eggs are set, take the pan off the heat.

4-5	eggs
	Salt
	Freshly ground black pepper
1	tblsp butter
3	tblsp heavy cream
3/4	cup grated Gruyère or Swiss cheese

When the label says sugar free, that means the item has less than 0.5 grams of sugar per serving. The term "low sugar" isn't regulated and may or may not mean what you expect.

Carefully transfer the egg mixture to an oven-proof dish, spoon the cream over the eggs, and sprinkle them with the cheese. Broil until golden. Cut the omelet in half, slide onto plates, and serve at once with hot buttered toast.

2 servings

Light egg white omelet

Nutritional facts per serving: 92 calories; 1.9g carbohydrates; 0mg cholesterol; 0g total fat; 0g fiber; 19.2g protein; 298.9mg sodium

3   egg whites

1   tblsp water

Dash salt

Dash freshly ground black pepper

Whisk egg whites and water together until mixture whitens and is light and foamy. Add salt and pepper.

Spray a 6" to 7" sauté pan with nonstick vegetable spray. Heat the pan over medium heat until a drop of water sizzles when sprinkled in the pan. Pour in the egg whites, and tilt pan to distribute them. Using a heatproof rubber spatula, briskly stir the egg mixture until soft-set but still moist. Smooth out the egg mixture, and allow it to cook until the bottom is set but the top is still somewhat shiny, about 1 minute.

Run the spatula under the edge of the omelet to loosen it. Fill as desired and flip the sides of the omelet over, envelope style, to cover the filling. Tilt the pan, and roll the omelet over onto a plate. Serve immediately.

1 serving

An omelet made only from egg whites bypasses the fat and calories in egg yolks. Yet you'll be surprised at how good it tastes with healthy fillings like reduced-fat feta, turkey bacon, and roasted vegetables — especially garlic and onions.

Basic ready-for-fillings omelet

Nutritional facts per serving: 162 calories; 0.9g carbohydrates; 334.2mg cholesterol; 13.2g total fat; 0g fiber; 9.4g protein; 95.3mg sodium

Whisk together eggs, water, and salt. Heat butter in a skillet until it just starts to turn color. Add egg mixture. Move the skillet around, forward and backward, to allow the uncooked egg mixture to cover the skillet bottom. When the eggs start to solidify, place the cooked filling mixture of your choice on one side of the eggs. Fold the omelet over the filling, and slide onto a platter. Serve immediately.

3   eggs

1   tblsp water

Dash salt

1   tblsp butter

2 servings

Nutrition **Note**

Couch potatoes have a higher risk of diseases ranging from arthritis to cancer and beyond, authorities warn. According to some estimates, inactivity causes the deaths of 250,000 people a year in the United States. Experts call this threat Sedentary Death Syndrome (SeDS). You won't need a shot or pill to prevent SeDS — just find fun ways to get more active. Even small amounts of activity may help as long as you keep at it. A study by the Centers for Disease Control and Prevention suggests that inactive women over 65 could cut their risk of dying from cancer in half just by getting more active. Naturally, folks who are the most active reap the most benefits, but even moderate exercise may help.

Herbed button mushroom omelet filling

Nutritional facts per serving: 58 calories; 9.1g carbohydrates; 21.2mg cholesterol; 6.5g total fat; 9.2g fiber; 2.7g protein; 368.4mg sodium

Melt butter in a large skillet. Add onion, mushrooms, parsley, and basil. Sauté quickly until just done, 2 to 3 minutes. Season to taste with salt and pepper. Fill basic omelet with the mixture before turning out.

2 servings

1   tblsp butter

1   medium onion, chopped

1   cup small button mushrooms, sliced

1/2   tblsp finely chopped fresh parsley

1/2   tblsp finely chopped fresh basil or tarragon

Salt

Freshly ground black pepper

Nutrition **Note**   You could cut your chances of getting a cold or the flu this season just by eating breakfast. Professor Andy Smith of Cardiff University directed a study of 100 people in Wales. He found that people who had fewer colds were more likely to eat breakfast. Try this breakfast, and see if it helps you shoo away colds and flu.

- glass of orange juice

- quarter cantaloupe cut into chunks

- cup of low-fat yogurt or glass of low-fat milk fortified with live yogurt cultures

- bowl of hearty whole-grain cereal with low-fat milk, or two slices of whole-wheat toast

Mexican fiesta omelet filling

Nutritional facts per serving: 81.8 calories; 6.2g carbohydrates; 10.2mg cholesterol; 18.7g total fat; 5.1g fiber; 4.2g protein; 321.7mg sodium

Melt butter in a large skillet. Add cumin, and heat until fragrant. Add green onions, red bell pepper, tomato, and oregano. Season to taste with salt and pepper, and sauté quickly until just done, 2 to 3 minutes. Fill basic omelet with the mixture before turning out.

Top the filled omelet with the salsa and cheese.

2 servings

1	tblsp butter
	Dash ground cumin
2	green onions, chopped
1/2	red bell pepper, chopped
1	tomato, peeled and chopped
1	tsp chopped fresh oregano
	Salt
	Freshly ground black pepper
1	cup salsa
4	ounces grated Monterey Jack cheese

Hard-boiled eggs can be easier with these tips.

- Peel hard-boiled eggs perfectly. As soon as they are cooked, put them in ice water for one minute. Then put them back into boiling water for 10 seconds. Remove the eggs, crack the shells all over, then start peeling them at the large end. The combination of heat and cold makes peeling a snap.

- Save energy and make perfect hard-boiled eggs. Using a pot with a tight lid, cover your eggs with water, add a pinch of salt, and bring to a rolling boil. As soon as the water is boiling rapidly, turn off the heat and allow the pot to stand, unopened, for 10 minutes before removing your eggs. This allows the eggs to finish cooking without cracking and breaking.

Basil brunch eggs with cream cheese

Nutritional facts per serving: 199 calories; 1.4g carbohydrates; 311.6mg cholesterol; 16.9g total fat; 0g fiber; 9.9g protein; 146.4mg sodium

Melt butter in a medium skillet. Add eggs and cook over medium heat for about 2 minutes or until eggs begin to thicken. Add remaining ingredients. Continue cooking, stirring constantly until eggs are loosely set. Serve immediately.

3-4 servings

1   tblsp butter

6   eggs, well-beaten

1   3-ounce package cream cheese, softened and cut into small pieces

2   tblsp chopped fresh basil

Salt

Whip up unbelievably fluffy omelets and scrambled eggs by adding a "secret" ingredient — one-fourth teaspoon of cornstarch for every egg. Beat well, cook as usual, and serve this light-as-a-feather dish with pride.

Snappy cheese and egg enchilada

Nutritional facts per serving: 408 calories; 69.6g carbohydrates; 214.4mg cholesterol; 9.2g total fat; 8.4g fiber; 15.2g protein; 510.2mg sodium

Preheat oven to 350 degrees. Spray a 6" x 9" casserole with nonstick spray.

Line casserole dish with 1 1/3 of the tortillas. Mix eggs and milk together. Pour into a nonstick skillet, and stir over medium heat until eggs are firm but not set. Pour them over tortillas. Cover with another layer of tortillas and sprinkle half of the Monterey Jack and cheddar cheeses over the tortillas. Spread with the salsa or chili, and top with remaining tortillas. Sprinkle with remaining cheeses and optional cilantro. Bake until cheese is bubbly and eggs set, about 20 minutes.

4	extra large flour tortillas
4	large eggs
2	tblsp milk
1/4	pound grated Monterey Jack cheese
1/4	pound grated sharp cheddar cheese
3/4	cup salsa or chili
3	tblsp fresh cilantro (optional)

4 servings

Sometimes eggs lay around in your refrigerator for eons before you realize they're past their prime. To test an egg for freshness, fill a cup with water, and add 2 teaspoons of salt. Gently place the egg in the water. If it sinks, it's still fresh. If it floats, toss it. Or place it in the bottom of a bowl of cold water. If it lies on its side, it's fresh. If it stands at an angle, it's at least three days old. If it stands on end, it's at least 10 days old.

Spicy goat cheese tortilla

Nutritional facts per serving: 389 calories; 43.1g carbohydrates; 20.8mg cholesterol; 18.2g total fat; 2.4g fiber; 13g protein; 606.1mg sodium

Preheat broiler. Brush a baking sheet with oil, or spray with nonstick cooking spray.

Heat 1 tablespoon of the oil in a nonstick skillet. Add tortillas one at a time, and fry on one side until speckled with brown, 1 minute or less. Turn and fry the second side. Repeat, adding oil as needed until all the tortillas are toasted, stacking them on a plate. (The tortillas can also be crisped in the oven but will not be quite as tasty.)

Break the cheese into chunks, and sprinkle it over the tortillas. Cover the cheese with some of the sausage, cilantro if using, hot peppers, and the tomato if using. Place tortillas on the prepared baking sheet and broil until bubbly, about 3 minutes. Serve whole for entree portions, or halve or quarter to make appetizer portions.

6 servings

1-3	tblsp vegetable oil
8-10	corn or flour tortillas (4-6 if using large flour tortillas)
8	ounces Montrachet or other soft goat cheese
1/2	pound hot chicken sausage, crumbled and cooked
1-3	tblsp chopped fresh cilantro (optional)
	Small hot peppers, such as jalapeños, seeded and chopped
1	tomato, peeled, seeded, and chopped (optional)

Nutrition **Note**

Not all cheese comes from the milk of cows. Sometimes called chevre, cheese made from goat's milk provides small amounts of many nutrients including vitamin A.

Tomato and sweet pepper piperade

Nutritional facts per serving: 268 calories; 16.7g carbohydrates; 425mg cholesterol; 15.8g total fat; 3.6g fiber; 15.3g protein; 259.7mg sodium

Heat oil in a heavy frying pan. Add onions and garlic, and cook over medium heat until soft and golden. Add bell peppers and cook 15 minutes. Add tomatoes and basil. Cover and cook until very soft. Remove the cover and add the eggs. Stir gently until lightly cooked and scrambled but not hard. Season to taste with salt and pepper. Serve with the toast.

6-8 servings

3   tblsp olive oil, butter, or drippings

2   onions, chopped

4   garlic cloves, chopped

3   large red bell peppers, sliced into 1/4" x 3" strips

1   green bell pepper, sliced into 1/4" x 3" strips

1   pound tomatoes, seeded and chopped

2   tblsp chopped fresh basil or thyme

16   eggs, beaten lightly

Salt

Freshly ground black pepper

4   slices bread, toasted and brushed with butter or oil and garlic

Nutrition **Note**   Even though most breakfast fare can be high in cholesterol, saturated fat, sodium, and calories, you can make breakfast healthier. To start the day right, try hot or cold cereal, preferably with 1 percent or skim milk. Add natural juice; a tasty bagel, English muffin, or toast without butter; and delicious fruit.

Orange-flavored French toast

Nutritional facts per serving: 319 calories; 27.5g carbohydrates; 157.7mg cholesterol; 20.6g total fat; 2.1g fiber; 6.8g protein; 212.2mg sodium

Beat eggs into the orange juice, then add cream and ginger, and combine completely. Melt butter in a large heavy frying pan until bubbling. Soak bread slices thoroughly in the egg mixture. Slide each slice carefully into the bubbling butter. Fry one side until golden brown. Turn and cook other side until golden. Serve topped with the orange slices and sprinkled with sugar and nutmeg.

4 servings

2	eggs
1	cup freshly squeezed orange juice
1/4	cup heavy cream
1/4	tsp ground ginger
1/4	cup butter, preferably unsalted
8	slices Italian or French bread, thickly sliced, preferably a bit stale
1	orange, sliced and the slices halved
	Confectioner's or brown sugar
	Freshly grated nutmeg

Nutrition **Note**   Before you begin any exercise, talk with your doctor about the best activities for you. Here are a few good questions to ask.

- Are there any exercises or activities that would be particularly helpful to me? Are there any sports or exercises I should avoid?

- Do I have any health conditions — or do I take any medications — that could affect my exercise plans?

- Is it safe for me to do the exercises that I have planned?

- How can I find out whether I'm exercising hard enough? How can I keep from exercising too hard?

Sunrise French toast

Nutritional facts per serving: 354 calories; 2.5g carbohydrates; 309.9mg cholesterol; 35g total fat; 0g fiber; 7.6g protein; 85mg sodium

To make the batter, beat together eggs, milk, vanilla, and salt if using. Melt butter in a large skillet. Dip each slice of bread into the batter, turn to soak, and let soak 10 to 15 minutes. Fry the bread in the skillet over medium heat until very lightly browned. Turn once.

Keep the cooked slices warm in a 250-degree oven while frying the remaining slices. Serve warm, sprinkled with confectioner's sugar and topped with butter and jam, if desired.

2	eggs
1/2	cup milk
1/2	tsp vanilla
	Salt (optional)
2-3	tblsp butter
4	slices bread, preferably a dense, homemade type
	Confectioner's sugar (optional)
	Butter (optional)
	Jam (optional)

Variation: 1/2 cup light or heavy cream may be substituted for the 1/2 cup of milk.

2 servings

Does your grandchild want to help when you're preparing a holiday meal? Give him a very special job. Fill a plastic jar half full of heavy whipping cream, and secure the lid. Explain to your little one that you're counting on him to make "magic" butter for the meal, but it will take a lot of work. Show him how to shake the jar with a rhythm, and suggest a magical chant such as "Milk is for cookies, butter is for bread. Milk go away, send butter instead." Before long you'll have creamy "magic" butter for your meal.

Fruit-filled oven-baked pancake

Nutritional facts per serving: 154 calories; 26g carbohydrates; 61.2mg cholesterol; 4.7g total fat; 2g fiber; 2.4g protein; 42mg sodium

---

Preheat oven to 425 degrees.

Sift flour with salt, sugar, and nutmeg. Combine eggs, milk, and vanilla, and pour into the flour mixture. Stir until batter is just blended. Melt butter in a 9" nonstick skillet or a 9" round cake pan, coating bottom and sides. Pour the batter into the hot pan, and bake for 15 to 20 minutes, or until golden brown. The pancake puffs and rises on the outside edges, but collapses when removed from the oven.

Fold edges over in a scalloped fashion. Dust with sugar, then sprinkle with lemon juice. Fill or garnish with fresh fruit, and sour cream if desired. Cut into wedges and serve immediately.

8 servings

1/2	cup flour
	Pinch salt
1	tsp sugar
	Pinch freshly grated nutmeg
2	eggs, lightly beaten
1/2	cup milk
1	tsp vanilla
2	tblsp butter
1/4	cup confectioner's sugar
1/4	lemon, juiced
4	cups sliced strawberries and bananas
	Low-fat sour cream (optional)

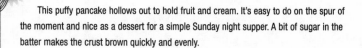

This puffy pancake hollows out to hold fruit and cream. It's easy to do on the spur of the moment and nice as a dessert for a simple Sunday night supper. A bit of sugar in the batter makes the crust brown quickly and evenly.

Light and creamy yogurt cheese

Nutritional facts per cup: 39 calories; 4.4g carbohydrates; 3.7mg cholesterol; 1g total fat; 0.1g fiber; 3.3g protein; 43mg sodium

Empty yogurt into a piece of cheesecloth. Tie it well, then suspend it over a dish, and let drain overnight in the refrigerator. Remove the yogurt cheese to a covered container. It will keep, covered, for one week or so in the refrigerator.

1   16-ounce container plain yogurt

1 cup

This is a super low-calorie substitute for cream cheese. One cup of low-fat yogurt has 140 calories while one cup of cream cheese has 790 calories. That's a whopping 650-calorie difference. If you don't have cheesecloth, use three coffee filters placed in a strainer over a bowl. Cover and refrigerate for 24 hours. Once you've tried making regular yogurt cheese, you can try interesting variations. For herb cheese, add 3 to 4 tablespoons of fresh chopped basil, thyme, or other herbs. For a sweet spread, add cinnamon. Spread it on a bagel, or use it as a dip for chips, crackers, or veggies.

Festive red and green salad

Nutritional facts per serving: 170 calories; 13.8g carbohydrates; 0mg cholesterol; 12.7g total fat; 3.9g fiber; 4.1g protein; 188.7mg sodium

Wash lettuce and spinach, and tear into small pieces. Combine with mushrooms, onions, pecans, and cherries. Pour dressing over to taste. Toss well and serve.

4 servings

1	small head Bibb, Boston, radicchio, leaf, or Romaine lettuce (or combination)
1/2	pound fresh spinach
1/2	cup sliced fresh mushrooms
4	green onions, thinly sliced
1/3	cup toasted pecan pieces
1/4	cup dried tart cherries
8	tblsp raspberry vinaigrette dressing

Nutrition **Note**

Cherries are delicious, vitamin-packed, and proven to relieve arthritis pain even better than aspirin, ibuprofen, and other drugs — with no stomach upset or other side effects. The same natural compounds that give cherries their red color — anthocyanins — also stop your body from making certain hormone-like substances that cause pain and inflammation. In lab studies, anthocyanins have proven to be about 10 times more effective than aspirin at relieving joint pain and swelling. Experts say about 20 cherries should do the trick. Or you can try the dried variety — just three pack the same amount of pain-relieving punch.

Oriental-style celery with walnuts

Nutritional facts per serving: 59 calories; 3.1g carbohydrates; 0mg cholesterol; 5.1g total fat; 1.2g fiber; 1.6g protein; 167.8mg sodium

---

Remove leaves and tough ends of the celery, and string if necessary. Slice on the diagonal. If the celery is large and tough, drop the slices into a pot of boiling water, return just to boiling, and drain.

Mix together soy sauce, vinegar, sesame oil if desired, and sugar to taste. Mix the walnuts with the celery in a large bowl. Pour the sauce over; toss well to combine. Serve warm, at room temperature, or chill.

4 servings

4	ribs celery
1	tblsp low-sodium soy sauce
1	tblsp rice or white wine vinegar
1/8	tsp sesame oil (optional)
	Sugar
1/4	cup coarsely chopped walnuts

Nutrition **Note**

Walnuts can help you squirrel away nutrients for better health. Loaded with unsaturated fat, vitamin E, and ellagic acid, walnuts can help lower cholesterol, fight cancer, and boost your brainpower. Use walnuts for baking or cooking, throw them in a salad, or just munch on them for a crunchy snack. As tasty and nutritious as walnuts are, they aren't the perfect food. Walnuts are a common source of food allergies. Another problem with walnuts, and all nuts for that matter, is that they limit the amount of iron your body absorbs. But you can fix this easily by getting an additional 50 milligrams of vitamin C — the amount in half a cup of orange juice.

Refreshing cucumber and yogurt salad

Nutritional facts per serving: 58 calories; 6.5g carbohydrates; 3.7mg cholesterol; 2.2g total fat; 0.5g fiber; 3.7g protein; 44.3mg sodium

---

Sprinkle sliced cucumbers with salt. Let stand in strainer 15 minutes or longer to release the bitter juices. Rinse well and dry.

In a blender or food processor, mix together the remaining ingredients. Combine with cucumbers in a bowl and refrigerate.

2 servings

2   cucumbers, peeled and sliced

Salt

1   cup plain yogurt

1   garlic clove, chopped or crushed

1   tblsp fresh mint (optional)

3   tblsp lemon juice

1   tsp canola oil

Freshly ground black pepper

Nutrition **Note**
Scary bacteria like *Salmonella* and *E. coli* can cause intestinal infections or diarrhea, but yogurt can help treat and perhaps prevent these miseries. Here's how it works. More than 400 different kinds of bacteria live in your digestive tract. Some are good ones, called probiotics, that help keep harmful bacteria in check. However, a round of antibiotics, a bout of food poisoning, or various illnesses often kill a lot of your good bacteria. The result can be intestinal upset, including diarrhea. You can help your body maintain the delicate balance between good and bad bacteria by eating yogurt. With its wealth of probiotics, cool and creamy yogurt is a natural way to re-stock your inventory of good bacteria.

Marinated cucumber-red onion salad

Nutritional facts per serving: 53 calories; 12.5g carbohydrates; 0mg cholesterol; 0.3g total fat; 2.6g fiber; 1.6g protein; 6mg sodium

Slice the cucumbers and onion. Dissolve sugar, if using, in the vinegar, and pour over the cucumbers, red onion, green onions, and sesame seeds. Add salt and pepper to taste. Marinate at least 2 hours before serving.

4 servings

3	English cucumbers, peeled
1	red onion, peeled
6	tblsp sugar (optional)
1/2	cup cider vinegar
2	green onions, chopped
3	tblsp sesame seeds
	Salt
	Freshly ground black pepper

Treat minor cuts and scrapes with convenient remedies from your kitchen.

- Don't go bananas hunting for an ordinary bandage. A banana peel will do. So will a slice of raw potato. Just tape it over your scratch.

- Wet tea bags soothe shaving nicks and other small cuts. They also work great for sunburn.

- Honey keeps wounds clean, kills bacteria, and prevents scarring. Spread honey on a bandage rather than directly on your skin.

- Cinnamon kills bacteria, numbs pain, and stops bleeding. After you wash and dry your cut, shake on some cinnamon powder and cover with a bandage.

- Save those little packets of ketchup and mustard you get in fast-food restaurants. Keep them in the freezer and use them as miniature ice packs for tiny injuries.

Easy chickpea-veggie salad

Nutritional facts per serving: 251 calories; 27.2g carbohydrates; 6.3mg cholesterol; 12.6g total fat; 7.4g fiber; 9.3g protein; 381.6mg sodium

Combine chickpeas, lentils, carrots, and onions. Toss together in a bowl. Whisk together lemon juice, balsamic vinegar, and oil. Season to taste with salt and pepper. Pour over vegetables, toss well, cover, and refrigerate for at least 2 hours, or overnight.

To serve, place 2 leaves of lettuce on each salad plate. Add feta and chopped cilantro to the marinated vegetables, and toss gently to mix. Divide vegetables between 4 salad plates. Garnish each plate with a sprig of cilantro and serve immediately.

4 servings

1	cup canned, cooked chickpeas, drained
1	cup cooked brown lentils
1/4	cup grated raw carrots
1/3	cup chopped green onion
	Juice of 1 lemon
1 1/2	tblsp balsamic vinegar
3	tblsp olive oil
	Salt
	Freshly ground black pepper
1	head Boston or Bibb lettuce, washed and patted dry
3	tblsp crumbled feta cheese
1	tblsp chopped fresh cilantro
4	sprigs fresh cilantro (optional)

Make this recipe work even better with these tips.

- Use low-fat feta cheese for fewer calories and less fat.

- When tossing a salad, place the bowl in the sink. Vegetables that fly over the edge of the bowl won't land on the counter top or floor. The cleanup will be a lot quicker.

Eggplant salad with raisins and pine nuts

Nutritional facts per serving: 397 calories; 25.3g carbohydrates; 0mg cholesterol; 33.4g total fat; 6g fiber; 4.7g protein; 11.6mg sodium

Cut eggplant into 1/2" cubes, leaving skin on. Cook eggplant in a large sauté pan until tender and lightly brown. Remove. Heat 1 1/2 teaspoons oil in the pan, add onions and celery, and sauté 5 minutes. Add garlic and cook a few minutes more.

To make dressing, combine vinegar, salt and pepper to taste, thyme, and basil. Add oil and mix well. Add eggplant and toss. Cover with plastic wrap and marinate for several hours.

One hour before serving, add raisins, pine nuts, and red peppers. Toss thoroughly to mix. Refrigerate until serving time.

4 servings

1	eggplant, about 1 1/2 pounds
1 1/2	tsp olive oil
1	onion, cut in 1/2" cubes
1/2	rib celery, sliced
1	garlic clove, chopped or crushed
1/3	cup wine vinegar
	Salt
	Freshly ground black pepper
1	tsp chopped thyme
1	tsp chopped fresh basil
1	cup olive oil
1/4	cup seedless raisins, plumped in warm water 10-15 minutes and drained
1/4	cup pine nuts
3	red peppers, sliced thin

Nutrition **Note**

Biotin is a B vitamin that helps your health in all kinds of ways — especially if you're diabetic. Biotin helps digest fats and carbohydrates. It also displays insulin-like activity in lowering blood sugar. In various tests, blood sugar levels in diabetics were cut in half, while insulin levels stayed the same. To bite into more biotin, eat peanut butter, eggs, cereals, nuts, and legumes.

Quick Italian vegetable salad

Nutritional facts per serving: 227 calories; 22.2g carbohydrates; 0mg cholesterol; 14.6g total fat; 4.4g fiber; 4.5g protein; 189.7mg sodium

Whisk together oil, vinegar, oregano, basil, and garlic powder. Add salt and pepper to taste. Toss with vegetables, except lettuce.

Place Romaine lettuce on 4 salad plates or on one platter. Arrange vegetables on lettuce. Sprinkle with grated Parmesan cheese, if desired.

4 servings

1/4	cup olive oil
1/4	cup red wine vinegar
1	tsp dried oregano
1	tsp dried basil
1/2	tsp garlic powder
	Salt
	Black pepper
1/4	pound zucchini, sliced
1	small yellow bell pepper, sliced
4	green onions, chopped
1	pint cherry tomatoes, halved
1	small can chickpeas, drained and rinsed
1	small head Romaine lettuce, sliced
	Grated fresh Parmesan cheese (optional)

Nutrition **Note** Here's how you can feel just as full on fewer calories. Try eating more "low-density" foods, like produce, whole grains, and legumes, and cut down on "high-density" fatty, sugary foods. You'll feel just as full, but you'll save hundreds of calories.

Grated beet salad

Nutritional facts per serving: 128 calories; 4.1g carbohydrates; 0mg cholesterol; 12.2g total fat; 1.3g fiber; 1.8g protein; 167.3mg sodium

To make the dressing, combine vinegar, lemon juice, mustard, and oil, and whisk until creamy. Sprinkle parsley over, and mix lightly.

Pour the dressing over the beets, and season to taste with salt and pepper. Cover and refrigerate. When chilled, top with chives, and serve.

4 servings

2	tblsp wine vinegar
1	tblsp lemon juice
2	tblsp Dijon mustard
3	tblsp canola oil
1	tblsp finely chopped parsley
2	cups cooked or canned beets, grated
	Salt
	Freshly ground black pepper
2	tblsp chopped chives

Nutrition **Note** The next time you're craving a sugary treat, trounce high-fat temptation with the sweetness of beets. They have the highest sugar content of any vegetable. In fact, 40 percent of the world's refined sugar comes from beets. Yet, unlike sugary desserts, this brightly colored root is low in calories and high in nutrients. Beets are loaded with potassium, magnesium, beta carotene, and folate — a valuable B vitamin. It's fabulous nutrients like these that protect your heart and help prevent cancer. When it comes to a sugary treat that's healthy, beets are hard to beat.

Marinated vegetable medley

Nutritional facts per serving: 152 calories; 7.6g carbohydrates; 0mg cholesterol; 13.9g total fat; 1.6g fiber; 1.2g protein; 8.7mg sodium

Cut vegetables into your choice of shapes — wedges, slices, etc. Whisk together vinegar and oil. Add salt and pepper to taste. Add garlic. Toss with vegetables, place in a shallow dish, cover, and refrigerate for up to 6 hours.

When ready to serve, toss with basil. Serve as is or on a bed of lettuce.

4 servings

1	medium cucumber
1	small sweet onion
1	pint cherry tomatoes
1/4	cup cider vinegar
1/4	cup olive oil
	Salt
	Black pepper
2	garlic cloves, finely chopped
2	tblsp chopped fresh basil

Experiment with these easy ways to eat more fruits and vegetables.

- Make fancy, colorful sandwiches. Don't settle for just meat and bread anymore. Dress them up with lettuce, tomato, cucumbers, sliced carrots, and green or red peppers.

- Instead of high-calorie, high-fat desserts, branch out to fruit. Eat old favorites, but try new varieties, too.

- Keep a bag of dried fruits or fresh sliced veggies at hand for snacking throughout the day.

- Leave meat out of one meal twice a week and add more vegetables instead. If that doesn't appeal to you, try this. Add an extra serving of produce at each meal until you reach six a day.

Orange-mustard asparagus and veggies

Nutritional facts per serving: 69 calories; 12.4g carbohydrates; 0.2mg cholesterol; 1g total fat; 6.1g fiber; 7.1g protein; 214.9mg sodium

Blanch asparagus for 4 minutes and drain. Blanch broccoli for 2 minutes and drain. Toss together asparagus, broccoli, and red pepper. Set aside.

For the sauce, mix sugar, vinegar, cornstarch, beef stock, orange peel, orange juice, Dijon, mustard seeds, and 1 tsp Worcestershire sauce. Season to taste with salt and pepper. Add more Worcestershire, if desired. Simmer until thick and creamy, about 4 to 5 minutes.

Pour over vegetables and refrigerate for 2 hours before serving. Serve chilled or at room temperature.

4 servings

1	pound asparagus, peeled
1	cup broccoli florets
1	red bell pepper, thinly sliced
1	tsp sugar (optional)
1	tblsp red wine vinegar
1 1/2	tsp cornstarch
1/4	cup beef stock
	Grated peel and juice of 1 orange
1	tblsp Dijon mustard
1/2	cup mustard seeds
1-2	tsp Worcestershire sauce
	Salt
	Freshly ground black pepper

Use these tips to help you get the most value when you buy broccoli.

- When you buy expensive fresh vegetables, be sure you use every part you can. Broccoli stems can be peeled and cut into small strips, then cooked with the broccoli florets. Eat as is or puree in a blender to add to soup stock.

- If your recipe calls for just a few broccoli or cauliflower florets, buy them in the super-market salad bar. You won't have leftover parts that might go to waste, and you'll save preparation time as well.

Ribboned Oriental vegetable salad

Nutritional facts per serving: 68 calories; 12g carbohydrates; 0mg cholesterol; 1.9g total fat; 3.2g fiber; 2.1g protein; 57.9mg sodium

Mix zucchini, red onion, red bell pepper, green onions, carrots, and water chestnuts. Separately, whisk together the sesame seeds, sherry vinegar, soy sauce, sesame oil, sugar, and season to taste with salt and pepper. Pour over vegetables and toss gently. Let vegetables sit for at least 15 minutes and up to several hours before serving at room temperature.

6 servings

1	large zucchini, halved and cut into 3" matchsticks
1	red onion, thinly sliced
1	red bell pepper, thinly sliced
6	green onions, thinly sliced
2	large carrots, peeled and cut into ribbons
1	8-ounce can sliced water chestnuts, drained
2	tblsp sesame seeds
1/4	cup sherry vinegar or rice wine vinegar
1/4	cup soy sauce
1	tsp dark Oriental sesame oil
1-2	tblsp sugar (optional)
	Salt
	Freshly ground black pepper

Nutrition **Note** Disturbing new data suggests iodine deficiency is on the rise. Even though most Western countries add iodine to salt to prevent iodine deficiency, iodine intakes are dropping as people cut back on salt for health reasons. Instead of eating more salt, just make sure you use iodized salt when you do sprinkle it on. If you're on a no-salt diet, add iodine from whole foods. High-powered iodine sources include seafood, sea vegetables, low-fat dairy foods, and spinach.

Cool jicama-tomato salad

Nutritional facts per serving: 63 calories; 5.2g carbohydrates; 3mg cholesterol; 4.5g total fat; 1.8g fiber; 1.8g protein; 53.7mg sodium

Make a bed of red leaf lettuce on a large platter. Spread sliced red onions over the lettuce. Mound the cherry tomato halves over the onions, and sprinkle with jicama strips. Top with chopped cilantro and bacon, if desired.

To make the vinaigrette, whisk together garlic, mustard seeds, red wine vinegar, olive oil, and lime peel and juice. Season to taste with salt, pepper, and sugar, if needed. Pour over the salad, and serve immediately.

8 servings

8   red leaf lettuce leaves

1   red onion, thinly sliced

3   cups halved cherry tomatoes

1   jicama, peeled and cut into matchstick strips

2   tblsp chopped fresh cilantro

3   slices turkey bacon, fried, drained, and crumbled (optional)

2   garlic cloves, chopped

1   tsp mustard seeds

2   tblsp red wine vinegar

2   tblsp olive oil

Grated peel and juice of 1 lime

Salt

Freshly ground black pepper

Sugar

Nutrition **Note**   The yummy jicama, pronounced HEE-kama, may look like a potato or a turnip, but it's mildly sweet and slightly crunchy.

A single medium jicama gives you 49 percent of your recommended dietary allowance (RDA) for iron, 21 percent of your potassium RDA and over 100 percent of the vitamin C you need each day.

Chilled asparagus with spicy Oriental sauce

Nutritional facts per serving: 86 calories; 5.7g carbohydrates; 0mg cholesterol; 6.9g total fat; 1.1g fiber; 1.6g protein; 457mg sodium

In a small bowl, combine green onions, soy sauce, rice wine vinegar, sesame oil, olive oil, garlic, sugar, chili oil, and red pepper flakes, Mix thoroughly, chill, and pour over the cooked and chilled asparagus just before serving.

6 servings

3	green onions, chopped
3	tblsp soy sauce
2	tblsp rice wine vinegar
2	tblsp sesame oil
1	tblsp olive oil
4	garlic cloves, chopped
1	tblsp sugar
1/4	tsp chili oil
1/2	tsp dried red pepper flakes
2	pounds asparagus, peeled and blanched

Nutrition **Note**

You look forward to your favorite delicious spicy dinner, but that meal always causes heartburn to blaze. Try drinking a cool glass of water about an hour before that spicy meal. After all, you get heartburn when the acid in your stomach backs up into your esophagus and irritates it. Water helps wash the acid out, giving your stomach a fighting chance to do its job properly. Drinking water an hour before a meal — or an hour after — can help keep your stomach from bloating. And that may help prevent the acid overflow that results in heartburn. Besides, drinking water can also help antacids and other medicines do their jobs faster and more efficiently.

Red rice salad on cabbage leaves

Nutritional facts per serving: 341 calories; 47.4g carbohydrates; 0mg cholesterol; 14.7g total fat; 2.8g fiber; 5.9g protein; 37.3mg sodium

Combine rice, tomato juice, and broth. Bring to a boil, reduce to a simmer, and cook until rice is tender. Drain in colander.

Whisk together oil, vinegar, and tomato paste. Season with salt and pepper to taste. Toss rice with enough to coat. Core, seed, and chop tomato. Add vegetables and toss. Season with salt and pepper as needed.

Serve at room temperature or cold on cabbage leaves.

4 servings

1	cup raw converted rice
1	cup low-sodium tomato juice
1	cup low-sodium chicken broth
1/4	cup canola oil
1/4	cup cider vinegar
1	tblsp tomato paste
	Salt
	Black pepper
1	ripe tomato
1	small green pepper, chopped
4	green onions, chopped
	Outer green leaves of a cabbage (optional)

Nutrition **Note**   Try these ideas and you may be surprised at how easily you add more fruits and vegetables to your diet.

- Put spinach on your sandwich instead of lettuce. A study found that people couldn't tell the difference, and spinach is more nutritious.

- Restaurants often pretty up your plate with parsley or kale. Eat these garnishes right along with your meal.

- Instead of butter or sour cream, top that baked potato with salsa.

Zesty coleslaw

Nutritional facts per serving: 137 calories; 29.5g carbohydrates; 4.1mg cholesterol; 1.8g total fat; 6.6g fiber; 4.6g protein; 300.8mg sodium

In a large bowl combine cabbage, carrots, onion, cucumber, radishes, parsley, dill, and cilantro.

Whisk together mayonnaise, yogurt, honey and vinegar. Slowly pour over slaw, tossing until it is coated to your taste. Season with salt and pepper. Cover and refrigerate for up to 2 hours.

4 servings

1	small head green cabbage, finely sliced
1	medium carrot, peeled and grated
1	small red onion, grated
1	small cucumber, unpeeled, finely sliced
4	red radishes, grated
1/3	cup finely chopped parsley
1 1/2	tblsp finely chopped fresh dill or 3/4 tsp dill weed
1 1/2	tblsp finely chopped fresh cilantro
1/2	cup fat-free mayonnaise
1/2	cup low-fat plain yogurt
2	tblsp honey
2	tblsp apple cider vinegar
	Salt
	Freshly ground black pepper

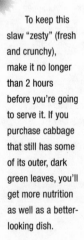

To keep this slaw "zesty" (fresh and crunchy), make it no longer than 2 hours before you're going to serve it. If you purchase cabbage that still has some of its outer, dark green leaves, you'll get more nutrition as well as a better-looking dish.

Crunchy rainbow slaw with pecan topping

Nutritional facts per serving: 306 calories; 20.5g carbohydrates; 0mg cholesterol; 25.4g total fat; 7.2g fiber; 4.1g protein; 39.2mg sodium

To make the dressing, whisk together oil, balsamic vinegar, and cider vinegar. Add salt and pepper to taste.

Toss cabbage, celery, and apple, slowly adding the dressing. You may not need all of it. Drain off any extra if you put too much. Sprinkle with pecans and serve.

2 servings

2	tblsp canola oil
1	tblsp balsamic vinegar
1	tblsp cider vinegar
	Salt
	Freshly ground black pepper
1	small green cabbage, thinly sliced
4	ribs celery, thinly sliced
1	Granny Smith apple, unpeeled, finely chopped
1/2	cup toasted pecan pieces

Remember these tips to help make this recipe easier and even better.

- Don't be tempted to grab just any old variety of apple. Granny Smith apples work best for uncooked dishes because their high citric acid content keeps them from browning quickly.

- When time is short, speed up your slaw-making by buying packages of prechopped or sliced cabbage available at the grocery store.

- For the crunchiest cabbage salads — like cole slaw — soak wedges of cabbage in salted ice water for an hour. Drain well and continue with your recipe.

Make-ahead overnight slaw

Nutritional facts per serving: 167 calories; 16.5g carbohydrates; 0mg cholesterol; 11.2g total fat; 5.7g fiber; 3.5g protein; 472.2mg sodium

Place cabbage in a large bowl. Cover with layers of onion, then peppers, then celery. Sprinkle sugar to cover entire top.

Combine oil, vinegar, mustard, celery seed, salt, and pepper in a small saucepan, and bring to a boil. Pour over cabbage mixture. Do not stir. Cover and refrigerate overnight.

When ready to serve, toss all ingredients in the bowl. Add parsley and toss to combine. Check salt and pepper and season more if needed. Drain well and serve.

4 servings

1	small head green cabbage, grated
1/2	large yellow onion, grated
1/2	large green bell pepper, chopped
1 1/2	ribs celery, diced
2 1/2	tblsp sugar (optional)
3	tblsp canola oil
1/4	cup cider vinegar
1/2	tsp Dijon mustard
1/2	tsp celery seed
3/4	tsp salt
1/2	tsp black pepper
1/2	cup finely chopped fresh parsley

Unlike the usual mayonnaise-dressed slaw, you can make this recipe the day before you serve it.

Mixed veggie coleslaw with boiled dressing

Nutritional facts per serving: 44 calories; 10g carbohydrates; 0mg cholesterol; 0.4g total fat; 3.1g fiber; 1.8g protein; 27.3mg sodium

In a food processor or by hand, shred cabbage, onion, and carrot. Place vegetables in a glass bowl or crock with a tight fitting lid. Sprinkle with 2 tablespoons of the sugar and the celery seeds.

In a small saucepan, bring salt, dry mustard, oil, vinegar, and 1 tablespoon of the optional sugar to a boil. Lower the heat and simmer for a minute or so, whisking occasionally. Remove from heat, and pour dressing over vegetables.

1	small head green cabbage
1	half onion, peeled
1	half carrot, peeled
3	tblsp sugar (optional)
1/4	tsp celery seeds
	Salt
1/4	tsp dry mustard
2	ounces canola oil
2	ounces white vinegar

Toss lightly and let stand, covered, for at least 4 hours, then refrigerate. Toss again before serving.

4 servings

Remember these tips anytime you decide that salad seems right for tonight.

- If you're tired of your oil and vinegar dressing separating, add a bit of dry mustard or paprika to your recipe. This helps slow down separation.

- Don't toss out that almost-empty ketchup bottle. Pour in a little salad oil and your favorite vinegar, and give it a shake. You'll have a great homemade salad dressing.

Traditional nicoise salad

Nutritional facts per serving: 251 calories; 5.2g carbohydrates; 13.2mg cholesterol; 20.6g total fat; 1.2g fiber; 12.3g protein; 175.6mg sodium

Break up tuna and spread on the bottom of a bowl, top with green beans, sprinkle with some of the optional herbs, then the cucumber.

Whisk mustard, vinegar, and olive oil together to make the dressing. Drizzle some of the salad dressing over the cucumber layer.

If desired, make a lattice of the anchovies, and put the olives in the lattice diamonds. Rim the salad with tomato quarters, rounded sides up. Brush tomatoes with the dressing, and spoon the remaining dressing over the entire salad. Garnish with more of the herbs, if desired.

4 servings

6	ounces canned tuna packed in water
1/2	pound cooked green beans or peas
	Chopped mixed herbs (optional)
1	cucumber, sliced 1/8" thick
1	tblsp Dijon mustard
2	tblsp vinegar
5	tblsp olive oil
	Salt
	Freshly ground black pepper
	Anchovies, drained (optional)
	Black olives (optional)
1	pound tomatoes, quartered

Nutrition **Note**

As the years pass, you may notice your senses of taste and smell seem to be fading. If your lost sense of smell persists for longer than two weeks, talk to your doctor. But if she says it's just part of growing older, help perk up those slumped senses by adding more seasoning to your food. Good choices include allspice, cinnamon, vanilla extract, ginger, thyme, oregano, paprika, basil, pepper (black and red), and dill. You can also try garlic, onions, vinegar, Worcestershire sauce, and lemon.

Green beans with orange vinaigrette

Nutritional facts per serving: 278 calories; 6.3g carbohydrates; 0mg cholesterol; 28.3g total fat; 2.3g fiber; 1.5g protein; 91.5mg sodium

Cook green beans quickly in boiling water until just barely tender, 7 to 10 minutes. Drain and rinse with cold water to refresh. May be cooked in advance and refrigerated.

Puree orange juice, grated peel, red pepper, green onion, garlic, mustard, and vinegar in a food processor until smooth. With the processor running, add oil in a thin, steady stream until dressing is thick and emulsified. Season to taste with salt, pepper, and sugar. Serve warm or at room temperature.

4 servings

1	pound green beans, ends removed
1	ounce orange juice
	Grated peel of 1 navel orange
1/2	red bell pepper, roasted, peeled, and seeded
2	green onions
1	garlic clove
2	tblsp coarse-grained Dijon mustard
1	ounce red wine vinegar
1/2	cup peanut oil
	Salt
	Freshly ground black pepper
	Sugar (optional)

If you're willing to clip, collect, and sort, many claim you can save as much as $2,000 a year on groceries. Just think, even if you only spend $100 a week, it's possible to shave 15 percent off your yearly grocery bill simply by clipping coupons. To make the most of coupon shopping, make a list, organize your coupons, read the fine print, watch out for expiration dates, and never buy something simply because you have a coupon for it.

New potatoes and green beans in vinaigrette

Nutritional facts per serving: 283 calories; 10g carbohydrates; 0mg cholesterol; 27.1g total fat; 4.2g fiber; 2.7g protein; 21.6mg sodium

Boil beans in salted water until still crunchy, 7-10 minutes. Remove from heat, drain, and immediately rinse with cold water to stop the cooking and set the color. Meanwhile, boil whole, unpeeled new potatoes in salted water until done, 20-30 minutes. Drain.

Make vinaigrette by whisking oil into the vinegar, mustard, and garlic. Add salt and pepper to taste. While the potatoes are still hot, peel quickly and toss them in half the vinaigrette, adding the herbs if you wish.

1/2	pound green beans, ends removed
1	pound new potatoes
1/4	cup white or red wine vinegar
1/2	cup olive oil
1	tsp Dijon mustard
1	garlic clove, crushed
	Salt
	Freshly ground black pepper
	Chopped fresh herbs such as basil or tarragon (optional)

If serving warm, stir green beans with 2 tablespoons of vinaigrette in a saucepan, and warm gently before adding to the potatoes. If serving cold, simply toss cooked beans with 2 table-spoons of dressing, and gently mix with the potatoes. Drizzle the dressing as desired, and serve lukewarm or cold.

Be sure your vegetables are hot when tossed in the vinaigrette. Hot vegetables absorb flavor quickly, so when they have cooled the flavor is even more enhanced.

4 servings

Snappy bean salad

Nutritional facts per serving: 119 calories; 19.4g carbohydrates; 10mg cholesterol; 2.8g total fat; 7.3g fiber; 5.6g protein; 343.7mg sodium

Blanch beans in a large pot of boiling water for 8 minutes. Drain, refresh under cold water, and drain again.

In a large bowl, toss together green beans, cherry tomatoes, kidney beans, black olives, jalapeño pepper, ginger, and dill.

Whisk together mustard, balsamic vinegar, and olive oil. Season to taste with salt, pepper, and sugar. Mix with the vegetables, and let marinate in the refrigerator for at least 2 hours before serving. Toss gently just before serving.

6 servings

2   cups green beans, ends removed

2   cups halved or quartered cherry tomatoes

1   15-ounce can kidney beans, rinsed and drained

1/2 cup sliced black olives

1   jalapeño pepper, chopped

1   tblsp chopped fresh ginger

2   tblsp chopped fresh dill

2   tsp Dijon mustard

1/4 cup balsamic vinegar

1   tblsp olive oil

Salt

Freshly ground black pepper

Sugar

Nutrition **Note** A new study from the USDA claims red kidney beans are a leading source of antioxidants — disease-fighting defenders of your health. These fiber-rich beans even contain phytoestrogens — special plant chemicals that may help you fight the symptoms of menopause. Just be sure to soak the raw beans at least five hours and boil them for a minimum of 10 minutes, so you can be sure they're safe to eat.

Summer red, white, and green salad

Nutritional facts per serving: 156 calories; 14.9g carbohydrates; 0mg cholesterol; 10.5g total fat; 5.4g fiber; 3.1g protein; 46.6mg sodium

Bring a saucepan of water to a boil over medium-high heat. Add green beans, reduce heat to Medium, and simmer until just tender, about 4 to 5 minutes, depending on the size of the green bean. Drain and run under cold water to stop further cooking. Drain well and place on paper towels to dry. They may be wrapped in plastic wrap and refrigerated for up to 24 hours.

When ready to serve, combine green beans, onion, and tomatoes. Whisk together the oil, vinegar, mustard, and salt and pepper to taste. Add to the vegetables and toss. Add parsley and toss. Put in a serving bowl, or arrange on a platter, and serve.

1/2   pound green beans, ends removed

1/2   sweet onion, thinly sliced

1   large, vine-ripened tomato, seeded and chopped

1 1/2   tblsp olive oil

1 1/2   tsp red wine vinegar

1/2   tsp Dijon mustard

Salt

Freshly ground black pepper

3   tblsp chopped parsley

2 servings

Try making this salad as soon as the new Vidalia onions and local tomatoes come in at the farmers' market. You won't regret it. If you can't find a Vidalia onion, substitute any other sweet onion. To spruce up this dish for parties or entertaining, toss the vegetables separately in the dressing, and arrange them in rows or circles.

Triple greens and grapefruit salad

Nutritional facts per serving: 347 calories; 15.2g carbohydrates; 0mg cholesterol; 31.9g total fat; 6.8g fiber; 4g protein; 226mg sodium

Toss together the greens, radicchio, endive, onion, basil, and grapefruit segments. Separately, whisk together the mustard, vinegar, lime juice, olive oil, sugar, salt and pepper to taste, and pine nuts. Just before serving, toss the greens with the dressing.

4 servings

4	cups torn salad greens
1	head radicchio, separated into leaves
1	head Belgian endive, separated into leaves
1/2	red onion, thinly sliced
1	tblsp chopped fresh basil
1	pink grapefruit, peeled and cut into segments
2	tblsp Dijon mustard
1/3	cup red wine vinegar
2	tablespoons lime juice
1/2	cup olive oil
1	tblsp sugar (optional)
	Salt
	Freshly ground black pepper
2	tblsp lightly toasted pine nuts

Nutrition **Note** Any time your doctor prescribes a new medication, ask whether you can still eat grapefruit. Grapefruit juice can affect the way your body handles certain drugs. Sometimes it blocks absorption, and other times it makes your body absorb the drug faster. Even medications you already take could be affected by grapefruit, so ask your doctor about them, too.

Fruity spinach walnut salad

Nutritional facts per serving: 343 calories; 28g carbohydrates; 0mg cholesterol; 25.5g total fat; 4.9g fiber; 5g protein; 306.2mg sodium

Combine spinach, oranges, strawberries, mushrooms, and walnuts in a large bowl. Place all dressing ingredients except oil in a blender or food processor. While blending, add the oil in a slow steady stream until the dressing is mixed thoroughly and slightly thick. Pour over salad.

4 servings

3	cups fresh spinach, washed and torn into small pieces
2	medium oranges, peeled, sectioned, and cut into chunks
1	cup sliced fresh strawberries
1	cup sliced fresh mushrooms
1/2	cup walnut pieces
1/4	cup sugar
1	tblsp sesame seeds
1/2	tsp poppy seeds
1/2	tblsp minced onion
1/8	tsp Worcestershire sauce
1/2	tsp salt
1/2	tsp dry mustard
1/8	tsp paprika
1/4	cup red wine vinegar
1/4	cup vegetable oil

Nutrition **Note**

Eating foods rich in antioxidants and omega-3 fatty acids may be the best nutritional decision you can make to prevent the devastating effects of Alzheimer's disease. Apples, oranges, strawberries, blueberries, spinach, and walnuts are all good choices.

Citrus-stuffed avocado salad

Nutritional facts per serving: 224 calories; 23.5g carbohydrates; 0mg cholesterol; 15.6g total fat; 6.5g fiber; 2.7g protein; 10.6mg sodium

Combine fruit chunks in a bowl. Mix lemon juice with the honey, and pour over the fruit. Stir gently and allow to marinate for 1 hour. Just before serving, peel and halve the avocados, removing the pit. Brush the cut surface with additional lemon juice. Fill the avocado cavities with fruit mixture.

6 servings

1 cup orange sections, cut into chunks

1 cup grapefruit sections, cut into chunks

1 cup pineapple wedges

2 tblsp lemon juice

2 tblsp honey

3 ripe avocados

Lemon juice

Nutrition **Note**

Avocados are rich in folate, one of the very important, water-soluble B vitamins. Since folate is not stored in your body, but either used or flushed out through your kidneys, you don't have to worry about overloading on it, but you do need to replace it often. Folate fights both high blood pressure and Alzheimer's disease by neutralizing homocysteine, a destructive amino acid. It is also essential for making DNA. Without it, you could end up with broken chromosomes, one risk factor for cancer. No wonder a folate deficiency seems to increase your risk of breast and colon cancers. Folate is mostly destroyed during cooking or processing, so eating raw folate-rich foods — like avocados — provides the healthiest dose.

Sunny navel orange and red onion salad

Nutritional facts per serving: 183 calories; 15.7g carbohydrates; 0mg cholesterol; 13.7g total fat; 3.4g fiber; 2g protein; 4.5mg sodium

3	tblsp red wine vinegar
4	tblsp olive oil
	Salt
	Freshly ground black pepper
1	garlic clove
4	seedless oranges
1	small red onion, thinly sliced
1	large head Boston lettuce

Whisk together vinegar and oil. Add salt and pepper to taste. Mash the garlic clove slightly to release its flavor, and add to the oil-vinegar mixture.

Peel the oranges and slice them in rounds. Layer the sliced oranges and onion slices in a glass or ceramic bowl. Pour the dressing over them, cover, and refrigerate for at least 3 hours, or overnight.

Separate the leaves of lettuce. Wash, pat dry, and refrigerate in a plastic bag to crisp.

When ready to serve, drain the oranges and onions, but reserve dressing. Taste the dressing because the sweetness of the oranges usually changes the need for seasoning. Add salt and pepper to taste.

Make 4 lettuce cups on a platter or individual salad plates. Divide the oranges and onions between them, sprinkle with more dressing if desired, and serve.

4 servings

Nutrition **Note**

Discover a little-known plant nutrient called beta cryptoxanthin, and you may help lower your chances of developing painful osteoarthritis. Get this powerful antioxidant from orange and green veggies, where it gangs up with fellow antioxidants lutein and zeaxanthin to shrivel your osteoarthritis odds.

Succulent strawberries with balsamic vinegar

Nutritional facts per serving: 82 calories; 20.3g carbohydrates; 0mg cholesterol; 0.5g total fat; 3.3g fiber; 0.9g protein; 5.5mg sodium

Wash strawberries with their green caps still on, and dry on paper towels. You can do that several hours ahead, put them in a bowl, cover, and refrigerate. Thirty minutes before serving, remove green caps from strawberries. If the berries are large, slice in half. Toss with vinegar and pepper. Add sugar to taste.

1	quart ripe strawberries
2 1/4	tsp balsamic vinegar
1 1/8	tsp freshly ground black pepper
3	tblsp light brown sugar

Divide berries between 4 serving bowls, cover with plastic wrap, and leave out at room temperature for 30 minutes. Toss gently just before serving.

4 servings

Nutrition **Note**
Strawberries are a top-notch cancer fighter. Research proves that strawberries act as antioxidants and cut down on free radical harm. They reduce the damage wreaked by cancer-causing substances and hinder the development of tumors. Strawberries owe much of this power to ellagic acid, a natural plant chemical that's in only a handful of fruits. But that's not all. Berries contain many potential protectors like vitamins C and E, folic acid, various carotenoids, and anthocyanins. All of these substances work together to help fight cancer.

Mellow peach and melon salad

Nutritional facts per serving: 118 calories; 21.7g carbohydrates; 0mg cholesterol; 3.5g total fat; 3.3g fiber; 3.1g protein; 14.5mg sodium

Combine peaches, orange juice, orange peel, and sugar, if using. Chill for at least 30 minutes. Combine the melon and mint with the peaches, and toss lightly.

To toast almonds, spread on a metal baking sheet, and bake in a 300-degree oven for 10 minutes, tossing once or twice, until golden. Sprinkle the toasted almonds on the fruit, and serve immediately.

4 servings

2 large peaches, peeled, pitted, and sliced

Peel of 1 orange, cut into thin strips

Juice of 1 orange

1 tsp sugar (optional)

1 cantaloupe, cubed

3 tblsp chopped fresh mint

2 ounces sliced toasted almonds

Nutrition **Note** — Watch out for mold in your home. It can quadruple your risk of getting rheumatoid arthritis. What's more, mold and mildew may trigger inflammation in your respiratory system, leaving you more vulnerable to colds. The biggest risks are the patches of fungus you can actually see. Not only will they put you in danger of getting more viral infections, but they also weaken your resistance to bronchitis, pneumonia, and allergies. To help prevent mold, keep your windows closed and use an air conditioner — and perhaps even a dehumidifier — to keep the temperature under 70 degrees Fahrenheit and the humidity at less than 50 percent.

Summer-fresh tomato-basil vinaigrette

Nutritional facts per serving: 137 calories; 3.9g carbohydrates; 0mg cholesterol; 13.8g total fat; 0.9g fiber; 0.7g protein; 6.6mg sodium

---

Process the tomato, olive oil, garlic, and shallots in a food processor or blender. Add basil and process just enough to cut it into tiny pieces. The dressing will not be completely smooth but should have a little texture. Season to taste with salt and pepper.

4 servings

1 large ripe tomato, peeled, cored, and seeded

1/4 cup olive oil

1 garlic clove, finely chopped

2 tsp chopped shallots

6 tblsp chopped fresh basil

Salt

Freshly ground black pepper

Nutrition **Note**

Don't skip your pills because they're tough to get down. Try these helpful tips to help you swallow pills more easily.

- Chew some food, then place the pill in your mouth with the food, and swallow — or take the pill in a spoonful of applesauce.

- Drink some water to wet your throat, place the pill on the back of your tongue, and take several more swallows of water.

- Resist the temptation to tilt your head back when swallowing. Instead, bring your head forward so your chin nearly touches your chest.

Golden honey-mustard dressing

Nutritional facts per serving: 133 calories; 3.8g carbohydrates; 0mg cholesterol; 13.6g total fat; 0.1g fiber; 0.2g protein; 24.7mg sodium

Combine all ingredients in a jar with a tight-fitting lid. Close and shake well. Refrigerate. Makes about 1 cup dressing.

8 2-tablespoon servings

1	garlic clove, finely minced
1	tblsp Dijon mustard
1	tblsp honey
1/4	cup balsamic vinegar
	Juice of 1/2 lemon
1/2	cup extra-virgin olive oil
1	tsp tarragon

Don't be fooled by reduced fat salad dressings. They can still be packed with calories — many from hidden sugars. For the best low-fat, low-calorie eating, make your own salad dressing with more vinegar and less oil. Choose flavored vinegars or lemon juice for added zing. Sprinkle herbs and spices on your "rabbit food" for extra zest. Try oregano, basil, ginger, mint, or dill. And finally, go wild with healthy dressing ingredients that offer a lot of taste — like honey, spicy mustard, or fruited yogurt.

Stuffed chicken with apricots and pine nuts

Nutritional facts per serving: 471 calories; 43.4g carbohydrates; 68.4mg cholesterol; 18.9g total fat; 4.6g fiber; 36.8g protein; 82.7mg sodium

Preheat oven to 375 degrees.

Mix together garlic, apricots, almond-water mixture, nuts, and spices in a small bowl. Set aside.

Butterfly each chicken breast (slice 3/4 of the way through horizontally so you can open it up and lay flat). Place a heaping spoonful of the apricot mixture on each breast and fold to close. Secure edges with toothpicks if you wish. Place chicken breasts in a greased, ovenproof dish. Add honey to the remaining apricot mixture, and pour over chicken. Bake for 45 minutes.

2 boneless chicken breasts

2 garlic cloves, crushed

1/2 cup chopped, dried apricots

1/4 tsp almond extract mixed with 2 1/2 tsp water

1/2 cup pine nuts, chopped

Pinch Chinese 5 spice powder

Pinch turmeric

2 tblsp honey

2 servings

Nutrition **Note**   This one sweet little fruit is loaded with as many nutrients as you'll find in your multivitamin — beta carotene, iron, fiber, vitamin C, several B vitamins, lycopene, potassium, magnesium, and copper. That makes apricots the nutrient super-hero of the produce aisle. Eat them often to battle cancer, high blood pressure, memory loss, and cataracts. You'll get even more nutrient power concentrated in dried apricots and can also enjoy them out of season in jams, spreads, and nectars.

Cheesy chicken divan

Nutritional facts per serving: 365 calories; 13.9g carbohydrates; 114.6mg cholesterol; 17.5g total fat; 0.4g fiber; 36.4g protein; 265.9mg sodium

---

Preheat oven to 375 degrees.

Blanch broccoli florets in boiling, salted water until just tender, about 2 minutes. Drain. Dry on paper towels. Sprinkle lightly with salt and pepper.

Take the meat off the chicken, and chop into generous bite-size pieces. In a medium saucepan, heat butter. Whisk in flour. Gradually whisk in milk and cook, stirring continuously, until thickened. Whisk in nutmeg and cayenne pepper. Stir in cheddar cheese until melted. Add more milk if sauce is too thick. Season to taste with salt and pepper.

Place broccoli in a baking dish. Pour half the sauce over it. Top with the chicken, then the remaining half of the sauce.

1	head broccoli, cut into florets
	Salt
	Freshly ground black pepper
1	3 1/2- to 4-pound whole roasted chicken
2	tblsp butter
3	tblsp flour
2	cups whole milk
1/4	tsp nutmeg
1/4	tsp cayenne pepper
4	ounces white cheddar cheese, shredded
1/4	cup toasted bread crumbs
1/4	cup freshly grated Parmesan cheese

Mix bread crumbs and Parmesan cheese together, and sprinkle over the top. Bake for 20 minutes, or until crumbs are golden brown, and dish is hot through.

4 servings

Never serve dry chicken again. Simply stuff a whole apple inside the chicken, then roast as usual. Throw away the apple, and serve your moist and tender chicken with pride.

Delightful chicken parmigiana

Nutritional facts per serving: 412 calories; 31.1g carbohydrates; 81.1mg cholesterol; 14.9g total fat; 2.5g fiber; 37.6g protein; 1127mg sodium

Preheat oven to 375 degrees.

Place chicken breasts between 2 sheets of plastic wrap, and pound them to 1/2" thickness.

Whisk together the egg and water, and place in a shallow dish. Place the flour in another shallow dish. In a third shallow dish, combine bread crumbs with 1/2 teaspoon of the basil, oregano, pepper, and Parmesan cheese.

Dredge breasts in the flour. Dip them in the egg mixture, turning to coat all sides. Then coat them with the breadcrumbs. Let sit on a wire rack for 15 minutes.

Heat olive oil in a large skillet over medium-high heat. Sauté the breasts for about 2 minutes on each side, or until golden brown. Transfer them to a shallow baking dish.

4	4-ounce boneless, skinless chicken breasts
1	egg, lightly beaten
1	tblsp water
1/2	cup all-purpose flour
1/2	cup dried bread crumbs
2	tblsp plus 1/2 tsp chopped fresh basil
1/4	tsp dried oregano
1/4	tsp black pepper
1/4	cup grated fresh Parmesan cheese
2	tblsp olive oil
1	15-ounce can tomato sauce
2	cloves garlic, finely chopped
2	tblsp chopped fresh parsley
2	ounces Provolone cheese, grated

In a medium bowl, whisk together the tomato sauce, garlic, the remaining 2 tablespoons of basil, and the parsley. Pour over the chicken. Top each with grated Provolone. Bake until chicken is cooked through, and cheese is bubbling and brown, about 15 minutes.

4 servings

Chicken florentine stir-fry

Nutritional facts per serving: 262 calories; 10.1g carbohydrates; 73.7mg cholesterol; 10.6g total fat; 4.2g fiber; 32.7g protein; 251.2mg sodium

Heat oil in a large frying pan. Add garlic, stirring to spread evenly. Add chicken and cook about 5 minutes, stirring occasionally, or until done. Remove chicken and garlic, and set aside.

Wipe mushroom caps clean with a wet towel. Discard stems. Cut caps into slices. Add mushrooms, onions, and pepper to pan, and cook, stirring occasionally, until tender. Add more olive oil if needed.

Add the spinach and cook, stirring with other vegetables, about 2 minutes more, or until wilted. Add the garlic and chicken, and stir to mix well. Cook just long enough to heat through. Sprinkle with salt and pepper to taste. Remove to a serving dish, and sprinkle with cheese.

2	tblsp olive oil
4	garlic cloves, thinly sliced
4	4-ounce boneless, skinless chicken breasts, cut into slices
2	shiitake mushroom caps
1	medium onion, sliced
1	small red bell pepper, sliced
2	bunches fresh baby spinach
	Salt
	Freshly ground pepper
3	tblsp grated Romano cheese

4 servings

Nutrition **Note** You want to lower your risk of heart attack, but you cherish the taste and texture of cheese. Instead of giving up cheese completely, either try low-fat cheese or switch to Parmesan or Romano. While they have as much fat as other cheeses, they're more flavorful so you can use less. Limit yourself to no more than 2 ounces of regular cheese a week, and you'll limit your risk for a heart attack, too.

Chicken, mushroom, and wild rice casserole

Nutritional facts per serving: 306 calories; 32.5g carbohydrates; 58.4mg cholesterol; 10.4g total fat; 3g fiber; 21.7g protein; 95.3mg sodium

Preheat oven to 350 degrees.

Take the meat off the chicken, and chop into generous bite-size pieces.

Rinse wild rice under cold water. Bring chicken broth to a boil. Add wild rice and simmer for 30 minutes, or until tender. Drain, but reserve broth.

Heat butter in a large frying pan over medium heat. Add onions, bell pepper, and mushrooms and sauté, stirring occasionally, for about 5 minutes, or until tender. Remove vegetables and set aside.

Whisk flour into the remaining butter. Add more broth or water if necessary to the reserved chicken broth to make 2 cups. Whisk this into the flour. Add thyme, oregano, Worcestershire, Tabasco, and salt and pepper to taste. Simmer uncovered for 10 to 15 minutes, or until it thickens to sauce consistency.

1	3-pound whole roasted chicken
3	cups low-sodium chicken broth
1 1/2	cups uncooked long-grain wild rice
4	tblsp butter
1	small onion, chopped
1	small red bell pepper, chopped
1/4	pound shiitake mushroom caps, wiped clean and sliced
4	tblsp all-purpose flour
1/2	tsp dried thyme
3/4	tsp dried oregano
1	tblsp Worcestershire sauce
1/4	tsp Tabasco
	Salt
	Black pepper

Mix the chicken, rice, and vegetables together. Add as much sauce as desired, and place everything in a baking dish. Cover and bake for 20 minutes, or until hot though.

4 servings

Zippy chicken pilau

Nutritional facts per serving: 433 calories; 41.7g carbohydrates; 97.3mg cholesterol; 12.8g total fat; 1.2g fiber; 35.2g protein; 426.5mg sodium

Take the meat off the chicken, and chop into bite-size pieces.

Heat butter in a large Dutch oven over medium-high heat. Add onions and garlic, and sauté for about 5 minutes, or until tender. Add rice and celery, stirring until rice is light brown, about 6 minutes. Stir in salt and pepper, Worcestershire sauce, and Tabasco. Add chicken broth, and bring to a boil. Cover, reduce heat to Low, and cook until rice is done, about 30 minutes (do not remove cover during cooking time). Stir in chicken, cover, turn off heat, and let sit for 5 minutes, or until chicken is hot through.

4 servings

1	3 1/2- to 4-pound whole roasted chicken
1 1/2	tblsp butter
1/2	medium onion, chopped
1	clove garlic, chopped
1	cup raw converted rice
1/4	cup chopped celery
1/2	tsp salt
1/4	tsp pepper
1/2	tsp Worcestershire sauce
	Dash Tabasco
2 1/2	cups low-sodium chicken broth

To cut your risk of food poisoning, thaw chicken in the refrigerator, in cold water, or in the microwave. You can thaw a 4-pound chicken in the refrigerator in about 24 hours, but thawing cut-up parts only takes 3 to 9 hours. Thawing in cold water is even quicker. Place the chicken in its original wrap — or a water-tight plastic bag — in cold water. Change water often. Thawing the whole chicken takes about 2 hours. For speedy thawing of raw or cooked chicken use the microwave. Thawing time will vary.

Crispy stuffed chicken breast

Nutritional facts per serving: 332 calories; 1.7g carbohydrates; 116.4mg cholesterol; 16.3g total fat; 0.1g fiber; 42.5g protein; 1119mg sodium

Preheat oven to 400 degrees. Set a rack on a baking sheet, and spray it with nonstick cooking spray.

Separate the skin from the meat on the side of each chicken breast to create a pocket. Into each pocket, press two basil leaves, a slice of Provolone, and a slice of turkey bacon (folded in half to fit if necessary). Tuck the ends of the breast in to make the breasts round up.

Lightly beat egg whites. Add garlic salt, salt, and pepper. Combine bread crumbs with basil, oregano, cheese, and pine nuts, if using. Dip breasts in egg whites, turning to coat all sides, then coat with breadcrumbs. Let them sit on a wire rack for 15 minutes.

Bake breasts for 25 minutes or until crumbs are golden brown, and chicken is cooked all the way through. Serve immediately with fresh lemon wedges.

4 servings

4	4-ounce boneless chicken breasts with skin on
12	leaves fresh basil
4	slices Provolone cheese
4	slices cooked turkey bacon
2	egg whites, lightly beaten
1/4	tsp garlic salt
1/4	tsp salt
1/4	tsp freshly ground black pepper
1	cup bread crumbs
1/2	tsp chopped fresh basil
1/4	tsp dried oregano
1/4	cup grated Parmesan cheese
1/4	cup pine nuts, finely chopped (optional)
	Lemon wedges

This recipe works well with a fresh light tomato sauce (see page 319).

Spiced chicken piquant

Nutritional facts per serving: 254 calories; 8.4g carbohydrates; 66.3mg cholesterol; 12.1g total fat; 1.6g fiber; 28.2g protein; 163.3mg sodium

Mix olive oil, oregano, salt, and pepper together in a shallow dish or bowl. Add chicken, toss, cover, and refrigerate 8 hours or overnight, turning once.

Preheat oven to 325 degrees. Spray a nonstick frying pan with nonstick vegetable spray.

Sauté chicken breasts over medium-high heat just until lightly golden. Remove breasts from pan, and place in a casserole dish large enough to hold them in one layer. Lightly cover with aluminum foil, and bake for 6 minutes, or until cooked through.

Add onions and garlic to the frying pan, and cook over medium-high heat until just tender, about 2 minutes. Add red wine vinegar, and briskly simmer until the liquid has almost evaporated, about 2 minutes.

Add chicken broth, tomatoes, tarragon, and Tabasco, and simmer for 2 minutes. Dissolve cornstarch in water, and add. Bring to a boil. Season with salt and pepper to taste. Pour sauce over the baked chicken, sprinkle with chives and parsley, and serve immediately.

4 servings

3	tblsp olive oil
1/4	tsp dried oregano
1/8	tsp salt
1/4	tsp freshly ground black pepper
4	4-ounce boneless, skinless chicken breasts
1/2	small yellow onion, chopped
1	garlic clove, finely chopped
1/4	cup red wine vinegar
1/2	cup low-sodium chicken broth
1	20-ounce can diced tomatoes and juice
1/2	tsp dried tarragon
	Dash Tabasco
1	tsp cornstarch
2	tsp water
	Salt
	Freshly ground black pepper
1	tblsp chopped fresh chives
1	tblsp chopped fresh parsley

Glazed chicken with blueberry sauce

Nutritional facts per serving: 229 calories; 26.3g carbohydrates; 66.3mg cholesterol; 1.8g total fat; 2.1g fiber; 27.2g protein; 82.5mg sodium

Whisk together orange juice, vinegar, garlic, and brown sugar. Put the chicken into a glass or plastic container, add the marinade, and toss to cover chicken well. Cover and refrigerate for 1 hour, turning chicken over once.

To make sauce, place blueberries, orange zest, apple juice, and honey in a small saucepan, stir well, and bring to a boil. Simmer until berries soften and liquid cooks down slightly. Remove from heat while berries remain intact and are shiny.

Preheat the grill. Drain chicken breasts but reserve the marinade. Brush the grate with oil. Grill breasts for about 6 minutes on each side, or until done, basting with the marinade when you turn them and once toward the end of cooking time for final glaze. Serve each piece of chicken with warm blueberry sauce.

3/4	cup fresh orange juice
2	tblsp red wine vinegar
2	garlic cloves, finely minced
2	tblsp brown sugar
4	4-ounce boneless, skinless chicken breasts
	Canola oil
1	pint blueberries, washed
1	tsp orange zest, finely chopped
2	tblsp apple juice
1	tblsp honey

4 servings

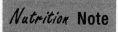 **Note**

Don't let urinary tract infections make you blue. Scientists know *E. coli* bacteria cause many urinary tract infections (UTIs). Like cranberries, blueberries contain antioxidants that make bacteria powerless to attach themselves to your cells and start multiplying. The secret to fewer UTIs — more blueberries.

Lemon chicken-vegetable medley

Nutritional facts per serving: 277 calories; 12.1g carbohydrates; 66.3mg cholesterol; 12.2g total fat; 2.2g fiber; 29.1g protein; 88.2mg sodium

Whisk together water, 1 tablespoon of oil, and 2 tablespoons of lemon juice. Whisk in cornstarch. Add ginger, garlic, and lemon zest, and mix well. Add chicken. Toss to combine well, cover, and refrigerate for 15 minutes.

Cook snow peas in boiling water for 2 minutes. Drain well. Heat the remaining 2 tablespoons of oil in a large frying pan over medium-high heat. Add the chicken mixture, green onions, and red pepper. Sprinkle with salt and pepper. Cook, stirring constantly, until chicken is just firm, 3 to 5 minutes. Add chicken broth and bring to a boil. Add snow peas, toss to combine, and heat through. Add the remaining 2 tablespoons of lemon juice, season to taste with salt and pepper, and serve immediately.

4 servings

1	tblsp water
3	tblsp canola oil
4	tblsp fresh lemon juice
2	tblsp cornstarch
1	tsp finely chopped fresh ginger
1	garlic clove, finely chopped
1	tblsp lemon zest
1	pound boneless, skinless chicken breasts, cut into 1/4" thick strips
	Salt
	Black pepper
1/2	pound snow peas, cut in half on the diagonal
2	cups chopped green onions
1/2	cup chopped red bell pepper
1/2	cup low-sodium chicken broth

It's important to remove the tendon from each chicken breast and to cut the strips to a uniform thickness. The length isn't crucial.

Low-cal chicken caesar

Nutritional facts per serving: 244 calories; 8.2g carbohydrates; 66.3mg cholesterol; 11.8g total fat; 1.3g fiber; 27.8g protein; 123.1mg sodium

---

Put olive oil, lemon juice, Worcestershire sauce, mustard, garlic, and pepper in a food processor, and blend. Rub the mixture on both sides of the chicken breasts, and refrigerate uncovered for 30 minutes.

Preheat oven to 400 degrees.

Lightly pat any excess marinade off the breasts. Roast breasts for about 6 minutes on each side, or until cooked through. Place four lettuce leaves on each plate. Slice chicken, and place one breast on the lettuce on each plate. Garnish with lemon slices. Add croutons and Parmesan, if desired.

4 servings

3	tblsp olive oil
1 1/2	tblsp fresh lemon juice
1	tsp Worcestershire sauce
1	tsp Dijon mustard
2	garlic cloves, finely chopped
1/4	tsp black pepper
4	4-ounce skinless, boneless chicken breasts
1	head Romaine lettuce, washed and drained
1	lemon, thinly sliced
	Croutons (optional)
	Fresh Parmesan cheese (optional)

Nutrition **Note**

You've given up every dairy product you can think of but still experience symptoms of lactose intolerance — especially digestive troubles. To put an end to discomfort from milk products, learn how to catch the disguised milk in food labels. Even if a label doesn't list eggs, cheese, yogurt, or milk, you may find these milk by-products in lots of foods: casein, sodium caseinate, lactose, and whey. What's more, about 20 percent of all prescription drugs and 6 percent of all over-the-counter products contain lactose. Make sure you read all food and drug labels carefully, and ask your pharmacist about any medication you're not sure of.

Mediterranean chicken and vegetables

Nutritional facts per serving: 467 calories; 11.5g carbohydrates; 128.6mg cholesterol; 29.6g total fat; 2.6g fiber; 33.8g protein; 144.6mg sodium

Heat olive oil in a Dutch oven or heavy frying pan on Medium-high. Add chicken and cook, turning, for about 10 minutes or until chicken is brown on all sides. Remove chicken, and add onion and garlic. Cook, stirring frequently, for 3 to 4 minutes, or until they begin to soften. Drain off oil and discard.

Add tomatoes, bell pepper, olives, and wine. Stir to combine. Add chicken. Cover, reduce temperature to Low, and cook chicken for 30 to 40 minutes, or until done.

Remove chicken to a serving platter. Add tomato paste to the liquid in the Dutch oven, and stir to thicken. When hot through, add rosemary and basil. Season to taste with salt and pepper. Spoon over and around the chicken, and serve.

4 servings

1	3-pound broiler-fryer, cut-up
3	tblsp olive oil
1	small onion, chopped
2	garlic cloves, finely chopped
4	large tomatoes, chopped
1	small green bell pepper, sliced
1/2	cup sliced black olives
1/2	cup white wine
3	tblsp tomato paste
1/2	tsp finely chopped fresh rosemary
1	tsp finely chopped fresh basil
	Salt
	Freshly ground black pepper

Italian-style chicken-sausage medley

Nutritional facts per serving: 341 calories; 20.3g carbohydrates; 117.5mg cholesterol; 15.1g total fat; 0.4g fiber; 29.6g protein; 430.6mg sodium

Prick the sausages all over with a fork. Heat a large skillet. Add sausages, and brown on all sides. Drain on paper towels, and slice into 1-inch pieces. Set aside.

Add chicken to the skillet, skin side down. Brown, turn, and brown on the other side. Remove. Add mushrooms, and sauté briefly. Return chicken and sausages to the skillet, and add bell pepper, garlic, wine, salt, ground peppers, and oregano. Bring to a boil. Reduce heat and simmer, covered, 20 minutes, until chicken and sausages are cooked through.

Serve over pasta, and sprinkle with parsley.

6 servings

1/2	pound hot Italian turkey sausage
1	2 1/2-pound chicken, cut up
1/2	pound fresh mushrooms, sliced
1	large red bell pepper, cut into thin strips
2	garlic cloves, chopped
1/2	cup dry white wine
	Salt
1/4	tsp ground cayenne pepper
	Freshly ground black pepper
1/4	cup finely chopped fresh oregano
1	pound pasta, cooked
1/3	cup finely chopped fresh parsley

Nutrition **Note** — Research suggests orange juice is an effective appetite suppressant. In a Yale University study, overweight men who drank OJ ate nearly 300 fewer calories at lunch. Overweight women consumed an average of 431 fewer midday calories. To reap these benefits, drink a glass of OJ a half-hour to an hour before a meal. You'll eat fewer calories during the meal and still feel comfortably full.

Marvelous chicken marinara

Nutritional facts per serving: 348 calories; 7.9g carbohydrates; 106mg cholesterol; 21.2g total fat; 1.3g fiber; 31.2g protein; 751.6mg sodium

Heat oil in a large heavy skillet until sizzling. Add chicken pieces, skin side down. Brown, turn, and brown other side. Add vinegar, and boil briefly to reduce. Add broth. Cover and simmer until chicken is cooked, about 30 minutes. Stir in marinara sauce, olives, and oregano, and cook together 2 to 3 minutes.

4 servings

3	tblsp olive oil
8-10	chicken thighs with skin or 1 3-pound chicken, cut up
2	tblsp red wine vinegar
1/2	cup chicken broth or stock, fresh or canned
	Salt
	Freshly ground black pepper
1 1/2	cups marinara sauce (see page 319)
8	ounces black olives, pitted (optional)
2	heaping tblsp finely chopped fresh oregano or basil

Nutrition **Note**

Try these tips for better slumber.

• Relax for 30 minutes before you turn in.

• Wake up the same time every day, no matter when you fall asleep — and try to avoid daytime napping.

• If you don't drift off after a half hour, get out of bed.

• Keep your bedroom dark and quiet.

• Wear comfortable, loose clothes to sleep in.

Colorful chicken, vegetables, and rice

Nutritional facts per serving: 191 calories; 27.4g carbohydrates; 0mg cholesterol; 6.2g total fat; 2.6g fiber; 6.9g protein; 597.2mg sodium

---

Preheat oven to 325 degrees.

Heat oil in a large skillet. Add chicken pieces, skin side down, and cook until just pale golden in color. Turn and brown. Remove. Add onion and green pepper to the skillet. Cook until soft. Add tomato, garlic, 1/4 cup of the lemon juice, bay leaf, salt, and hot sauce, if using. Mix well and cook until mushy.

Dissolve the optional saffron in 1 cup hot chicken broth, and combine with 1/4 cup lemon juice. Pour into skillet, add parsley, and stir well. Arrange chicken in a heatproof casserole, and pour the vegetable mixture over it. Cover and cook over medium heat until chicken is tender, about 15 minutes. Add rice and stir to distribute it evenly in the casserole. Add remaining chicken broth and stir once carefully. Bring to a boil and cover. Bake for 20 minutes. Remove from oven. Garnish with peas, pimiento strips, and parsley. Sprinkle generously with remaining lemon juice diluted to taste with water. Cover and allow to stand 15 minutes. Remove bay leaf before serving. This dish can also be made with dry white wine instead of lemon juice.

6 servings

2	ounces olive oil
1	3-pound chicken, cut into 8 pieces
1	onion, finely chopped
1/2	medium green bell pepper, finely chopped
1	large ripe tomato, peeled, quartered, seeded, and finely chopped
2	garlic cloves, chopped
3/4	cup lemon juice, divided
1	bay leaf, crumbled
1	tblsp salt
	Dash hot sauce (optional)
	Pinch saffron (optional)
4	cups chicken broth or stock, divided
1	heaping tblsp finely chopped fresh parsley
2	cups long-grain rice
1	cup cooked peas
1	pimiento, cut in strips
	Chopped parsley

Fast and easy blackberry chicken

Nutritional facts per serving: 354 calories; 55.2g carbohydrates; 68.4mg cholesterol; 1.6g total fat; 0.8g fiber; 27.6g protein; 102.3mg sodium

Preheat the broiler. Spray a roasting pan with nonstick spray. Place the rack 8" from the broiler.

Place chicken breasts in a resealable plastic bag. Add blackberry preserves. Season with salt and pepper. Coat the chicken, remove, and place chicken in the roasting pan. Broil 8 minutes on each side, or until cooked through and nicely crusted.

4 | chicken breasts, boned and skinned

1 | cup blackberry preserves, beaten to soften

Salt

Freshly ground black pepper

4 servings

Nutrition **Note**

The end to your sinus headaches may be in sight. If you constantly suffer from sinus headaches, but over-the-counter (OTC) painkillers don't help, your "sinus" headache could actually be a migraine. Migraines usually need much stronger medicine than OTC medicines. To see if you might be a migraine sufferer, ask yourself three questions. Do your "sinus" headaches happen often? Are your headaches interfering with your daily life? Do your headaches get worse over time? If you answered yes, yes, and no, your mystery headaches could be migraines. Watch for other symptoms like light sensitivity, pain on one side of your head, nausea, or throbbing pain. Visit your doctor if these symptoms sound all too familiar. Then you can begin to get the proper treatment for your headaches.

Tender apple and onion chicken pot pie

Nutritional facts per serving: 384 calories; 25.8g carbohydrates; 68mg cholesterol; 21.5g total fat; 1.8g fiber; 21.9g protein; 364.9mg sodium

Preheat oven according to directions on the pie crust.

Melt butter in a large saucepan over medium heat. Add garlic and ginger, and cook for 2 to 3 minutes, or until just tender. Stir in flour until smooth. Reduce heat to Medium, and gradually whisk in the chicken broth. Cook, stirring, until it thickens to sauce consistency.

Add onion and apple chunks. Let simmer for about 5 minutes, stirring regularly, until just tender. Add lemon juice, thyme, salt, and pepper, and mix well. Add the chicken.

Spoon into a deep, 10" ceramic or glass pie dish. Lay the thawed pie crust over the top of the dish. Trim and crimp the edges. Cut several slits in the center of pie. Set the pie on a baking sheet, and place in the oven on the middle rack. Bake according to crust directions, until the pie bubbles around edges and top is golden brown. You can use freshly poached chicken for this recipe, or speed things up by using leftovers from a roasted chicken.

2	tblsp butter
2	garlic cloves, finely chopped
1	tblsp fresh ginger, finely chopped
3	tblsp all-purpose flour
2	cups low-sodium chicken broth
1	small onion, cut into chunks
1	medium Granny Smith apple, cut into chunks
2	tblsp lemon juice
1/2	tsp dried thyme
1/8	tsp salt
1/2	tsp freshly ground pepper
2	cups chopped cooked chicken
1	frozen deep-dish pie shell, thawed

Nutrition **Note**

A new study has discovered that Granny Smith apples are a potent source of the antioxidants that help you stay healthy.

4 servings

Oven-baked chicken and pepper kebabs

Nutritional facts per serving: 266 calories; 4.3g carbohydrates; 68.4mg cholesterol; 15.1g total fat; 1.2g fiber; 27.8g protein; 217.5mg sodium

---

Whisk together the olive oil, vinegar, oregano, and garlic salt. Put the pieces of chicken into a glass or plastic container, add the marinade, and toss to cover chicken well. Cover and marinate overnight.

Preheat oven to 400 degrees. Line 2 baking pans with foil.

Place peppers on 1 sheet. Drain chicken well. Sprinkle lightly with salt and pepper. Place chicken on the other baking sheet. Bake both pans 4 to 5 minutes. You may need to take smaller pieces of chicken out a little sooner.

4	tblsp olive oil
2	tblsp red wine vinegar
3/4	tsp dried oregano
3/4	tsp garlic salt
1/2	pound boneless, skinless chicken breasts cut into cubes
1	small red bell pepper, cut into squares
1	small yellow bell pepper, cut into squares
	Salt
	Freshly ground black pepper

Skewer as follows: 1 square of yellow pepper, 1 piece of chicken, 1 square of red pepper, the second piece of chicken. Serve warm or at room temperature.

4 servings

This cooking technique is called "oven-sautéing." Instead of sautéing the chicken in butter or oil, you achieve almost the same effect without any fat by baking the pieces in a 400-degree oven. What's more, you'll love the convenience of cooking all the items at one time — and you can easily remove pieces of chicken or peppers that happen to cook faster than the others.

Louisiana-style chicken jambalaya

Nutritional facts per serving: 290 calories; 20.1g carbohydrates; 79.4mg cholesterol; 11.5g total fat; 4g fiber; 26.6g protein; 633.7mg sodium

---

Heat oil in a soup pot. Sauté onion, celery, green pepper, and garlic until just tender. Add seasonings, tomatoes with their juice, tomato paste, chicken stock, and wine, and stir well.

Add the sausage and chicken. Simmer for 30 minutes. Taste for seasonings, and add more if desired. Ladle over hot plain long-grain rice or Seasoned-just-right Creole rice (see page 195).

4 servings

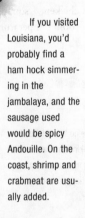

If you visited Louisiana, you'd probably find a ham hock simmering in the jambalaya, and the sausage used would be spicy Andouille. On the coast, shrimp and crabmeat are usually added.

1	tsp canola oil
1	small onion, chopped
1/3	cup chopped celery
1/2	small green bell pepper, chopped
2	garlic cloves, finely chopped
1	bay leaf
1/4	tsp each cayenne pepper, black pepper, dried oregano, and dried thyme
2	15-ounce cans diced or crushed tomatoes
4	ounces tomato paste
3/4	cup low-sodium chicken stock
1/4	cup dry white wine
1/2	pound spicy chicken or turkey sausage, cooked and drained
1/2	pound cooked, boned chicken, chopped in generous bite-size pieces

Hot seasoned chicken and vegetable pitas

Nutritional facts per serving: 395 calories; 45.5g carbohydrates; 70.2mg cholesterol; 9.4g total fat; 7.1g fiber; 34.4g protein; 738.1mg sodium

Heat oil in a large frying pan over medium-high heat. Add chicken and stir-fry about 2 minutes, or until lightly browned. Add onion, celery, bell pepper, salt, and pepper. Cook for about 5 minutes, stirring occasionally, until chicken is done and vegetables are tender. Add mayonnaise, mustard, and horseradish, stirring constantly, for about 1 minute, or until heated. Season to taste with salt and pepper.

To serve, line pita bread halves with lettuce and tomatoes, and stuff with the hot chicken mixture.

4 servings

2	tblsp canola oil
4	4-ounce boneless, skinless chicken breasts, cut into slices
1	medium sweet onion, sliced
1	cup sliced celery
1	small red bell pepper, sliced
1/2	tsp salt
1/4	tsp pepper
3	tblsp low-fat mayonnaise
2	tblsp Dijon mustard
1	tsp prepared horseradish sauce
	Salt
	Freshly ground black pepper
2	small tomatoes, sliced
8	Romaine lettuce leaves
4	large whole wheat pita breads, cut in half

Nutrition **Note** Pantothenic acid — or vitamin B5 — has been called the "anti-stress" vitamin. You need it to keep your adrenal gland healthy and functioning properly and to help stimulate antibody production. Hearty whole grains are a great way to get more vitamin B5.

Soft chicken tacos with homemade salsa

Nutritional facts per serving: 430 calories; 30.4g carbohydrates; 96.5mg cholesterol; 15.4g total fat; 5.2g fiber; 40.7g protein; 163.3mg sodium

---

In a medium bowl, stir together tomatoes, scallions, garlic, lime juice, jalapeño pepper, cilantro, and olive oil to make the salsa. Season to taste with salt and pepper. Refrigerate.

Mix the refried beans and cayenne pepper, and heat in the microwave or on the stove. Heat the tortillas on the grill. Put out the tortillas, refried beans, salsa, chicken, cheese, and lettuce, and have everyone fill and roll their own tacos.

4 servings

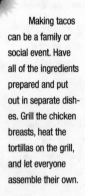

Making tacos can be a family or social event. Have all of the ingredients prepared and put out in separate dishes. Grill the chicken breasts, heat the tortillas on the grill, and let everyone assemble their own.

3/4	pound fresh tomatoes, chopped
2	scallions, finely chopped
2	garlic cloves, finely chopped
2	tblsp fresh lime juice
1	small jalapeño pepper, finely chopped, or to taste
1	tblsp finely chopped fresh cilantro
1	tblsp olive oil
	Salt
	Freshly ground black pepper
1	cup refried beans
1	tsp cayenne pepper, or to taste
4-8	soft flour tacos, depending on size
4	4-ounce boneless, skinless grilled chicken breasts, sliced
1	cup pepper jack cheese or cheddar cheese, grated
1 1/2	cups Romaine lettuce, shredded

Mexican chicken with summer vegetables

Nutritional facts per serving: 213 calories; 14.2g carbohydrates; 66.3mg cholesterol; 4.4g total fat; 2.8g fiber; 29.7g protein; 102.8mg sodium

In a large frying pan, heat oil over medium-hot heat. Add chicken breasts and brown both sides. Remove chicken. Add garlic, onion, bell pepper, and jalapeño pepper, and cook for about 3 minutes, stirring, or until just tender. Add chicken broth and tomato juice, and bring to a boil. Add cumin, and season to taste with salt and pepper. Return chicken to the pan. Simmer for 8 to 10 minutes, or until chicken is tender through.

Add corn and tomato. Simmer for 2 to 3 minutes, or until corn and tomato are just lightly cooked. Stir in jicama and cilantro. Serve with tortilla chips, if desired.

4 servings

2   tblsp canola oil

4   4-ounce boneless, skinless chicken breasts

1   garlic clove, minced

1   small onion, sliced

1/4   cup chopped green bell pepper

1   small jalapeño pepper, finely chopped, or to taste

1   cup low-sodium chicken broth

4   ounces low-sodium tomato juice

1/2   tsp ground cumin

  Salt

  Freshly ground black pepper

3/4   cup fresh corn kernels, cut from cob

1   large ripe tomato, chopped

1/2   cup chopped jicama

2   tblsp chopped fresh cilantro

  Tortilla chips (optional)

Spanish-style sautéed chicken breast

Nutritional facts per serving: 255 calories; 13.9g carbohydrates; 66.3mg cholesterol; 9.3g total fat; 3.1g fiber; 29.1g protein; 209.6mg sodium

4	4-ounce boneless, skinless chicken breasts
1/4	cup flour
1/2	tsp black pepper
2	tblsp olive oil
1/2	small onion, chopped
2	garlic cloves, finely chopped
4	tblsp freshly squeezed lemon juice
1	tsp finely chopped lemon zest
2	tblsp capers
1	cup canned artichoke hearts, drained and chopped
1/4	cup roasted red peppers, drained and chopped
1/4	cup pitted and chopped green olives
1 1/2	tblsp fresh parsley, chopped

Place chicken breasts between 2 sheets of plastic wrap, and pound into an even thickness. Combine flour and black pepper. Dredge chicken in flour, patting off any excess.

Heat olive oil in large skillet over medium heat. Add chicken breasts to pan, sautéing until golden, about 4 minutes each side. Remove chicken breasts and keep warm. Add onion and garlic, and cook for 5 minutes, or tender.

In small bowl, stir together lemon juice, lemon zest, capers, artichoke hearts, red peppers, and olives. Add the lemon juice mixture to the skillet, continuing to stir until hot, scraping any brown bits off the bottom of the pan. Season to taste with salt and pepper. Spoon some sauce over each chicken breast, sprinkle with parsley, and serve immediately.

Nutrition Note

According to a new USDA study, artichoke hearts are one of the top 5 vegetable sources of antioxidants. Only red beans, kidney beans, and pinto beans scored better.

4 servings

Tex-Mex chicken and black beans

Nutritional facts per serving: 383 calories; 13.4g carbohydrates; 100.5mg cholesterol; 20g total fat; 2.8g fiber; 35.8g protein; 780.5mg sodium

Take the meat off the chicken, and chop into bite-size pieces.

Heat olive oil in small frying pan over medium heat. Add onion, red bell pepper, garlic, and poblano pepper, and cook for about 5 minutes, stirring occasionally, until tender. Add black beans, chicken broth, bay leaf, cumin, and chili powder. Season to taste with salt and pepper. Cook on low temperature, uncovered, about 5 minutes. Add the chicken and simmer for 10 minutes. Ladle over hot rice. Sprinkle with cheddar cheese, if desired. Remove bay leaf before serving.

Serve this dish with Seasoned-just-right Creole rice (see page 195) or plain, hot long-grain rice.

4 servings

1	3 1/2- to 4-pound whole roasted chicken
2	tblsp olive oil
1/2	small onion, chopped
1/2	small red bell pepper, chopped
2	garlic cloves, finely chopped
1	small poblano pepper, finely chopped, or to taste
1	15-ounce can black beans, drained and rinsed
1/4	cup low-sodium chicken broth
1	bay leaf
1/2	tsp cumin
1/4	tsp chili powder
	Salt
	Freshly ground black pepper
1/2	cup grated sharp cheddar cheese (optional)

Bite-size chicken-tomato salad

Nutritional facts per serving: 442 calories; 14.7g carbohydrates; 85.7mg cholesterol; 29.6g total fat; 5.7g fiber; 32.3g protein; 112.2mg sodium

Take meat off the chicken, and chop into bite-size pieces.

Toss lettuce, tomato, and onion in 3/4 cup of the dressing. Add salt and pepper to taste. Mound on the plates. Toss chicken in the remaining 1/4 cup dressing. Chop the avocado, and toss it in the lemon juice to prevent browning. Sprinkle the chicken, avocado, and bacon on top of the salads. Sprinkle with parsley and blue cheese, if desired. Serve immediately.

4 servings

1	3 1/2- to 4-pound whole roasted chicken
4	cups chopped romaine lettuce
2	cups chopped tomato
1/4	cup chopped red onion
1	cup tomato-basil vinaigrette (see page 101)
	Salt
	Freshly ground black pepper
1	avocado
2	tblsp fresh lemon juice
4	slices crisp turkey bacon, chopped
1/4	cup chopped fresh parsley
1/4	cup blue cheese crumbles (optional)

Nutrition **Note**

Eating high fat avocados may help lower your total cholesterol without cutting "good" HDL cholesterol. Although the avocado is high in fat — 30 grams per fruit — it's mostly monounsaturated fat. This fat helps protect good HDL cholesterol, while wiping out the bad LDL cholesterol that clogs your arteries. An avocado also contains fiber and a plant chemical called beta sitosterol. Both help reduce cholesterol. That's three reasons why avocados are a heart-smart step to a healthier you.

Curried fruit and chicken salad

Nutritional facts per serving: 382 calories; 35.3g carbohydrates; 88.3mg cholesterol; 13.6g total fat; 3.4g fiber; 30.9g protein; 153.7mg sodium

Take meat off the chicken, and chop into bite-size pieces. Combine chicken, grapes, apple, scallions, and 3 tablespoons of the almonds in a bowl.

Put oil, lime juice, mayonnaise, and chutney in a food processor, and process until almost smooth. Add curry powder, salt, and pepper to taste. Combine with the chicken mixture and refrigerate.

Separate lettuce leaves, wash, and drain on paper towels. When ready to serve, divide lettuce between four plates, and place a portion of salad on each. Sprinkle the remaining sliced almonds over the salad, and garnish with mango slices.

4 servings

1	3 1/2- to 4-pound whole roasted chicken
1	cup grape halves
1	medium Granny Smith Apple, chopped
2	scallions, chopped
4	tblsp toasted sliced almonds
1/4	cup canola oil
1/4	cup fresh lime juice
2	tblsp low-fat mayonnaise
3	tblsp mango chutney
	Curry powder
	Salt
	Freshly ground black pepper
1	head Boston lettuce
1	mango, peeled and sliced

Nutrition **Note**

Grape skins contain resveratrol, a plant estrogen that may help against heart disease and cancer. In your body, resveratrol fights inflammation and prevents blood clots, both of which help you against heart disease. But that's not all resveratrol can do. University of Illinois researchers found that this plant estrogen foils cancer by acting as an antioxidant and fighting inflammation, cell mutation, and tumors. In fact, experts link eating more grapes to a lower risk of oral cancer.

Florida chicken salad

Nutritional facts per serving: 426 calories; 28g carbohydrates; 85.7mg cholesterol; 216g total fat; 6.6 g fiber; 31.7g protein; 95.2mg sodium

Take meat off the chicken, and chop into generous bite-size pieces. Combine chicken, onion, cucumber, and orange sections in a bowl.

Combine vinegar and orange juice. Slowly whisk in olive oil. Add zest and herbs, and season to taste with salt and pepper. Pour over the chicken mixture and toss well. Serve immediately.

4 servings

1	3 1/2- to 4-pound whole roasted chicken
1	small red onion, sliced
1	cucumber, unpeeled, finely chopped
4	seedless oranges, peeled and sectioned
2	tblsp red wine vinegar
2	tblsp fresh orange juice
4	tblsp olive oil
2	tblsp orange zest, chopped
1/2	cup finely chopped fresh parsley
1/2	cup finely chopped fresh chives
1/2	cup finely chopped fresh mint
	Salt
	Freshly ground black pepper

Save money, time, and electricity by keeping an inventory on the door of your refrigerator. When you return from the grocery store, make a list of all the food items you store inside. Also note the date. As you use things up cross them off the list. With this method you can plan meals at a glance without having to dig around in the fridge.

Greek isles chicken salad

Nutritional facts per serving: 407 calories; 9g carbohydrates; 110mg cholesterol; 25.3g total fat; 3g fiber; 36.7g protein; 315.3mg sodium

Take the meat off the chicken, and chop into bite-size pieces. Combine chicken, tomatoes, bell pepper, cucumber, scallions, and olives. Toss to mix well.

Whisk together the wine vinegar and oil. Add oregano and thyme, and season to taste with salt and pepper. Pour over the chicken mixture. Cover and refrigerate until well chilled.

At serving time, divide the spinach between four plates, and place a portion of salad on each. Sprinkle with feta.

4 servings

1	3 1/2- to 4-pound whole roasted chicken
2	large tomatoes, chopped
1	small green bell pepper, chopped
1	cucumber, chopped
2	scallions, chopped
1/4	cup sliced, pitted Kalamata olives
4	tblsp olive oil
4	tblsp red wine vinegar
1/4	tsp dried oregano
1/4	tsp dried thyme
	Salt
	Freshly ground black pepper
1	bunch curly spinach, washed and stemmed
1/4	cup reduced-fat feta crumbles

Nutrition **Note** Iron deficiency is the most common nutritional deficiency in the world. Iron is not absorbed very well from the foods you eat, but vitamin C helps you absorb iron better. Talk to your doctor before you try iron supplements because iron overload is dangerous.

Tropical island grilled chicken salad

Nutritional facts per serving: 371 calories; 32.6g carbohydrates; 66.3mg cholesterol; 14.8g total fat; 6.3g fiber; 30.8g protein; 243.9mg sodium

Process the honey, lime juice, ginger, garlic, soy sauce, and sesame oil in a food processor until pureed. With the processor running, slowly add canola oil to emulsify. Remove to a container, and chill 1 hour before using. Stir before using.

Preheat the grill. Season chicken breasts with salt and pepper. Brush breasts with oil. Place them on the grill, and cook for 3-5 minutes on each side, or until cooked through. Remove to let rest 5 minutes before slicing.

Meanwhile, toss the peppers, spring onions, and cabbage with the dressing. Mound onto plates. Slice the chicken breasts and place on top. Garnish with mango and cilantro sprigs. Sprinkle sesame seeds on top, and serve immediately.

4 servings

2 tblsp honey

4 tblsp fresh lime juice

2 tsp grated ginger

1 garlic clove, finely chopped

1 tblsp light soy sauce

2 tsp sesame oil

2 tblsp canola oil

4 4-ounce boneless, skinless chicken breasts

Salt

Freshly ground black pepper

1 tblsp olive oil

1 small yellow bell pepper, thinly sliced

1 small red bell pepper, thinly sliced

4 spring onions, sliced

1 small head cabbage, thinly sliced

1 fresh mango, sliced

1/2 cup cilantro sprigs

2 tblsp toasted sesame seeds

Elegant chicken-pear salad

Nutritional facts per serving: 362 calories; 7.7g carbohydrates; 66.3mg cholesterol; 24.9g total fat; 1.4g fiber; 29.6g protein; 83.9mg sodium

Whisk together the vinegar and honey. Slowly whisk in olive oil. Add salt and pepper to taste.

Place pears in a medium bowl, and gently toss with the salad dressing to prevent them from browning. Combine arugula and watercress. Remove pears from the dressing, and toss dressing with the greens.

Divide the greens between 4 plates. Place one breast, slices fanned out, on each plate. Arrange pears between slices of chicken. Sprinkle with walnuts and blue cheese.

4 servings

3	tblsp white wine vinegar
1	tblsp honey
4	tblsp olive oil
	Salt
	Freshly ground black pepper
4	pears, sliced
4	4-ounce grilled boneless, skinless chicken breasts, sliced to fan out
1	bunch arugula, rinsed
1	bunch watercress, rinsed
1/4	cup toasted chopped walnuts
1/4	cup blue cheese crumbles (optional)

Impress your friends with fancy rolled sandwiches. First, trim the crust off half a loaf of thin sandwich bread. Next, mix cream cheese with various shades of food coloring, and spread a different color on each bread slice. Stack them in groups of four layers, and use a cheese slicer to cut dainty sandwiches as you would a jelly roll.

Crunchy turkey salad

Nutritional facts per serving: 413 calories; 30.8g carbohydrates; 84.4mg cholesterol; 18.4g total fat; 3.4g fiber; 31.1g protein; 337.4mg sodium

Cook rices according to package directions. Drain well. Combine wild rice, white rice, celery, scallions, apples, walnuts and turkey.

Combine sour cream and mayonnaise. Whisk in vinegar, cumin, sage, and thyme. Season to taste with salt and pepper. Add as much of this dressing as desired to the turkey mixture. Cover and refrigerate for at least one hour. When ready to serve, toss with fresh parsley.

4 servings

This recipe is especially good when made with smoked turkey and some added sherry wine vinegar. Use only as much mayonnaise as you prefer.

1/4 cup raw wild rice

1/4 cup raw converted rice

1/2 cup chopped celery

2 scallions, chopped, green tops included

1 small Granny Smith apple, cored and chopped, skin on

1 small Fugi, Gala, or other crisp red eating apple

1/4 cup toasted chopped walnuts

1 pound cooked, chopped turkey

2 tblsp low-fat sour cream, or to taste

1/2 cup low-fat mayonnaise

2 tblsp apple cider vinegar

1/8 tsp each ground cumin and ground sage

Pinch dried thyme

Salt

Freshly ground black pepper

4 tblsp chopped fresh parsley

Saucy grilled chicken salad

Nutritional facts per serving: 394 calories; 11.7g carbohydrates; 95.7mg cholesterol; 22.4g total fat; 4.9g fiber; 37.1g protein; 276.4mg sodium

Preheat the grill.

Place chicken breasts between 2 sheets of plastic wrap, and pound them to an even thickness. Brush both sides with olive oil, and sprinkle with salt and pepper. Grill for about 5 minutes on each side, or until done. Remove chicken from grill, and set aside.

Toss greens with as much of the vinaigrette as desired (refrigerate any left over) and divide them between four plates. Slice the chicken breasts, and arrange each on top of the greens on each plate. Sprinkle with cheese, if using, and cilantro. Top with a spoonful of sour cream, if desired.

4 servings

4	4-ounce boneless, skinless chicken breasts
	Olive oil
	Salt
	Freshly ground black pepper
1	pound baby mixed field greens
	Tomato-basil vinaigrette (see page 101)
1/2	cup grated pepper-jack cheese (optional)
2	tblsp chopped fresh cilantro
	Low-fat sour cream (optional)

Take a large zip-top freezer bag, and fill it with cold water. Zip it shut and lay it flat in your freezer on a baking sheet. Then, next time you need crushed ice, take the bag from your freezer, and drop it on a hard floor until the ice is broken up.

Perfectly pan-seared duck breasts

Nutritional facts per serving: 348 calories; 0.5g carbohydrates; 132mg cholesterol; 23.8g total fat; 0.1g fiber; 31.4g protein; 127.1mg sodium

Trim off any excess fat from the duck breasts. Score the skin in a criss-cross pattern, not cutting through to the meat. Mix garlic, pepper, sage, and olive oil. Toss the breasts in this, cover, and marinate for at least 1 hour, or overnight.

Preheat oven to 425 degrees.

4	duck breasts, skin on
1	garlic clove, finely chopped
1	tsp freshly ground black pepper
1	tsp dried sage
4	tblsp olive oil
	Salt

Heat a heavy-bottomed ovenproof sauté pan over medium heat. Lightly sprinkle the duck breasts with salt. Place them in the hot pan skin-side down, and sauté for about 5 minutes to render the fat. If the skin is getting too brown, lower the heat.

Turn breasts so the skin is up, and place them in the hot oven. Roast the breasts for 4 to 5 minutes for medium-rare. Remove from pan, and let breasts rest in a warm place for 10 minutes, keeping the skin-side up so they will remain crisp.

4 servings

Some meat departments carry duck breasts with the skin on now, but the whole ducks available from the grocery store are frozen. Buy them several days in advance to allow them to thaw in the refrigerator. Cut the breasts out of a whole duck just like you would cut the breasts out of a chicken. You want the bones out but the skin left on. Use the legs and thighs to make a good stew or gumbo.

Spicy crisp Cornish hens

Nutritional facts per serving: 268 calories; 2.4g carbohydrates; 112.8mg cholesterol; 12.3g total fat; 0.3g fiber; 35.3g protein; 106.1mg sodium

---

2	Cornish hens
	Juice of 2 lemons
2	garlic cloves, crushed with 1 tblsp salt
1	tblsp freshly ground black pepper
1-2	tsp ground cayenne or hot ground pepper
1	tblsp paprika
1	tblsp butter, melted

Split and butterfly the hens by cutting down the backbone and opening the hens, leaving the breast attached. Squeeze lemon juice over the hens. Mix garlic, peppers, and paprika, and add to the melted butter. Pour over the hens. If possible, let them sit overnight, uncovered, in the refrigerator.

Prepare the grill. Place hens, breast side up, on the grill. Cover the grill, and cook hens for 50 minutes, until crisp. Or bake the hens in a 350-degree oven, skin side up, for 50 minutes or until done. Don't turn. If the skin is not crispy, place chicken under the broiler to crisp the skin and brown, watching carefully so that it doesn't burn.

6 servings

Skinless chicken is lower in fat, but the skin seals in flavor, vitamins, and moisture. So cook it first, then remove the skin. Looking for another way to cut fat? Use whipped butter or margarine instead of sticks. Although you can't use it for cooking or baking, the whipped variety will spread better on bread and rolls, making it easier to use less.

Easy roasted Cornish hens

Nutritional facts per serving: 356 calories; 0.7g carbohydrates; 168.4mg cholesterol; 25.6g total fat; 0.1g fiber; 28.7g protein; 82.6mg sodium

Split hens down the backbone so that each half has a breast, thigh and leg. Combine olive oil, pepper, and garlic, and rub it on the hens. Refrigerate for 15 minutes.

Preheat oven to 350 degrees, or fire up the grill for a medium fire. If roasting in the oven, spray a baking pan and rack with nonstick vegetable spray.

2	Cornish hens (about 1 1/2 pounds each)
2	tsp olive oil
1/2	tsp freshly ground black pepper
2	garlic cloves, finely chopped

Roast hens for 10 to 15 minutes on each side, or grill hens for about 10 minutes on each side, or until juices run clear.

4 servings

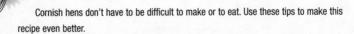

Cornish hens don't have to be difficult to make or to eat. Use these tips to make this recipe even better.

- To make Cornish hens far less trouble to eat, split them in half and roast or grill the halves. That makes them much easier to handle at the table. Just remember you'll have to plan ahead so you can decide how many halves you want to serve per person.

- Cornish hens are usually sold frozen. Thaw them in the refrigerator.

- Try warm Apricot honey-mustard sauce (see page 322) with this Cornish hen recipe.

Quick beef and vegetable stir-fry

Nutritional facts per serving: 314 calories; 17.5g carbohydrates; 74.8mg cholesterol; 15.8g total fat; 4.5g fiber; 27g protein; 433.1mg sodium

Preheat grill and spray wok with nonstick cooking spray. (You can prepare this dish in a deep skillet on the stove if you prefer.)

Combine soy sauce, cornstarch, and water in a small bowl, and set aside. Pour broth into wok and allow to heat. Add celery to wok and stir-fry for 1 minute. Add broccoli and stir-fry another minute. Add beef strips and cook 1 minute. Add peppers and zucchini and stir-fry for about 30 seconds. Add bean sprouts and the soy sauce mixture. Stir thoroughly until the sauce thickens. Serve immediately over steamed rice.

4 servings

2	tblsp low-sodium soy sauce
2	tblsp cornstarch
1/4	cup water
1/4	cup beef broth
1	1-pound beef sirloin cut into finger-length, thin strips
3	ribs celery, sliced
1 1/2	cups broccoli flowerets
1	green pepper, cut in thin strips
1	red pepper, cut in thin strips
2	zucchini, halved lengthwise and sliced
1	cup bean sprouts

You can change how nutritious your food is just by the way you cook it.

- Never fry your meat — especially in oil. Instead, grill away any unhealthy fat.

- Microwave, steam, or stir-fry your vegetables, and you won't boil away their vital nutrients. Steaming, especially, cuts down on all that chopping, peeling, and constant stirring.

- If you must boil vegetables, use very little water, and don't overcook them. This will keep them nutritious and delicious.

Sumptuous sirloin and vegetable medley

Nutritional facts per serving: 355 calories; 12.6g carbohydrates; 74.8mg cholesterol; 23.5g total fat; 3.1g fiber; 24.5g protein; 253.1mg sodium

Heat olive oil in a large skillet until hot. Add steaks, and sauté quickly on high heat, approximately 2 minutes per side. Set aside on a plate, and cover with foil to keep warm.

Add onion and bell pepper to the same pan, reduce heat to Medium, and cook until soft, about 10 minutes. Add garlic, tomatoes with juice, and wine vinegar, and cook until thick and most of the liquid has evaporated, about 7 minutes.

Add the drained spinach. Heat through, 2 to 3 minutes, and then return meat to the pan. Cover and reheat quickly until the meat is hot. Season with salt and pepper to taste, and serve.

4 servings

1/4 cup olive oil

4 4-ounce thin boneless sirloin steaks, pounded to 1/3" thickness

1 onion, sliced

1 red bell pepper, sliced

4 garlic cloves, chopped

1 16-ounce can whole peeled tomatoes with juice, broken into large pieces

1 tblsp red wine vinegar

1 12-ounce box frozen chopped spinach, defrosted and well drained

Salt

Freshly ground black pepper

Nutrition **Note** Beef up on vitamin B12 to help banish a scary threat to your brain. A study showed that people with vitamin B12 deficiency may permanently lose brain power unless the deficiency is caught early. Add vitamin B12 with chicken liver or sardines, sirloin steak, tuna packed in water, and cottage cheese.

Savory marinated flank steak

Nutritional facts per serving: 351 calories; 33.9g carbohydrates; 58.8mg cholesterol; 12.7g total fat; 1.3g fiber; 25.2g protein; 1356.5mg sodium

Place steak in a plastic bag or in a shallow glass dish. Mix all marinade ingredients and pour over steak. Place in refrigerator and marinate for 3 to 6 hours. Turn steak from time to time. Grill for 15 to 20 minutes, turning once. Slice thinly across the grain and serve.

4-5 servings

1/2	cup pineapple juice
1/2	cup low-sodium soy sauce
1/2	cup plum sauce
1/2	cup low-sodium ketchup
1/4	cup sliced green onions
2	tblsp minced garlic
2	tblsp minced fresh ginger
3	tblsp chopped cilantro
1	1-pound beef flank steak

Dodge dangerous bacteria while grilling your favorite foods. Don't leave marinating meat out on the counter. Put it in the fridge to keep bacteria from multiplying. Never reuse marinade after it's been on raw meat or fish. And always use clean plates and utensils to remove cooked foods from the grill — never the same ones you used for the raw meat.

Rancher's red-wine-marinated London broil

Nutritional facts per serving: 347 calories; 1.7g carbohydrates; 58.8mg cholesterol; 25.5g total fat; 0g fiber; 22.5g protein; 82mg sodium

1/2	cup red wine
1/4	cup red wine vinegar
1/4	cup olive oil
1	garlic clove, chopped
1/4	tsp red pepper flakes
1	bay leaf
1/4	tsp dried thyme
1	1-pound flank steak
	Salt
	Freshly ground black pepper

Combine wine, wine vinegar, olive oil, garlic, pepper flakes, bay leaf, and thyme. Coat both sides of the flank steak with the marinade. Cover with plastic wrap and refrigerate, turning occasionally, for at least 3 hours or overnight.

Preheat the grill or broiler.

Sprinkle both sides of the steak with salt and pepper. Grill or broil the steak for 4 minutes on each side for rare or 5 minutes for medium-rare, basting with the marinade. Remove from grill or oven, lightly cover with foil, and let juices settle for 5 minutes before slicing. Remove bay leaf before serving.

4 servings

London broil is a fancier name for flank steak. Flank steak, hanger steak, and skirt steak are all cuts of beef that are full of flavor, but they're also tough because they come from the chest and side of the steer. For best results, marinate flank steak first to make it more tender. Then just grill or roast it to rare or medium-rare, and slice it thinly. And remember, you must slice flank steak across the grain.

Top-choice herb-seasoned steaks

Nutritional facts per serving: 242 calories; 1.1g carbohydrates; 78.2mg cholesterol; 15.3g total fat; 0.6g fiber; 23.8g protein; 62mg sodium

Combine thyme, rosemary, oregano, and garlic. Season to taste with salt and pepper. Rub steaks on both sides with the herb mixture.

Heat butter and oil over high heat in a frying pan. Add the steaks and cook 3 to 5 minutes. Turn the steaks and cook the other side for 3 to 5 minutes for rare steaks.

4 servings

1   tblsp chopped fresh thyme

1   tblsp chopped fresh rosemary

1   tblsp chopped fresh oregano

1   garlic clove, finely chopped

Salt

Freshly ground black pepper

4   tenderloin or filet mignon steaks, 1" - 1 1/2" thick

1   tblsp butter

1   tblsp oil

Nutrition **Note**   Juicy beef tenderloin is a super source of the zinc you need to help your senses stay sharp. Zinc plays a part in sense functions, including your sense of taste and smell. It also helps keep your vision keen by helping maintain levels of sight-saving vitamin A. And it's particularly important in night vision. Zinc is found in more than 60 enzymes in your body and assists those enzymes in performing many important tasks. You need it for your body to produce DNA for cell growth, which helps speed wound healing. Zinc even helps strengthen your immune system. When you're not in the mood for beef tenderloin, get zinc from other good sources like fortified cereals, crabs, and oysters.

Tangy tomato-lemon beef with gremolata

Nutritional facts per serving: 284 calories; 8.2g carbohydrates; 78.1mg cholesterol; 12.5g total fat; 1.9g fiber; 34.1g protein; 80.1mg sodium

Divide meat into four pieces, preferably thick slices.

Heat oil over medium-high heat in a heavy frying pan. Add onion and half the garlic, and cook until soft, 4 to 5 minutes. Stir in tomatoes, tomato paste, half the lemon peel, and the meat. Top with half the chopped basil, and heat quickly.

Season to taste with salt, pepper, and sugar.

Remove meat to a hot platter, stir the tomato mixture, and pour over the meat. In a small bowl, mix together the remaining garlic, basil, and lemon peel to make gremolata, and sprinkle over the meat.

4 servings

1	1-pound cooked eye of round
1/4	cup olive oil
1	large onion, sliced
2	garlic cloves, chopped
1	16-oz can Italian plum tomatoes, drained, juices reserved
1	tsp tomato paste
	Grated peel of 1 lemon
2	tblsp chopped fresh basil, or dried to taste
	Salt
	Freshly ground pepper
	Sugar (optional)

Use these tips when creating beef dishes.

- Try something exotic to tenderize your meat. Kiwi — that cute, little green fruit — contains the enzyme actinidin, which works great on tough meat and lends an interesting flavor.

- Next time you're broiling meat, put a couple of slices of bread in the drip pan. The bread will soak up the grease, resulting in less smoking and less chance of the grease catching fire.

Saucy lemon-lime pot roast

Nutritional facts per serving: 418 calories; 24.7g carbohydrates; 332mg cholesterol; 32.1g total fat; 12.8g fiber; 12.3g protein; 88.2mg sodium

---

Place roast in a zipper-type plastic bag with garlic, lime juice, and lemon juice. Marinate several hours or overnight in the refrigerator. Remove and pat meat dry, reserving the marinade.

Heat oil in a Dutch oven, add meat, and brown on all sides. Add the broth and marinade, bring to a boil, and reduce heat. Simmer, covered, until meat is tender, 1 1/2 to 2 hours.

Remove meat, and degrease the liquid. Add tomatoes. Boil until thick, about 15 minutes, adding flour if necessary to thicken. Slice the meat, cover with sauce, add herbs, and heat through. Top with the grated rinds.

4 servings

1	2-pound chuck roast, trimmed of all fat
2	garlic cloves, chopped
	Juice and grated rind of 3 limes
	Juice and grated rind of 2 lemons
2	tblsp canola oil
1 1/2	cups canned beef broth
1	16-ounce can tomatoes, chopped
2	tblsp flour (optional)
1	tblsp rosemary
	Salt
	Freshly ground black pepper

Forget throwing out frozen foods attacked by freezer burn. Preventing it is as simple as 1-2-3. First wrap your food in a layer of plastic wrap or aluminum foil. Then slide it inside a locking freezer bag. Finally, remove absolutely all the air left inside the bag, since this is what causes those leathery spots on frozen food. Remember, freezer burn doesn't make your food unsafe, just unappetizing.

Texas beef and black bean enchiladas

Nutritional facts per serving: 492 calories; 56.6g carbohydrates; 45.4mg cholesterol; 17.4g total fat; 10.7g fiber; 27g protein; 1052.8mg sodium

Preheat oven to 350 degrees. Coat a small baking dish with nonstick cooking spray.

Brown the ground beef and drain. Add onion and pepper, and cook for about 5 minutes or until vegetables are tender. Stir in half the taco sauce and all the seasonings, mixing well. Heat thoroughly then set aside.

Lay tortillas out flat, and arrange 2 or 3 spoonfuls of beans down the center of each. Top with beef mixture and shredded cheese to taste. Roll up the tortillas and place them seam-side down in the baking dish. Pour remaining taco sauce over all, and bake for 30 minutes or until heated through. Serve with lettuce and tomato.

4 servings

1/2	pound lean ground beef
1/4	cup chopped onion
1/4	cup diced green pepper
1	cup taco sauce
1	tsp chili powder
1/2	tsp garlic salt
1/2	tsp ground cumin
1	16-ounce can black beans, rinsed and drained
4	8" whole-wheat tortillas
1/2	cup low-fat shredded cheese
2	cups shredded lettuce
1	small tomato, diced

Here are some tips that will cut fat, calories, and cholesterol. After cooking ground meat, blot it with paper towels, then put it in a colander and rinse with hot water. You've just "bathed" out about half the fat. Or microwave your hamburger patties for one to three minutes, then pour off the liquid and grill as usual. Choose reduced-fat or fat-free cheeses to top that hamburger, and pair it with oven-roasted potatoes instead of French fries.

Great Georgia chili

Nutritional facts per serving: 216 calories; 18.2g carbohydrates; 53.1mg cholesterol; 4.7g total fat; 4.7g fiber; 25.9g protein; 283.5mg sodium

Spray a large heavy-bottomed frying pan with nonstick vegetable spray. Add olive oil, and heat on Medium. Add onion, garlic, bell pepper, and banana pepper, cover, and cook over medium heat, stirring occasionally, until just tender, about 3 minutes. Add ground turkey, and cook until no longer pink. Season lightly with salt and pepper to taste.

Add chili powder, cumin, and bay leaf, and stir to mix well. Cook for 2 minutes, stirring, to meld flavors with meat. Add tomatoes and kidney beans. Reduce heat to Low, and simmer 30 minutes, stirring occasionally. Season to taste with salt, pepper, and Tabasco. Remove bay leaf before serving.

To spice up this low-heat chili, add jalapeños, hot peppers, hot sauce, or chili powder. To make it thicker, just cook it longer. This chili is best when cooked the day before serving — allowing time for the flavors to meld.

1	tblsp olive oil
1/2	large yellow onion, chopped
2	garlic cloves, chopped
3/4	cup chopped green bell pepper
1	small banana pepper, chopped
3/4	pound ground turkey
	Salt
	Freshly ground black pepper
1 1/2	tsp hot chili powder
1/4	tsp cumin
1	bay leaf
1	14-ounce can tomatoes, diced, with juice
1	8-ounce can kidney beans with liquid
	Tabasco

Serve immediately, or cool, cover, and refrigerate up to 2 days, or freeze up to 3 months.

4 servings

Deluxe honey-mustard pork tenderloin

Nutritional facts per serving: 171 calories; 0.9g carbohydrates; 73.6mg cholesterol; 7.5g total fat; 0.1g fiber; 24.1g protein; 321mg sodium

Whisk together 1 1/2 teaspoons of the olive oil with the honey, lime juice, orange juice, cumin, mustard, Tabasco, salt, and pepper. Put the pork tenderloin in a glass or plastic dish, add the marinade, and turn to make sure it is coated on all sides. Refrigerate for 1 hour, turning once.

Heat the remaining 1 1/2 teaspoons of olive oil over medium heat in a frying pan. Add the tenderloin and cover. Cook until deeply brown, turning every 5 to 6 minutes for 18 to 20 minutes. Temperature should be 150 degrees, and the center should be a little pink.

Remove the tenderloin from the pan, and let rest for 10 minutes before carving so the juices will settle. It will still continue to cook.

4 servings

3	tsp olive oil
1	tblsp honey
1 1/2	tsp fresh lime juice
1 1/2	tsp fresh orange juice
1	tsp cumin
1	tsp Dijon mustard
1/2	tsp Tabasco
1/4	tsp salt
1/4	tsp black pepper
1	1- to 1 1/2-pound pork tenderloin, fat and membrane removed

Because pork tenderloins have no fat to keep them juicy, you should marinate them to help prevent drying out. Pork can be a little pink in the center and still be completely safe to eat.

Glazed pork sauté with apples and peppers

Nutritional facts per serving: 413 calories; 12.5g carbohydrates; 225.8mg cholesterol; 15.3g total fat; 32.2g fiber; 18.2g protein; 569.3mg sodium

Heat 1 tablespoon of oil in a large pan, and add onions, apples, and peppers. Sauté 3 to 5 minutes, until slightly softened. Remove mixture and set aside.

Add the remaining oil to the pan with the pork. Brown the meat all over, about 5 minutes total. Remove pork from the pan, adding it to the onion mixture. Add the soy sauce, vinegar, and chicken broth to the pan, and bring to a boil. Cook until reduced and nearly syrupy, about 4 minutes. Add the pork and vegetables back into the pan, and toss well to coat. Season to taste with salt, pepper, thyme and parsley.

4 servings

2	tblsp olive oil
2	medium onions, sliced
1	Granny Smith apple, peeled, cored, and cut into 8 wedges
2	red or green bell peppers, sliced 1/2" thick lengthwise
1	1-pound pork tenderloin, sliced crosswise into 1/2" slices
1	tblsp low-sodium soy sauce
1/4	cup red wine vinegar
1/2	cup canned chicken broth
	Salt
	Freshly ground black pepper
2-3	tblsp chopped fresh thyme
1	tblsp finely chopped fresh parsley

Nutrition **Note** Although the B vitamins are separate substances, they often work together. For example, your body requires folate in order to absorb the other B vitamins. A deficiency in one could quickly lead to deficiencies in the others as well. Be sure to get a balanced intake of B vitamins because each contributes to your good health.

Succulent roasted pork tenderloin

Nutritional facts per serving: 273 calories; 33.4g carbohydrates; 73.6mg cholesterol; 4.1g total fat; 0.9g fiber; 25.8g protein; 1248.3mg sodium

Whisk together juice, soy sauce, mustard, thyme, garlic powder, and sugar. Put the pork tenderloin in a glass or plastic dish, and add the marinade ingredients, making sure it is coated on all sides. Cover and refrigerate, turning once, for 1 hour.

5 1/2	ounces low-sodium vegetable juice, such as V8®
1/2	cup light soy sauce
1	tblsp Dijon mustard
2	tsp dried thyme
1	tsp garlic powder
1/4	cup brown sugar
1	1-pound pork tenderloin, fat and membrane removed

To grill, heat the grill to Medium-hot. Grill the meat for 10 minutes on each side for medium. To roast, preheat the oven to 500 degrees. Put the meat on a baking sheet on a rack, and roast for 5 minutes. Reduce heat to 425 degrees, and roast for about 10 minutes more for medium, or longer for your desired degree of doneness.

Remove from grill or oven, and let juices settle for 10 minutes before carving.

4 servings

Nutrition **Note**   Vitamin B1 (thiamin) is required by every cell in your body to process energy. It even plays important roles in the function of your nerves, muscles, and heart. You need this vitamin for your nerves to carry signals from your brain to other parts of your body so it helps keep your brain and your body working efficiently. If you're feeling tired and a little forgetful, you may need more B1 in your diet. Fortunately, pork can be one good place to get it. Others include fortified cereals, enriched white rice, and black-eyed peas.

Hearty grilled lamb chops

Nutritional facts per serving: 344 calories; 1.7g carbohydrates; 149.6mg cholesterol; 12.6g total fat; 0.2g fiber; 47.4g protein; 155.7mg sodium

Combine wine, vinegar, oil, garlic, pepper flakes, thyme, salt, and pepper in a glass or plastic container. Place lamb chops in the marinade, and turn over to coat evenly. Cover and refrigerate for 1 hour.

Fire up the grill for a medium-hot fire, or preheat the oven to Broil.

When ready, remove chops from the marinade. Grill chops for 1 1/2 to 2 minutes on each side for rare to medium-rare or 2 1/2 to 3 minutes on each side for medium. If broiling, place chops on the pan, and place under the preheated broiler about 6 inches away from the element. Broil 2 to 3 minutes on each side for rare to medium-rare. Broil 2 1/2 to 3 1/2 minutes on each side for medium.

Remove chops from the grill or oven, lightly cover with aluminum foil, and let set in a warm place for 5 minutes before serving.

4 servings

1/2	cup white wine
2	tblsp white wine vinegar
4	tblsp olive oil
3	garlic cloves, smashed
1/2	tsp red pepper flakes
1	tblsp chopped fresh thyme, or 1 tsp dried thyme
	Salt
	Freshly ground black pepper
8	4-ounce lamb chops

Although 3- to 4-ounce lamb chops are the most common, the size of chops varies. Cooking time will vary slightly depending on the thickness of the chop.

Luscious rosemary-garlic lamb chops

Nutritional facts per serving: 210 calories; 0.6g carbohydrates; 72.4mg cholesterol; 12.4g total fat; 0.1g fiber; 23.3g protein; 72.8mg sodium

Preheat the grill or broiler.

To make garlic into a paste, peel the cloves and place on a cutting board. Use a metal spatula to mash. Add salt, rosemary, and olive oil to the garlic.

Remove any fat from the chops. Spread the garlic paste on both sides of the lamb chops. Grill or broil them 5 to 6 minutes per side over medium-high heat, or until desired doneness is reached. Season to taste with pepper.

6-8 lamb chops, 1 1/2" thick

2 garlic cloves

2 tsp kosher (coarse) salt

1 tblsp chopped fresh rosemary

2 tblsp olive oil

Freshly ground black pepper

4 servings

Meats are a major carrier of bacteria. Use proper handling and preparation to prevent them from making you sick.

- Wash your hands with warm soapy water for at least 20 seconds before and after handling raw meat. Clean cutting boards, knives, and other utensils in warm, soapy water as well as between uses.

- Clean up spilled juices with paper towels rather than a dishcloth or sponge that's likely to spread germs. And scrub countertops where meat has been prepared with a mixture of 1 tablespoon chlorine bleach to one quart of water.

- Thaw frozen foods in the refrigerator or microwave, not on the countertop.

Quick and delicious leg of lamb

Nutritional facts per serving: 434 calories; 0.0 g carbohydrates; 107.1 mg cholesterol; 38.7 g total fat; 0.0 g fiber; 21.7 g protein; 182.8 mg sodium

Take lamb out of the freezer 30 minutes before serving.

Heat enough of the butter and oil to cover the bottom of a large frying pan. With a sharp knife, cut thin (1/8" to 1/4" thick) slices of the lamb into the sizzling fat. Brown and turn. Brown the second side quickly.

Season to taste with salt and pepper, and serve immediately with jelly or sauce. Return any unused lamb to the freezer.

4 servings

1	1-pound boneless leg of lamb, fat trimmed, frozen
1/4	cup butter
1/4	cup oil
	Salt
	Freshly ground black pepper
1/4	cup loganberry or cranberry sauce or jelly (optional)

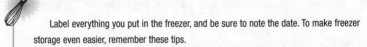

Label everything you put in the freezer, and be sure to note the date. To make freezer storage even easier, remember these tips.

- Masking tape works as well as the more expensive freezer tape. You can write on it, and it sticks tight. Cellophane tape, on the other hand, won't hold when frozen.

- Store your roll of clear plastic wrap in the freezer. It will unroll and tear more easily, and it won't stick to itself until it thaws out. Any time you have trouble getting it to stick to your bowl, try moistening the outer edge of the dish before you wrap it.

Flavorful chill-to-grill kebabs

Nutritional facts per serving: 410 calories; 25.8g carbohydrates; 321.5mg cholesterol; 16.9g total fat; 16.2g fiber; 33.7g protein; 821.4mg sodium

Preheat grill or broiler. If using wooden skewers, soak in water for 30 minutes to prevent burning.

Mix together oil, vinegar, dry mustard, soy sauce, thyme, and Worcestershire sauce. Season to taste with salt and pepper. Add the meat. Refrigerate, covered, as long as possible, 4 hours or up to overnight, turning occasionally. Remove meat from the marinade, and place on skewers, alternating with the tomato and squash.

Grill the skewers over medium-high heat on all sides for a total of 8 to 12 minutes, depending on the size of the meat chunks. Serve hot on a bed of Spiced couscous (see page 206) or wild rice.

4 servings

1/4	cup oil
1/2	cup apple cider vinegar
2	tsp dry mustard
2-4	tblsp soy sauce
1	tsp dried thyme
2	tsp Worcestershire sauce
	Salt
	Freshly ground black pepper
1	1-pound beef or lamb cut in 1" - 1 1/2" cubes
2	medium tomatoes, cut in eighths, or 16 cherry tomatoes
1	small yellow squash, cut in 1" chunks

Marinades don't just make grilled meats tastier — they make them healthier, too. Marinades can be up to 99 percent effective in preventing cancer-causing substances from forming while meat grills. Just make sure your marinade includes a flavoring like garlic or onion, a base (honey or oil), and, most importantly, an acidic liquid, like lemon juice or vinegar.

Prime veal scaloppine

Nutritional facts per serving: 326 calories; 7.9g carbohydrates; 125.6mg cholesterol; 21.8g total fat; 0.3g fiber; 23.8g protein; 99.6mg sodium

Spread a piece of wax paper on the counter. Season veal with salt and pepper. Dredge veal in flour, and shake off any excess.

Heat oil and 2 tablespoons of the butter in a large frying pan until sizzling hot. Add the veal — you may have to cook it in batches — and sauté on one side for 1 to 2 minutes or until browned. Turn and brown on the second side. Remove from pan, and keep warm on a serving platter. Repeat until all the meat is browned.

Add the rest of the butter to the pan, and cook over medium heat until it just begins to brown. Remove pan from the heat, and add lemon juice, parsley, and capers if using. Pour over the veal. Garnish with lemon slices, and serve immediately.

1/4 cup all-purpose flour

4 veal cutlets, pounded thin (about 1 pound)

Salt

Freshly ground black pepper

2 tblsp vegetable oil

4 tblsp butter

Juice of 2 lemons

2 tblsp chopped fresh parsley (optional)

2 tblsp capers (optional)

1 lemon, sliced

4 servings

Paillards is another name for a thinly pounded cut of meat, often chicken, that can be used in a scaloppine recipe. Pound paillards to slightly flatten them so they cook more quickly and uniformly. Simply lay the meat in a single layer on wax paper. Use a meat mallet, edge of a plate, or even a rolling pin to pound them slightly until they are about 1/4" thick.

Saucy grilled veal chops

Nutritional facts per serving: 412 calories; 2.7g carbohydrates; 181.6mg cholesterol; 20.7g total fat; 0.1g fiber; 46g protein; 208.7mg sodium

Combine red wine, vinegar, oil, garlic, pepper flakes, thyme, salt, and pepper in a glass or plastic container. Place veal chops in the marinade, and turn over to coat evenly. Cover and refrigerate for 1 hour.

Fire up the grill for a medium-hot fire, or preheat the oven to Broil. When ready, remove the chops from the marinade. Grill the chops for 1 1/2 to 2 minutes on each side for rare to medium-rare or 2 1/2 to 3 minutes on each side for medium.

To broil, place marinated chops on the pan, and place under the preheated broiler about 6" away from the element. Broil 2 to 3 minutes on each side for rare to medium-rare. Broil 2 1/2 to 3 1/2 minutes on each side for medium.

Remove chops from the grill or oven, lightly cover with aluminum foil, and let set in a warm place for 5 minutes before serving. Top with Smooth red bell pepper sauce (see page 325).

4 servings

1/2	cup red wine
2	tblsp red wine vinegar
4	tblsp olive oil
3	garlic cloves, smashed
1/2	tsp red pepper flakes
1	tblsp chopped fresh thyme, or 1 tsp dried thyme
	Salt
	Freshly ground black pepper
8	4-ounce veal chops
	Red pepper sauce

To trim fat without giving up beef entirely, choose beef cuts with loin or round in the name. Pick "choice" instead of "prime," and choose cuts graded USDA Select.

Light and easy homemade sausage

Nutritional facts per serving: 262 calories; 18.3g carbohydrates; 126.2mg cholesterol; 12.6g total fat; 0.3g fiber; 9.2g protein; 1289.7mg sodium

Steam apricots for 15 to 20 minutes, or until soft.

Break the sausage up with your fingers. Add apricots, onion, mustard, and tarragon, and combine lightly with your fingers. Mix in egg. Mix in bread crumbs. Gently shape the sausage into 12 patties. Refrigerate for 1 hour.

Preheat oven to 325 degrees.

Put the patties on a baking sheet with sides. Bake for 20 to 30 minutes or until browned and cooked through.

4	ounces dried apricots, chopped
1	pound bulk good-quality breakfast sausage
1/2	small onion, chopped
2	tblsp Dijon mustard
1	tsp dried tarragon
1	large egg, lightly beaten
1/2	cup fresh bread crumbs

12 servings

Nutrition **Note**

Use this recipe, and you may eat less processed sausage — a change that could help you feel better now and keep you well later. Here's the scoop. The sodium nitrites in processed sausage can cause some folks to have headaches. But even if you're not one of them, you should know that sausages are high in saturated fat. Over time, saturated fat helps shut down your arteries and contribute to high cholesterol, heart disease, and weight gain. Sausage may even contribute to your cancer risk. So, if you must have sausage, try for low-fat sausage, or use this recipe whenever you can.

Juicy sirloin steak and heart-of-palm salad

Nutritional facts per serving: 378 calories; 12g carbohydrates; 69.2mg cholesterol; 24.5g total fat; 4.3g fiber; 28.1g protein; 693.9mg sodium

Broil or grill sirloin about 15 minutes or until desired doneness. Cool and cut into thin slices. Place in a resealable plastic bag. Place the hearts of palm, tomatoes, carrots, and green onion in another resealable plastic bag.

In a small bowl or jar with lid, combine dressing ingredients: oil, vinegar, mustard, zest, dill, salt, and pepper. Whisk or shake until thoroughly mixed. Pour half the dressing over the meat and the other half over the vegetables. Seal the bags, and refrigerate 6 hours or overnight. Turn bags occasionally to distribute marinade evenly.

Divide the salad greens and mushrooms evenly between 4 plates. Arrange steak and vegetable mixture on top.

4 servings

1	1-pound boneless beef sirloin steak, 1" thick
1	14-ounce can hearts of palm, drained and diced
1	cup cherry tomatoes, halved
1/2	cup sliced carrots
1/4	cup sliced green onion
1/3	cup olive oil
1/4	cup white wine vinegar
2	tsp Dijon-style mustard
1/2	tsp lemon zest
1/2	tsp dried dill
1/2	tsp salt
1/4	tsp pepper
6	cups mixed salad greens
3/4	cup sliced fresh mushrooms

According to the Texas Beef Council, it only takes one glance to tell if that supermarket cut of beef is fresh. They say to look for meat with a bright, cherry-red color that is firm when you touch it, not soft. Make sure the package itself is cold, with no tears in the wrapping or too much liquid in the bottom. At the very least, you should check the sell-by date on the label.

Un"beet"able roast beef salad

Nutritional facts per serving: 439 calories; 3g carbohydrates; 91.7mg cholesterol; 43.7g total fat; 0.5g fiber; 32.8g protein; 117.1mg sodium

Toss together roast beef, beets, and onions.

To make dressing, combine vinegar, mustard, and garlic in a small bowl. Whisk in oil in a slow, steady stream. Season to taste with salt and pepper. Add to the beef and vegetables, and toss to coat. Refrigerate, covered, for 1 hour.

Defrost snow peas, and add half to the beef and vegetables, and toss gently. Put in serving bowl, and sprinkle with the remaining peas, parsley, and optional herb.

4 servings

1	1-pound rare roast beef, cut into 1/2" strips
1	4-ounce can whole beets, drained, cut into strips
1	bunch green onions, chopped
1/4	cup red wine vinegar
1	tsp Dijon mustard
1	garlic clove
2/3	cup canola oil
	Salt
	Freshly ground black pepper
1	6-ounce package frozen snow peas
2	tblsp chopped fresh parsley
1	tblsp chopped fresh oregano or thyme (optional)

Nutrition **Note** You may help prevent sinusitis by boosting your antioxidant levels. Danish scientists measured levels of the antioxidants glutathione and uric acid in the nasal linings of people with and without sinusitis. Those with sinusitis had significantly less glutathione and uric acid than healthy folks. So eating foods high in glutathione and purines may help.

Easy marinated salmon

Nutritional facts per serving: 303 calories; 4.1g carbohydrates; 62.4mg cholesterol; 21.3g total fat; 0.3g fiber; 23.1g protein; 319.4mg sodium

Combine all marinade ingredients. Place salmon in a resealable plastic bag, and pour marinade in. Close bag and refrigerate for 4 to 6 hours, turning occasionally to coat fish.

Spray grill rack with nonstick cooking spray and preheat grill. Remove salmon from marinade and grill until fish flakes with a fork, turning halfway through cooking.

4 servings

4	4-ounce salmon filets
1/4	cup peanut oil
1/2	tsp sesame oil
2	tblsp low-sodium soy sauce
2	tblsp balsamic vinegar
2	tblsp sliced green onion
1 1/2	tsp brown sugar
1	garlic clove, minced
3/4	tsp ground ginger
1/2	tsp crushed red pepper flakes

Nutrition **Note**
To keep your heart healthy, eat fish more often. A study on doctors found that those who ate at least one fish meal a week were 52 percent less likely to die from a sudden heart attack than those who ate fish less than once a month. It's the omega-3 fatty acids in fish that lower your blood pressure, reduce the stickiness of your blood, and help regulate your heartbeat. Fatty fish such as tuna, sardines, herring, mackerel, and salmon contain lots of omega-3.

Broiled salmon with Dijon mustard

Nutritional facts per serving: 344 calories; 6.2g carbohydrates; 100.4mg cholesterol; 18.4g total fat; 0g fiber; 33.8g protein; 850.4mg sodium

1	1-pound salmon filet, skinned and deboned
	Salt
	Freshly ground black pepper
1/4	cup Dijon mustard

Preheat broiler. Adjust rack so it is 4 to 5 inches from the heat source.

Place salmon in a roasting pan. Season with salt and pepper. Spread the Dijon mustard evenly over the top of the fish, place under the broiler, and cook 8 to 10 minutes for every inch of thickness, turning half way through.

Remove from oven, and cut into serving portions. Serve with boiled potatoes and spinach.

2 servings

Nutrition **Note**

If you're fed up with your arthritis, feed yourself more fatty fish. According to researchers, people with rheumatoid arthritis who eat fish containing omega-3 fatty acids have fewer tender joints and less morning stiffness. Add fish like salmon, mackerel, sardines, tuna, Pacific herring — and even anchovies — to your diet regularly. It may not be the ultimate cure for your arthritis, but it could be a delicious way to loosen up your joints.

Oriental baked salmon

Nutritional facts per serving: 221 calories; 1.1g carbohydrates; 73.7mg cholesterol; 10.1g total fat; 0.2g fiber; 29.7g protein; 851.3mg sodium

Preheat oven to 400 degrees. Grease a large ovenproof dish.

Heat oil in a small pan over medium heat. Add onion slices and sauté until soft, about 5 minutes. Transfer onions to the ovenproof dish, and top with the fish filet.

In a small mixing bowl, combine sesame oil, soy sauce, water, brown sugar and sherry if using, hot pepper sauce, and ginger. Pour over fish, and sprinkle with salt and pepper. Cover the baking dish tightly with aluminum foil. Bake 12 to 15 minutes or until just done — the salmon should be opaque, but not dry.

4 servings

1	tblsp canola oil
1	medium onion, sliced
1	1-pound salmon filet (or 1 1/2 pounds 1" thick steaks)
1/2	tblsp sesame oil
3	tblsp soy sauce
1	tblsp water
1	tsp brown sugar (optional)
2	tblsp dry sherry (optional)
1/4	tsp hot pepper sauce
1	tsp finely chopped fresh ginger
	Salt
	Freshly ground black pepper

Nutrition **Note** Replace the meat in your meals with fish, and your diet would look more like the ones in Asia. People in Asian countries have long been known for their low rates of heart disease, obesity, and many cancers. Eat like they do, and your health might benefit. According to the Asian food pyramid, most of your diet should consist of rice, noodles, bread, millet, corn, and other grains. The next level of the pyramid contains foods to eat daily — fruits, vegetables, nuts, legumes, and seeds. Small amounts of vegetable oil, fish, shellfish, and dairy products may also be eaten daily. Higher up the pyramid are sweets, eggs, and poultry, which should be eaten only weekly. Finally, red meat is advised just once a month.

Basil-parsley salmon with tomatoes

Nutritional facts per serving: 146 calories; 2.9g carbohydrates; 58.9mg cholesterol; 4.1g total fat; 0.8g fiber; 23.1g protein; 82.1mg sodium

Preheat oven to 400 degrees.

Sprinkle salmon with basil and parsley. Place in a roasting pan. Cover fish with tomato slices, leaving no flesh exposed. Season with salt and pepper. Roast 10 minutes per inch of thickness, including the tomatoes. Broil the last few minutes if desired.

2 servings

1   1-pound salmon filet, skinned and deboned

1   tblsp chopped fresh basil

1   tblsp chopped fresh parsley

2   tomatoes, peeled and thinly sliced, about 1/4" thick

Salt

Freshly ground pepper

Nutrition **Note**

Eating fish could literally help save your skin. Some antioxidant powers of fatty fish come from a substance called astaxanthin. This antioxidant finds and destroys free radicals that might damage your cells. Studies show it can protect you from skin cancer, too. The pinkish color of salmon as well as the lobster's redness come from astaxanthin — a natural protector against the sun's harmful ultraviolet rays. Since skin cancer has been linked to sunburns, it's wise to protect yourself as much as possible. When mice were fed astaxanthin in their diets, then exposed to ultraviolet radiation — similar to the rays of the sun — their skin was less damaged than mice that weren't fed the antioxidant. So think pink, and eat a little more salmon. You may be doing yourself more good than you know.

Easy grilled side of salmon

Nutritional facts per serving: 424 calories; 0.7g carbohydrates; 116.8mg cholesterol; 28.3g total fat; 0g fiber; 39.4g protein; 117mg sodium

Whisk together olive oil, lemon juice, and herbs. Lay the salmon out flat in a shallow dish. Coat both sides with the marinade. Sprinkle both sides lightly with salt and pepper. Cover with plastic wrap, and refrigerate for 30 minutes.

Preheat the grill to Medium-high. Place the salmon on the grill skin-side down. Grill the salmon for 5 minutes — slightly more if it is thicker than 1 inch. Carefully turn and grill it skin-side up for an additional 5 minutes.

Serve hot, or cool to room temperature and refrigerate. This can also be cooked under the broiler.

1	2-pound side of salmon, bones removed, skin on
2	tblsp olive oil
2	tblsp fresh lemon juice
1	tblsp chopped fresh dill, or tarragon, or basil
	Salt
	White pepper

4 servings

Try this simple formula to determine how long to grill or broil a fish.

1. Measure the piece of fish at its thickest point.

2. Cook it 10 minutes per inch for the first inch, five minutes on each side.

3. Add only 1 more minute per side for an additional inch, then test it.

To tell if a filet is cooked "well-done," insert a fork along the center indentation, and twist slightly. The filet should separate easily, and the flesh will be opaque.

Low-cal poached salmon

Nutritional facts per serving: 126 calories; 6.3g carbohydrates; 38mg cholesterol; 5.5g total fat; 0.2g fiber; 12.7g protein; 8.5mg sodium

Put 2 quarts of water in a frying pan. Add Old Bay seasoning and simmer for 10 minutes to infuse the water with the seasoning. Slide in the filets or steaks. Reduce heat to Low, and simmer for 10 minutes, or until the fish tests done.

2	tsp Old Bay seasoning
4	4-ounce salmon filets or 6-ounce salmon steaks
8	ounces plain yogurt
1	tblsp fresh lemon juice
2	tsp chopped fresh dill
	Zest of 1 lemon
	Dash paprika

To test a filet, insert a fork along the center groove, and twist slightly. The filet should separate easily. To test a salmon steak, insert the fork along the dorsal bone at the center of the steak, and twist slightly. The bone should separate easily from the meat. Remove fish from the water. Drain for a moment on paper towels. Mix the yogurt and lemon juice. Sprinkle fish with fresh dill. Garnish with lemon zest and paprika, and serve with the lemon yogurt mix.

4 servings

Nutrition **Note** Eat fatty fish for their health benefits, but don't let a balanced diet become "the one that got away." Some studies suggest that eating lots of fatty fish without a well-balanced diet could reduce the amount of vitamins A, C, and E available to you. And you need these powerful antioxidant vitamins to help defend you from disease. But don't eliminate the fish oils that work to protect your cells. Instead, aim for a balanced diet that includes both fatty fish and plenty of colorful foods rich in vitamins A, C, and E.

Marinated tuna steak sauté

Nutritional facts per serving: 345 calories; 8.9g carbohydrates; 76.4mg cholesterol; 15.3g total fat; 1.2g fiber; 41.4g protein; 70.6mg sodium

Mix half the oil with the ginger, onions, garlic, hot pepper sauce, and water. Place the tuna in a glass dish large enough to hold the steaks side by side. Pour the marinade evenly over them all. Cover and refrigerate for 1 hour.

Combine the flour, curry powder, salt, and pepper in a separate shallow bowl. Dredge the tuna steaks in the flour mixture until evenly coated. Heat the remaining oil in a large skillet over medium-high heat. Add tuna and sauté 3 to 4 minutes a side or until cooked through and golden brown.

4 servings

4	6-ounce tuna steaks, 3/4" thick
1/4	cup olive oil
1	tblsp grated fresh ginger
8	green onions, chopped
1	garlic clove, minced
1/4	tsp hot pepper sauce
1/4	cup water
1/2	cup all-purpose flour
1	tsp curry powder
	Salt
	Black pepper

Nutrition Note

Whether you hook them at the lake or at the supermarket, eating fish at least twice a week could sink your risk for heart disease and stroke. There's evidence, too, that fish could combat arthritis, diabetes, cataracts, Alzheimer's disease, depression, and a host of other age-related illnesses. If you're worried about your risk of cancer, take care to balance the amount of omega-3 and omega-6 fatty acids in your diet. Researchers believe having more omega-6 promotes the growth of cancerous tumors. Cut back on fried, fast, and processed foods — they're full of omega-6 fatty acids. And get two servings a week of cold-water fish like salmon, tuna, herring, and mackerel for their good fats.

Lemon grilled tuna steak

Nutritional facts per serving: 128 calories; 1.3g carbohydrates; 51.2mg cholesterol; 1.2g total fat; 0.1g fiber; 26.5g protein; 42.2mg sodium

Marinate the steaks in lemon juice for 30 minutes. Prepare a hot grill, brushing with oil if desired. Season tuna liberally with lemon juice, salt, and pepper. Cook the tuna on one side for 5 minutes, turn and cook for 5 minutes more on the other side. The steaks should be lightly brown on both sides, but do not overcook.

2   tuna steaks, 1 " thick

Juice of 2 lemons

Salt

Freshly ground black pepper

4 servings

Tuna is a wonderful fish, packed full of the omega-3 fatty acids that are so good for you. Buy the best tuna available. The color of good fresh tuna should range from pink to red. Like swordfish, tuna can overcook quickly and dry out. Tuna steaks are best when at least 1 " thick and cooked medium-rare — definitely no more well done than medium.

Three-herb marinated fresh tuna

Nutritional facts per serving: 458 calories; 1.5g carbohydrates; 76.4mg cholesterol; 29.6g total fat; 0.2g fiber; 40.1g protein; 65.6mg sodium

Mix together oil, wine, parsley, mint, and garlic. Pour over tuna steaks, cover, and refrigerate for 3 to 4 hours, turning at least once.

Prepare the grill. To cook, let the excess marinade drip off the tuna steaks. Cook steaks over high heat about 5 minutes per side for each inch of thickness. Turn once.

2 servings

1/4	cup canola oil
1/4	cup white wine
1	tblsp chopped fresh parsley
2	tblsp chopped fresh mint
2	garlic cloves, chopped
2	6-ounce tuna steaks, 1 1/2" - 2" thick

Nutrition **Note**

Tame triglycerides with tuna instead of aiming for zero fat in your heart-smart diet. After all, you want your triglycerides and LDL cholesterol to decrease while your HDL cholesterol goes up. But if you try to maintain a diet with less than 20 percent fat, your triglyceride levels can shoot up even as your good HDL cholesterol levels drop. The key to heart health is not to cut all fat, but to get the right kind of fat. The omega-3 essential fatty acids in fish like tuna, salmon, rainbow trout, and mackerel can bring down your LDL cholesterol numbers and keep your triglycerides under control.

Peppery ginger tuna steak

Nutritional facts per serving: 216 calories; 1.3g carbohydrates; 76.4mg cholesterol; 2.7g total fat; 0.1g fiber; 41.7g protein; 1069.2mg sodium

Preheat oven to 400 degrees.

Pat tuna steak dry, then sprinkle both sides lightly with olive oil. Mix together ginger, hot soy sauce, and wine. (Substitute low-sodium chicken broth for wine, if desired.) Pour some of the mixture into a shallow glass baking pan, lay the tuna steak in the pan, and pour on the remaining sauce mixture.

1	1/2 pound fresh tuna steak, 1" thick
1	tsp olive oil
1	tblsp chopped fresh ginger
1/4	cup hot soy sauce or soy sauce plus cayenne pepper to taste
1/4	cup white wine

Bake, uncovered, 10 minutes. (Cook 8 minutes per inch of thickness.) Remove any tough skin. Serve with a light pasta and green vegetable side dish.

2 servings

Nutrition **Note**

Seafood may help you see well for years to come. One study found that eating more fish — especially tuna — significantly slices your odds of macular degeneration, a condition that can lead to vision loss. Another study discovered that eating fish once a week netted the most protection. But remember this. According to the Massachusetts Eye and Ear study, fish and omega-3 fatty acids seem to lower your risk for macular degeneration, but only if your diet does not include much linoleic acid (omega-6 fatty acids). So pass up margarine, corn oil, and soybean oil, and eat more fatty fish like salmon, mackerel, herring, and tuna.

"Special occasion" grilled swordfish

Nutritional facts per serving: 168 calories; 0.4g carbohydrates; 44.3mg cholesterol; 7.9g total fat; 0.1g fiber; 22.4g protein; 102.1mg sodium

---

Fire up the grill to Medium-high. Combine olive oil, lemon juice, lime juice, cilantro, and basil in a small bowl, and brush on the swordfish steaks. Lightly sprinkle the steaks with salt and pepper. Grill them for 3 minutes per side, or until their centers are opaque. Remove from the grill and serve.

4 servings

4   4-ounce skinless swordfish steaks

2   tblsp extra virgin olive oil

1   tblsp fresh lemon juice

1   tblsp fresh lime juice

1   tblsp chopped fresh cilantro

1   tblsp chopped fresh basil

Salt

Freshly ground black pepper

Swordfish is great on the grill, but it intimidates people because it's as dry as the Sahara if you overcook it. Instead, cook it to medium-rare on the grill. The interior will continue to cook, so it will be a nice, juicy medium by the time you eat it. Just 3 ounces of swordfish will supply nearly all the selenium you need for the day. It's also a good source of iron, zinc, and two B vitamins. But remember to avoid serving swordfish if you or anyone else at the table is pregnant, nursing, planning to become pregnant, or feeding a young child. This fish can be very high in mercury. So save it for a treat, and don't eat it often.

Baked garlic-vinegar trout

Nutritional facts per serving: 269 calories; 5.8g carbohydrates; 101.6mg cholesterol; 11.9g total fat; 0.6g fiber; 33.6g protein; 52.3mg sodium

Heat oven to 400 degrees. Oil a 9" x 13" baking dish.

Rub both sides of fish filets with salt and pepper. Heat the tablespoon of oil and butter in a frying pan. Peel garlic cloves, and add them with the onion, sautéing until brown, about 10 minutes. Measure the filets. If they're not 1" thick, fold them in half or thirds, making them as close to 1" thick as possible, and place them in the baking dish. Top with rosemary and bay leaf and the sautéed garlic and onion.

4	rainbow trout filets
	Salt
1/2	tblsp cracked pepper
1	tblsp plus 1/2 cup olive oil
1	tblsp butter
16	garlic cloves
1	small onion, sliced
4	sprigs fresh rosemary
1	bay leaf
2	tblsp red wine vinegar

Whisk together the remaining 1/2 cup of olive oil with the red wine vinegar. Pour half of this mixture over the fish, bake 5 minutes, then pour the remaining mixture over the fish, and bake until fish flakes easily, 5 to 7 minutes longer. Total baking time should be 10 minutes per inch of thickness. Remove the bay leaf before serving.

4 servings

You're the best fish chef in three counties, but afterward, they can still smell the fish on your hands three counties away. Get rid of that lingering odor. Just dip a lemon wedge in salt, rub it on your hands, and rinse with water. Or wash them with toothpaste.

Trout filets on clever cucumber noodles

Nutritional facts per serving: 131 calories; 4.2g carbohydrates; 46.6mg cholesterol; 5g total fat; 0.8g fiber; 17.2g protein; 30mg sodium

Arrange filets in a heatproof dish. Top with lime juice, sesame oil, and cilantro. Season to taste with salt and pepper. Place the dish over a pot of simmering water, cover, and steam until the fish is opaque throughout, about 10 minutes.

Use a vegetable peeler to pare long strips from each cucumber half. Sprinkle them with salt, place in a strainer, and set aside for 10 minutes to drain. Rinse them, squeeze out the moisture, and mound on four plates. Place a trout filet on each cucumber "noodle" bed, and garnish with lime wedges.

4	3-ounce trout filets
	Juice of 2 limes
1/2	tsp sesame oil
2	tblsp chopped fresh cilantro
	Salt
	Freshly ground black pepper
2	cucumbers, peeled, halved lengthwise, and seeded
1	lime, cut into wedges

4 servings

Try these fishy tips for healthier seafood dinners you can enjoy.

- Only buy fish that are firm to the touch, have shiny, metallic skin, and show no signs of browning or slime. Make sure the fish is wrapped in a leak-proof package before you take it home.

- To reduce overall fat content without losing any omega-3, remove the skin from fish before cooking.

- Cook fish with moist heat to make the protein in it easier to digest.

Pistachio-crusted trout

Nutritional facts per serving: 388 calories; 11.4g carbohydrates; 83.7mg cholesterol; 22.1g total fat; 3.6g fiber; 37g protein; 80.3mg sodium

Preheat oven to 400 degrees.

In a large bowl, mix together pistachio nuts and flour, bread crumbs, lemon peel, rosemary, and salt and pepper to taste. Pat filets dry with a paper towel. Dip them first into the egg white mixture, then into the crumb mixture, pressing lightly so the coating will adhere. (May be done ahead to this point and refrigerated up to 4 hours.)

Place filets on a baking pan, and cook 10 minutes per inch of thickness, or until the fish is opaque. Serve at once with lemon wedges.

4 servings

1 cup pistachio nuts, finely chopped with 2 tblsp flour

1/2 cup fine, dry bread crumbs

1 tblsp grated lemon peel (no white attached)

2 tsp chopped rosemary

Salt

Freshly ground black pepper

4 6-ounce trout filets

2 egg whites beaten with 1 tblsp water

Lemon wedges

Nutrition **Note**   Trout can help you fight the vitamin B12 drought older adults often face. If you're over 50, your requirement for vitamin B12 totals 2.4 micrograms daily. That may not sound like much, but your body has a harder time absorbing it from food as you age. As a result, B12 deficiencies are all too common among older adults. So pay close attention to meeting your needs for this nutrient. Eating trout can help because just 3 ounces gives you well over 100 percent of the B12 you need. Trout is also a good source of vitamin B6, niacin, zinc, and potassium, so it's good for your health in more ways than one.

Baked Italian flounder

Nutritional facts per serving: 97 calories; 3.7g carbohydrates; 41.3mg cholesterol; 1.2g total fat; 0.6g fiber; 16.6g protein; 357.5mg sodium

Preheat oven to 400 degrees.

Arrange thawed filets in ungreased 13" x 9" x 2" baking dish. Sprinkle with paprika and salt. Place 1 tomato slice on each filet. Sprinkle with green onions and tarragon. Pour dressing over all. Bake uncovered until fish flakes easily with a fork, about 10 minutes.

4 servings

1	12-ounce package frozen flounder filets about 1" thick
	Paprika
	Salt
4	tomato slices, 1/2" thick
2	green onions, chopped
1/4	tsp dried tarragon
1/4	cup low-fat Italian salad dressing

Fish and tips:

- To keep raw fish fresh and free from odors, rinse it with fresh lemon juice and water as soon as you get home. Dry thoroughly, rewrap, and refrigerate.

- Get rid of fishy smells in your microwave fast and easy. Pour a bit of vanilla extract in a bowl, and microwave on High for one minute. Repeat if necessary.

- If you don't have vanilla, get out a lemon, and cut it in quarters. Place the lemon and a cup of water in a microwave-safe dish. Cook on High for three minutes.

Herb and citrus catfish

Nutritional facts per serving: 323 calories; 1.1g carbohydrates; 80mg cholesterol; 23.1g total fat; 0.1g fiber; 26.5g protein; 91.3mg sodium

Combine all ingredients except the fish and parsley. Place the filets in a glass or plastic baking dish, and pour the mixture over them. Cover and refrigerate. In 15 minutes, turn the fish. Refrigerate for another 15 minutes.

Preheat the broiler. Cover the broiling pan with aluminum foil, and spray the foil with nonstick spray. Broil catfish for about 3 minutes on each side, depending on the thickness. They should flake easily with a fork. Sprinkle with parsley, and serve immediately with lemon wedges, if desired.

4 servings

1	tsp fresh lemon juice
1	tblsp fresh lime juice
1	large garlic clove, crushed
1	tblsp apple cider vinegar
3	tblsp olive oil
1/4	tsp chopped fresh rosemary
1/4	tsp chopped fresh basil
4	6-ounce catfish filets
2	tblsp chopped fresh parsley
	Lemon wedges (optional)

Nutrition **Note**

This recipe adds the blockbuster power of garlic to the good-for-you gifts of fish — and that may be one winning combination for your heart. Medical researchers have discovered that this one-two punch lowers bad LDL cholesterol more and presents a better ratio of good to bad cholesterol than either food source alone. This is an exciting discovery for people trying to control their cholesterol without taking drugs. A garlic-fish combination may be just what the chef — and the doctor — ordered.

Zesty ginger grilled grouper

Nutritional facts per serving: 197 calories; 3.6g carbohydrates; 62.8mg cholesterol; 1.8g total fat; 0.2g fiber; 67.8g protein; 261.6mg sodium

Place fish steaks in a shallow bowl. Mix together soy sauce and fresh ginger, and pour it over the steaks.

Brush the grill with oil if desired. Heat the grill. When hot, remove the fish from the marinade and grill approximately 5 minutes on each side for each inch of thickness, depending on the heat. The grouper may break up into chunks, so be prepared to remove it with a slotted spatula or a fish spatula.

2   grouper steaks, 1 1/2" - 2" thick

2   tblsp soy sauce

1   slice fresh ginger, chopped

4 servings

Nutrition **Note** Add more fish to your diet, and you may reel in a better night's sleep. The amino acid L-tryptophan tells your body to produce more melatonin, which helps you sleep better. The best way to regulate your natural melatonin levels is to eat foods high in L-tryptophan. Your top options include fish, cheddar cheese, cottage cheese, pork, chicken, turkey, beans, eggs, figs, dates, beef, and oatmeal. Try eating tryptophan-rich foods about an hour before bedtime. Your melatonin levels may go up, and you may sleep more soundly.

Baked red snapper filets with stuffing

Nutritional facts per serving: 337 calories; 15g carbohydrates; 96.2mg cholesterol; 11.4g total fat; 4.6g fiber; 46.9g protein; 156.5mg sodium

Preheat oven to 350 degrees. Oil a baking dish. Rinse fish and pat dry, then brush with oil.

To make stuffing, melt butter in a skillet, and add onions and bell pepper. Cook until onions are nearly soft and the pepper still crunchy. Add tomato, herbs, olives, and salt and pepper to taste. Divide this mixture, and put half in the center of each filet. Roll up the filets from small side to large, skin side inside. Place in baking dish. Measure the thickness of the fish, and bake 10 minutes for every inch of thickness, about 30 to 40 minutes. Remove to a warm platter, or serve from the baking dish. Pour lemon juice over the fish, and decorate with lemon slices.

2 servings

2	6-ounce filets of red snapper
1	tsp olive oil
1	tblsp butter
3	green onions, chopped
1	small red bell pepper, chopped
1	tomato, peeled, seeded, and chopped
2	tblsp chopped fresh parsley
1	tsp chopped fresh basil (optional)
4	black olives, pitted and sliced (optional)
	Salt
	Freshly ground black pepper
	Juice of 1 lemon
1	lemon, sliced

Nutrition **Note**

Red snapper may be a good fish to eat and here's why. Fish are the main food sources of the toxins mercury and PCBs (polychlorinated biphenyls). The older and larger the fish, the more toxins it may have accumulated. But red snapper is a low-mercury fish. According to the Food and Drug Administration, most people are safe eating up to 14 ounces a week of low-mercury fish such as red snapper, fresh tuna, orange roughy, marlin, and others.

Heavenly halibut with ginger vegetables

Nutritional facts per serving: 156 calories; 5.6g carbohydrates; 36.3mg cholesterol; 2.7g total fat; 1.8g fiber; 25.8g protein; 345mg sodium

Cut each halibut steak into 4 pieces. Heat canola oil in a large skillet over high heat. Add fish to the skillet, and cook 5 minutes. Turn the fish, and add the ginger, soy sauce, sherry, red bell pepper, and carrot ribbons. Simmer 5 minutes to cook the vegetables slightly. (The fish should cook a total of 10 minutes per inch of thickness. If it is done before the vegetables, transfer to a warm plate while the vegetables finish cooking.)

Add the snow peas and bean sprouts, and cook 2 minutes longer. Toss well to coat vegetables with the sauce. Serve with cellophane noodles if desired.

4 servings

1	tblsp canola oil
2	1" thick halibut steaks, about 8 ounces each
1	tblsp finely chopped fresh ginger
1	tblsp soy sauce
1-2	tblsp sherry (optional)
1/2	cup julienned red bell pepper
1	carrot, peeled and cut into ribbons
1/2	cup snow peas
1/4	cup bean sprouts
	Cellophane noodles, rehydrated (optional)

Chinese cellophane noodles make a great accompaniment to this dish. These transparent noodles are made from ground mung beans. They are usually sold in a bundle and are brittle and hard in their dried state. Cellophane noodles rehydrate quickly in warm water and require no cooking.

Orange roughy Romano

Nutritional facts per serving: 235 calories; 2.9g carbohydrates; 65.6mg cholesterol; 11g total fat; 0.1g fiber; 29.5g protein; 524.8mg sodium

Thaw filets if frozen. Preheat oven to 350 degrees. Coat a 9" x 13" baking pan with nonstick spray.

Separate filets into 3 portions. Place in a single layer in greased baking pan. Combine sour cream, Romano cheese, lemon juice, hot pepper sauce, onions, and salt, and spread over fish. Sprinkle paprika on top. Bake 25-30 minutes, or until fish flakes easily with a fork.

3 servings

1	pound orange roughy filets
1/2	cup low-fat sour cream
1/4	cup Romano cheese
1 1/2	tsp fresh lemon juice
	Dash hot pepper sauce
3/4	tsp instant minced onions
1/4	tsp salt
1/4	tsp paprika

Nutrition **Note**   Heart attack symptoms can be surprisingly different depending on whether you're male or female. A man is more likely to have squeezing chest pressure that lasts more than 10 minutes; pain that spreads to the neck, jaw, shoulders, or arms — especially the left arm; and sweating, nausea, dizziness, or shortness of breath. But a woman is more likely to experience mild chest pain, breathlessness, dizziness or lightheadedness, and nausea or heartburn. Whether you're a man or woman, if you suffer any of these symptoms for more than 10 minutes, get immediate medical care.

Pompano in a salt crust

Nutritional facts per serving: 368 calories; 0g carbohydrates; 113.6mg cholesterol; 21.6g total fat; 0g fiber; 41.6g protein; 5598.4mg sodium

---

Preheat oven to 350 degrees. Cover a baking sheet with a 1/4" layer of kosher salt.

Kosher (coarse) salt

1 2- to 3-pound whole pompano, cleaned, fins trimmed

Freshly ground black pepper

Pat the fish dry. Season on each side with pepper to taste. Place fish on the baking sheet, and sprinkle generously with more salt to cover the fish entirely.

Bake until done, about 12 minutes per inch of thickness (including the salt crust), 25 to 30 minutes. Remove from oven, and let cool slightly on a rack.

Crack the salt layer with a knife. The skin and salt crust should be easily removed to expose 2 filets that will have separated from the spine during cooking. Gently remove the filets with a knife. Remove the spine, and repeat procedure for the remaining 2 filets. By peeling away the salt crust, you will eliminate most of the sodium in this dish.

4 servings

Nutrition **Note** Pamper your skin with pompano? It just might help. Pompano contains health-building omega-3 fats. Eat enough of these fatty fish, and you may like what you see in the mirror. That's because an added bonus of eating lots of fatty fish is healthier looking skin. If your skin is dry and rough, it could be a sign you need more oil. Eating foods with omega-3 fats should give your skin a healthy sheen.

Simple broiled lemon-herb fish

Nutritional facts per serving: 190 calories; 1.4g carbohydrates; 97.7mg cholesterol; 9.8g total fat; 0.1g fiber; 23.3g protein; 62mg sodium

---

Dip filets in the butter or oil. Place on a foil-lined baking sheet. Measure the filets' thickness. If less than 1/2", fold over. Broil until done, 10 minutes for each inch of thickness, turning halfway through the cooking time, if possible. When done, transfer to a warm platter using a spatula or pancake turner, and season with salt and pepper. Drizzle lemon or lime juice over filets, and sprinkle with herbs and paprika as desired.

4 servings

4   fish filets (1 1/4 - 1 1/2 pounds)

2   tblsp butter or oil (optional)

    Salt

    Freshly ground black pepper

1/4   cup fresh lemon or lime juice

1   tblsp fresh chopped herbs, such as rosemary, thyme, oregano, basil, or chives (optional)

1/4   tsp paprika (optional)

Buy your seafood from a seller that works hard at food safety, and you'll help protect your family from the risk of food poisoning. Use these tips from the FDA to help you choose.

- Notice how the fish are displayed. They should be in a case or under protective cover — and should literally be "on ice." Their ice bedding should be thick and show no signs of melting. What's more, each fish should be displayed belly down so that the ice drains away from it.

- Check that employees are wearing clean clothing and a hair covering.

- Watch to see whether employees wear disposable gloves to handle the fish and whether they change gloves after handling raw seafood.

Tilapia on stir-fry vegetables

Nutritional facts per serving: 406 calories; 26.1g carbohydrates; 98.7mg cholesterol; 16.8g total fat; 6g fiber; 38.1g protein; 762.6mg sodium

Cut filets into 1" pieces. Toss together tilapia and sesame oil. Set aside.

Heat oil in a wok or frying pan until hot. Add green onions, garlic, ginger, carrots, red bell pepper, and water chestnuts, and stir-fry for about 2 minutes. Add fish pieces, optional sherry, chicken broth, soy sauce, rice wine vinegar, sugar, and red pepper flakes. Cover and steam over medium heat about 5 minutes. Remove fish and vegetables from the wok and set aside.

Add orange juice and shredded cabbage, and stir-fry until the cabbage just begins to wilt. Place the cabbage on a platter, and top with the fish, vegetables, and chow mein noodles. Season to taste with salt and pepper.

Do your frozen fish fillets taste like they've been in your freezer since the ice age? Pour milk over them, and let them thaw in the refrigerator. They'll taste as fresh as today's catch.

4 servings

1	pound tilapia or other thick filets
1	tsp sesame oil
1	tblsp olive oil
6	tsp green onions, sliced into 1" pieces
2	garlic cloves, chopped
1	tblsp chopped fresh ginger
2	carrots, sliced 1/8" thick
1	red bell pepper, sliced (optional)
1	8-ounce can sliced water chestnuts, drained
2	tblsp dry sherry (optional)
1/2	cup low-sodium chicken broth
2	tblsp soy sauce
1	tblsp rice wine vinegar
1	tsp sugar
1/2	tsp red pepper flakes
2	tblsp orange juice
4	cups shredded red cabbage
1	cup chow mein noodles
	Salt
	Freshly ground black pepper

Gulf Coast shrimp pilau

Nutritional facts per serving: 515 calories; 43.3g carbohydrates; 210.8mg cholesterol; 24g total fat; 0.8g fiber; 28.8g protein; 347.6mg sodium

In a large skillet, heat butter and add celery and bell pepper. Cook until soft.

Meanwhile, sprinkle shrimp with Worcestershire sauce. Stir the shrimp in the flour, and add it to the vegetable mixture. Stir and simmer until the shrimp are cooked, about 5 minutes. Season with salt and pepper. Combine with hot cooked rice. Crumble the bacon and sprinkle on top.

4 servings

3	tblsp butter
1/2	cup finely chopped celery
2	tblsp chopped green bell pepper
2	cups medium shrimp
1	tblsp Worcestershire sauce
1	tblsp flour
	Salt
	Freshly ground black pepper
3	cups cooked white rice
4	slices crisp-cooked bacon

You'll be away from home for a week or two — perhaps on vacation. When you get back, how will you know if there has been an electrical power failure? This is important because food in the freezer could thaw, spoil, and refreeze without your knowing it. Before you leave, place a penny on top of an ice cube in a tray. When you return, if the penny is still on top, you'll know the ice didn't melt, and all is well. If the penny is on the bottom, chances are the power was off long enough for food to spoil.

Seasoned shrimp bell pepper stir-fry

Nutritional facts per serving: 159 calories; 7.2g carbohydrates; 2.7mg cholesterol; 14.2g total fat; 2g fiber; 2.6g protein; 519.2mg sodium

Heat a large frying pan or wok over medium-high heat. Add spinach and a few tablespoons of water, and cover until wilted, 3 to 5 minutes. Remove spinach to a warm plate and set aside.

Combine pepper strips, basil leaves, soy sauce, vinegar, garlic, and red pepper flakes. Heat the sesame and canola oils in the frying pan or wok over medium-high heat. Add the pepper mixture and cook, tossing and stirring, for 3 to 5 minutes. Add the shrimp, and cook until done, 3 to 5 minutes. Season to taste with salt and pepper. Serve on a bed of the lightly wilted spinach.

4 servings

1	pound prewashed baby spinach, largest stems removed
2	red bell peppers, cut in 1" strips
2	yellow bell peppers, cut in 1" strips
10	leaves fresh basil
2	tblsp soy sauce
2	tblsp rice wine vinegar
1	tblsp finely chopped garlic
1	tsp red pepper flakes (optional)
1	tblsp sesame oil
3	tblsp canola oil
1	pound large shrimp, peeled and deveined
	Salt
	Freshly ground black pepper

Nutrition **Note**

Shellfish may help people with diabetes get two important minerals – zinc and magnesium. If you're diabetic, consider adding top sources like shellfish, beans and whole grains to your diet.

Tangy curried shrimp

Nutritional facts per serving: 221 calories; 15.2g carbohydrates; 99.3mg cholesterol; 13.3g total fat; 2.8g fiber; 12.7g protein; 213.1mg sodium

Heat 3 tablespoons of butter in a large saucepan. Add flour and cook, stirring, for 5 minutes. Whisk in broth and stock, smoothing out lumps. Reduce the heat and simmer, stirring occasionally, for 30 minutes.

In a separate sauté pan, heat the remaining 2 tablespoons of butter. Add green pepper, green onion, and garlic, and cook for 3 minutes, stirring once. Stir in curry powder, tomatoes, and tomato paste. Add salt and pepper to taste.

Stir this mixture into the stock mixture, and simmer for 10 minutes or until it thickens. Add the shrimp, and cook until they turn pink and begin to curl. Fold in the chopped parsley. Serve over Currant and almond rice pilaf (see page 198).

4 servings

5	tblsp butter
1/4	cup flour
1	cup low-sodium chicken broth
2	tblsp strong shrimp stock (see page 340)
1	medium green bell pepper, chopped
4	green onions, chopped
2	garlic cloves, finely chopped
2	tblsp curry powder
1	cup diced tomatoes, including juice
1	tblsp tomato paste
	Salt
	Black pepper
1	pound medium shrimp, peeled and deveined
2	tblsp chopped fresh parsley

Nutrition **Note**

Shrimp can be part of a heart-healthy diet. Researchers at Rockefeller University found that a shrimp diet lowered the ratio of total to HDL cholesterol, and of LDL to HDL cholesterol. By keeping these levels in proportion, the good effects of shrimp cancelled out the bad.

Flavorful pan-seared sea scallops

Nutritional facts per serving: 216 calories; 3.6g carbohydrates; 34.6mg cholesterol; 14.3g total fat; 0.3g fiber; 17.7g protein; 169.6mg sodium

Combine 4 tablespoons of the olive oil with the bay leaves, thyme, garlic, and cayenne pepper. Add scallops and toss well. Cover and refrigerate for at least 2 hours, but not longer than 4 hours.

Pat scallops dry with paper towels. Lightly salt and pepper them. Heat the remaining tablespoon of olive oil in a large nonstick frying pan or skillet over medium-high heat until very hot. Quickly add half the scallops, one at a time. Do not pack the pan full. Sear

5	tblsp olive oil
2	bay leaves
2	tblsp chopped fresh thyme
3	garlic cloves, chopped
1/2	tsp cayenne pepper
1	pound sea scallops (approximately 28)
	Salt
	Freshly ground black pepper

scallops for 3 to 4 minutes. When they are ready, they will be easy to turn over without sticking to the bottom of the pan. Sear the other side for another 2 to 3 minutes. You want a firm scallop that is nicely brown on each side. Keep them warm in a 200-degree oven while you cook the second batch. Repeat the cooking procedure. Serve immediately.

4 servings

Pan-searing is a quick, hot cooking method that seals in the flavor. Never crowd the pan. The scallops may exude some water, so putting in too many will result in a juicy steaming instead of a nice searing.

No-mess herbed scallops

Nutritional facts per serving: 155 calories; 15.2g carbohydrates; 37.3mg cholesterol; 1.3g total fat; 2.8g fiber; 20.9g protein; 209.8mg sodium

Preheat oven to 450 degrees. Place four pieces of aluminum foil on a baking sheet.

Combine tomatoes, parsley, basil, and garlic. Separately combine the zucchini, carrot, and leek. Divide half the zucchini mixture among the 4 pieces of aluminum foil, top with half the tomato mixture divided among the 4 portions. Divide the scallops evenly among the 4 portions, and arrange them on top of the tomatoes. Season with salt and pepper, and sprinkle with lemon juice.

Layer the remaining zucchini mixture over the scallops, and top with the remaining tomato mixture. Cover each with another piece of foil, and fold the edges together to seal. May be assembled to this point up to 4 hours in advance. Bake 18 minutes. Transfer the unopened packets to dinner plates, and let your guests open them at the table. Just beware of the burst of steam.

4 servings

2   pounds Italian plum tomatoes, peeled, seeded, and chopped

2   tblsp chopped fresh parsley

2   tsp chopped fresh basil leaves

1   garlic clove, chopped

1   cup julienned or thickly grated zucchini

1   cup julienned peeled carrot

1   cup julienned leek (white only)

1   pound sea scallops, rinsed and patted dry

    Salt

    Freshly ground black pepper

    Fresh lemon juice

Portuguese clams with tomatoes

Nutritional facts per serving: 136 calories; 11.2g carbohydrates; 17.1mg cholesterol; 9.6g total fat; 3.1g fiber; 3.4g protein; 291.1mg sodium

Heat olive oil and butter in a large skillet over moderate heat. Add onions and green peppers, and sauté until soft, about 10 minutes. Add garlic, bay leaf, tomatoes and their liquid, and tomato sauce. Bring mixture to a simmer, cover, and simmer for 10 to 15 minutes.

Spoon mixture into a deep Dutch oven, and bring to a simmer. Add clams, cover tightly, and cook over medium heat, shaking occasionally, until clams open, about 10 to 15 minutes. Add spinach, and cover for 1 to 2 minutes until wilted. Ladle into shallow bowls, remove bay leaf, and sprinkle with parsley.

2 servings

If your sauce is too thick, add one-third cup white wine or chicken stock to thin it out. Or serve the thicker version over pasta or rice.

2   dozen littleneck or other small clams, scrubbed clean

1   tblsp olive oil

1   tblsp butter

2   small onions, thinly sliced

1   large green bell pepper, cut into thin strips

2   garlic cloves, chopped

1   small bay leaf

1/2 pound fresh or canned tomatoes with liquid, broken up

1   4-ounce can tomato sauce

1   6-ounce package prewashed baby spinach

1/4 cup coarsely chopped fresh Italian parsley

Spicy garlic steamed clams

Nutritional facts per serving: 143 calories; 13.5g carbohydrates; 27.9mg cholesterol; 4.7g total fat; 0.7g fiber; 10.9g protein; 380mg sodium

Heat olive oil over medium heat in a large frying pan or skillet. Add green onion, garlic, and red pepper flakes, and cook for 2 minutes, stirring. Add vinegar, and simmer for 1 or 2 minutes or until most of the liquid is gone. Add the V8 juice and clam juice, and bring to a simmer. Add the clams, cover the pan, and cook just until the shells open, about 5 minutes. Some take a little longer to cook than others, depending on size. Shake the pan to distribute the broth inside the open clams.

1	tblsp olive oil
1/4	cup finely chopped green onion
4	garlic cloves, finely chopped
1/2	tsp crushed red pepper flakes
4	tblsp red wine vinegar
3/4	cup low-sodium V8® juice
3/4	cup bottled clam juice
36	small clams (about 2 pounds)
1/4	cup chopped fresh parsley

Remove pot from the heat, and divide clams among four soup plates. Pour any remaining broth over the clams. Garnish with parsley. Serve immediately.

4 servings

Nutrition **Note**

Experts say you should get calcium from milk and dairy products, but you have trouble digesting milk. So eat extra helpings of other calcium sources like green leafy vegetables and high-calcium seafood. Try clams, oysters, or shrimp. Snack on canned sardines or salmon, including the bones. Calcium supplements are also available. While these may help if you can't have dairy products, avoid them if you can get calcium naturally. Just remember that you may need more than 8 ounces of shellfish to catch as much calcium as you'd get from 8 ounces of milk.

Seasoned mussels in lemon and wine

Nutritional facts per serving: 58 calories; 7.4g carbohydrates; 2.2mg cholesterol; 0.3g total fat; 2g fiber; 1.7g protein; 27mg sodium

Put the mussels in a large heavy pot with lemon juice, wine, and onion. Cover and heat them just until the shells open. Add basil, taste for seasoning, and add salt and pepper if needed. Serve hot with the cooking liquid and a halved lemon.

2 servings

2	dozen mussels, cleaned and scrubbed
	Juice of 1 lemon
3/4	cup white wine
1	small onion, chopped
2	tblsp chopped fresh basil
	Salt
	Freshly ground black pepper
1	lemon

Take a sheet of paper, and make a list of items you buy from the grocery store on a regular basis. Leave space for additional items you may want to add later. Make a note of the price you pay and the price you see in ads. You'll get a better handle on what an item should cost and recognize a good buy when you see one. Make photocopies of the list, and hang one on the refrigerator to remind yourself to check off the items you need. When shopping time rolls around, your list is practically done. The items not marked are also good reminders of essentials you may not have realized you need.

Flavorful wild rice and mushrooms

Nutritional facts per serving: 320 calories; 51.7g carbohydrates; 15.5mg cholesterol; 7.4g total fat; 4.7g fiber; 15.3g protein; 120.9mg sodium

Heat 1 tablespoon of butter and add the garlic and shallots. Add rice and cook for 5 minutes more, stirring frequently. Add chicken stock and simmer until the rice is tender, 30 to 40 minutes, stirring occasionally. Clean mushroom caps with a wet paper towel, remove stems, and slice. Heat the remaining tablespoon of butter, add mushrooms, and cook until tender, stirring frequently.

2	tblsp butter
1	garlic clove, chopped
1	shallot, chopped
1 1/2	cups wild rice, rinsed in cold water
3	cups chicken stock, home made or low-sodium
3/4	pound mushrooms

Drain the rice of any extra stock. Toss with the mushrooms until hot through, and serve.

4 servings

Nutrition **Note**

You may be at higher-than-usual risk for vitamin D deficiency if any of the following apply to you.

- You're an older adult. Your digestive system's ability to absorb vitamin D from food, and your skin's ability to convert vitamin D both decline as you age.

- You live in an area that gets little sunshine, you avoid sunshine, or you use sunscreen frequently.

- You have a condition that limits your ability to absorb fat — like liver disease, Crohn's disease, or sprue.

- You're lactose intolerant and avoid dairy products.

Seasoned-just-right Creole rice

Nutritional facts per serving: 205 calories; 39.4g carbohydrates; 7.8mg cholesterol; 3.2g total fat; 1g fiber; 3.7g protein; 36.1mg sodium

Preheat oven to 350 degrees.

Heat broth to a boil. Heat butter over medium heat, add onion, celery, and garlic, and cook for 2 minutes. Add rice and cook for 2 minutes. Add broth along with garlic powder, cayenne pepper, and black pepper to taste. Bring back to a boil.

Pour rice into a casserole dish, cover tightly with foil, and bake for 1 hour, or until rice is tender. Fluff rice with a fork before serving.

2 servings

1 1/4	cups low-sodium chicken broth
1	tblsp butter
3	tblsp finely chopped onion
3	tblsp finely chopped celery
2	garlic cloves, finely chopped
1	cup raw converted rice
	Garlic powder
	Cayenne pepper
	Black pepper

Nutrition **Note**

Standard processing of rice removes the grain's hull and underlying bran — stripping away a treasure trove of nutrients and fiber. But rice labeled "parboiled" or "converted" is soaked and pressure steamed before the hull and bran are removed. Thanks to this extra step, nutrients from the hull and bran layers are pulled into the rice you eat, instead of getting stripped away. So a cup of converted rice delivers a whopping third of your daily iron requirement, at least 35 percent of the recommended amounts for vitamins B3 and B6, and 75 percent of recommended selenium. That rice also gives you vitamin B1, vitamin B2, folate, zinc, and magnesium.

Lemon and spice rice

Nutritional facts per serving: 140 calories; 14.7g carbohydrates; 23.4mg cholesterol; 7.8g total fat; 0.4g fiber; 3g protein; 51.9mg sodium

Melt butter in a saucepan. Add salt, mustard seed, and turmeric, and stir until they are well blended. Add the rice and lemon juice and heat through, stirring constantly.

4 servings

1/4 cup butter

1 tsp salt

1/2 tsp black mustard seed

1/2 tsp turmeric

2 cups cooked white rice

Strained juice of 1/2 lemon

Nutrition **Note**

Turmeric is a golden spice that might be worth its weight in gold. One of the world's leading voices in herbal medicine, the German Commission E, touts turmeric as a cure for indigestion. Turmeric seems to prompt your liver to pump out more bile, an essential digestive fluid. If you don't have enough bile, you may feel bloated and sick to your stomach after a normal-sized meal. Turmeric is a key ingredient in curry dishes, so that's one way to get more turmeric in your diet. But you can also find the pure spice in the grocery store. Try sprinkling a half tablespoon on your food every day to help avoid that bloated, uncomfortable feeling. But talk to your doctor before you begin. Turmeric is strong enough that you should avoid it if you have certain conditions, like gallstones.

Brown rice almondine with cherries

Nutritional facts per serving: 314 calories; 48.3g carbohydrates; 5mg cholesterol; 10g total fat; 4.3g fiber; 10.2g protein; 70.8mg sodium

Carefully shake almonds in a small pan over medium heat until golden brown. Remove almonds and set aside. Add butter to the hot pan. Add the white part of the chopped green onions to the butter, and cook briefly until soft. Bring the chicken broth to a boil in a separate pot, and add the cooked onion and butter, dried cherries, and rice. Cook, covered, until the liquid is absorbed, about 45 to 60 minutes.

1/4	cup slivered almonds
1	tsp butter
1/4	cup chopped green onions, green part reserved
1/4	cup dried cherries
1/2	cup brown rice
1 1/4	cups low-sodium chicken broth

To serve, toss the hot rice with the almonds, and garnish with the chopped green onion tops.

2 servings

Nutrition **Note**

Not only are cherries deliciously sweet, they may also be a sweet deal for your heart. Cherries pack no less than 17 powerful antioxidant compounds. Hidden in the anthocyanins that tint cherries red, these antioxidants may protect against atherosclerosis and heart disease by preventing the build-up of plaque in your arteries. But that's not all. Cherries also provide fiber and potassium, two winning warriors in the battle against heart disease. Fiber has been shown to lower cholesterol and reduce the risk of heart disease and stroke. Potassium, too, shields you from stroke. It also fights heart disease by controlling your blood pressure so your heart doesn't have to work overtime.

Currant and almond rice pilaf

Nutritional facts per serving: 381 calories; 63.9g carbohydrates; 15.5mg cholesterol; 10.5g total fat; 3.1g fiber; 8.4g protein; 87.5mg sodium

Preheat oven to 350 degrees.

In a medium sauce pan, heat the butter, then add onion, garlic, and rice, and cook for 2 minutes. Add the stock and currants. Pour into a casserole, cover tightly with foil, and bake for 1 hour. Fluff rice with a fork, season with salt to taste, if desired. Sprinkle with almonds and serve.

4 servings

2	tblsp butter
1	small onion, chopped
2	garlic cloves, chopped
1 1/3	cups raw converted rice
1 1/3	cups chicken stock, home made or low-sodium
1/3	cup currants
1/3	cup toasted sliced almonds
	Salt

Nutrition **Note**

Get current on currants, and it could benefit your future health. A currant is a red, white, or black berry that grows on shrubs. Sweet red and white currants are just different colors of the same variety. A cup of these bright berries provides nearly 5 grams of fiber. But the healthiest currant may be the black currant. Half a cup of black currants brims with more than 100 milligrams of vitamin C — well over the recommended dietary allowance (RDA). It's also a good source of potassium and ellagic acid, a substance that fights cancer. This polyphenol has been shown to stop cancer in the lung, liver, skin, and esophagus of lab animals. Give currants a try, and find out what these delicious berries can do for you.

Savory Mediterranean baked rice

Nutritional facts per serving: 457 calories; 83.3g carbohydrates; 0mg cholesterol; 8.2g total fat; 4.3g fiber; 12g protein; 106.9mg sodium

Preheat oven to 350 degrees.

Heat broth to a boil. Heat olive oil over medium heat, add onion, garlic, and bell pepper, and cook for 2 minutes. Add the rice and cook for 2 minutes. Add the spinach, hot broth, oregano, and salt and black pepper to taste. Bring back to a boil.

Pour the rice into a casserole dish, cover tightly with foil, and bake for 1 hour, or until rice is tender. Add basil and toss to fluff the rice. Sprinkle with feta, if desired, and return to the oven for 2 minutes, or until feta is soft.

4 servings

2 1/2	cups low-sodium chicken broth
2	tblsp olive oil
1	small onion, finely chopped
2	garlic cloves, finely chopped
1	small bell pepper, cored and chopped
2	cups raw converted rice
1	10-ounce package frozen spinach, thawed and moisture squeezed out
1/4	tsp ground oregano
	Salt
	Freshly ground black pepper
3	tblsp chopped fresh basil
1/2	cup reduced-fat feta cheese crumbles, preferably basil and sun-dried tomato flavor (optional)

Nutrition **Note**

Following a Mediterranean-style diet might help you stay healthier. Eat lots of antioxidant-rich fresh fruits and vegetables, hearty whole-grain breads and pastas, and plenty of olive oil. Limit fish and chicken to a few times a week and red meat to several times a month. Eat dairy products sparingly — mainly cheese and yogurt.

Far East fried rice

Nutritional facts per serving: 169 calories; 26.4g carbohydrates; 70.8mg cholesterol; 4.2g total fat; 1.6g fiber; 5.8g protein; 196.3mg sodium

Heat oil in a large skillet over high heat. Add mushrooms, and sauté 1 to 2 minutes to coat and start cooking. Add the cooked rice, and stir-fry until rice is heated and oil is evenly distributed.
Mix the sherry, if using, and soy sauce. Add to rice and mix well. Stir in eggs and blend well. Add lettuce and cook, stirring 1 minute longer. Garnish with green onions.

6 servings

1   tblsp peanut oil

1   cup mushrooms, sliced

4   cups cooked rice, preferably made with chicken stock

1   tsp dry sherry (optional)

1   tblsp soy sauce

2   eggs, beaten

1   cup chopped red leaf or romaine lettuce

3   green onions, finely chopped

Nutrition **Note**   You're not the only one who has a tough time getting enough fiber into your diet. Although recommended amounts of fiber range from 21 to 38 grams per day, most Americans only get between 5 and 20 grams daily. You can easily add health-promoting fiber to your diet by switching from refined to whole-grain foods. Some people even say whole-grain breads and cereals have a richer taste, too. Don't be afraid to branch out from whole-wheat products either. Whole grains include hearty whole oats, old-fashioned oatmeal, nutty-flavored brown rice, natural popcorn, and sweet whole grain corn. If you want even more choices, consider millet, barley, buckwheat, bulgur, triticale, spelt, teff, and kamut.

Colorful brown and wild rice vegetable salad

Nutritional facts per serving: 354 calories; 50.9g carbohydrates; 0mg cholesterol; 15.1g total fat; 6g fiber; 7.7g protein; 399.2mg sodium

Bring a saucepan of water to a boil. Add snow peas, reduce heat, and simmer for 1 minute. Drain and place in a bowl of iced water to stop further cooking. When cool, drain well and place on paper towels to dry. They may be wrapped in plastic wrap and refrigerated for up to 24 hours.

Whisk together the mustard, vinegar, olive oil, salt, and pepper. Combine snow peas, corn, brown rice, wild rice, red bell pepper, celery, green onions, parsley, dill weed, and basil in a large bowl, and toss. Gradually add the dressing, tossing as you add. You may not need all of it. Season to taste with salt and pepper. Serve, or cover and refrigerate for up to 4 hours.

4 servings

1/4	pound snow peas, thinly sliced on the diagonal
	Kernels from 2 ears cooked fresh corn
1	tblsp Dijon mustard
1/4	cup red wine vinegar
1/4	cup olive oil
1/2	tsp salt
1/2	tsp freshly ground black pepper
1 1/2	cups cooked brown rice
1 1/2	cups cooked wild rice
1	small red bell pepper, diced
1/2	cup finely chopped celery
4	green onions, thinly sliced
1/4	cup finely chopped fresh parsley
1	tblsp chopped fresh dill or 1/2 tsp dried dill weed
1	tblsp chopped fresh basil or 1/2 tsp dried basil

Two-rice Italian vegetable salad

Nutritional facts per serving: 274 calories; 39.5g carbohydrates; 0mg cholesterol; 10.7g total fat; 3.1g fiber; 6.2g protein; 40.4mg sodium

Cook both kinds of rice according to package directions. Drain well. Combine rice and vegetables. Whisk together the oil, vinegar, and mustard. Season to taste with salt and pepper. Add to the vegetables and toss. Add parsley and chives, and toss. Check seasoning, and add salt and pepper, if desired. Put in a serving bowl, or arrange on a platter, and serve.

4 servings

1/2	cup raw wild rice
1/2	cup raw converted rice
2	scallions, finely chopped
1	large ripe tomato, seeded and chopped
1	zucchini, seeded and chopped
1/4	pound mushrooms, wiped clean and sliced
1	small red bell pepper, finely chopped
3	tblsp olive oil
3	tblsp red wine vinegar
1	tsp Dijon mustard
	Salt
	Freshly ground black pepper
4	tblsp chopped fresh parsley
4	tblsp chopped fresh chives

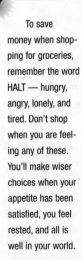

To save money when shopping for groceries, remember the word HALT — hungry, angry, lonely, and tired. Don't shop when you are feeling any of these. You'll make wiser choices when your appetite has been satisfied, you feel rested, and all is well in your world.

Tasty risotto with shrimp

Nutritional facts per serving: 246 calories; 16.9g carbohydrates; 20.8mg cholesterol; 14.3g total fat; 1.9g fiber; 13g protein; 459.9mg sodium

Melt olive oil in a large Dutch oven. Add garlic, onions, and green onions, and cook over medium heat for 2 minutes. Add lemon juice and rice, and cook for 2 to 3 minutes until the rice is coated with butter and begins to look opaque. Add the hot shrimp stock 1/2 cup at a time, stirring constantly, until the liquid has been absorbed by the rice. It should take about 20 to 25 minutes to cook the rice to a creamy consistency.

When you add the final 1/2 cup of stock, add the raw shrimp, thyme, and salt and pepper to taste. The shrimp will cook in about 3 minutes. Before serving, fluff with a fork, and sprinkle with the parsley and Parmesan, if desired.

6 servings

3	tblsp olive oil
3	garlic cloves, chopped
2	onions, chopped
4	green onions, chopped
2	tblsp fresh lemon juice
2	cups Arborio rice
6	cups shrimp stock (see page 286)
36	medium to large shrimp, peeled and deveined, shells reserved for stock
2	tsp finely chopped fresh thyme
	Salt
	Freshly ground black pepper
2	tblsp fresh parsley
6	ounces grated Parmesan cheese (optional)

Nutrition **Note**

According to an eye-opening study, our ancestors began eating spices because they prevent food poisoning. Garlic, onion, allspice, and oregano tested best in the study — killing 100 percent of all bacteria. Thyme, tarragon, cumin, and cinnamon weren't far behind.

Hearty bulgur pilaf

Nutritional facts per serving: 317 calories; 44g carbohydrates; 0mg cholesterol; 11.3g total fat; 5.1g fiber; 11g protein; 579.4mg sodium

Heat oil and butter in a large saucepan. Sauté onion and garlic for about 2 minutes or until soft. Stir in orzo, bulgur, and rice. Stir well and cook about 5 minutes or until golden brown. Add salt, pepper, and broth. Bring to a boil, then reduce heat. Cover and simmer for 15 to 20 minutes or until the liquid is absorbed and the grains are tender. Add water or more broth if the mixture becomes too dry. Stir in parsley and almonds.

3-4 servings

1 1/2	tsp olive oil
1 1/2	tsp butter or margarine
1/4	cup chopped onion
1/2	tsp chopped garlic
1/2	cup orzo
1/3	cup bulgur
1/4	cup long-grain white rice
1/2	tsp salt
1/2	tsp freshly ground pepper
1 1/2	cups chicken broth
1/2	cup minced fresh parsley
1/2	cup slivered almonds, toasted

Nutrition **Note**

This deliciously healthy grain is made from whole-wheat berries or kernels that have been steamed, dried, and cracked. It's one of the oldest recorded types of foods, and you'll find it in many Middle Eastern recipes. It has a hearty, nutty flavor and is a good source of insoluble fiber, protein, magnesium, iron, manganese, and B vitamins. Add bulgur to your menu as a nice change from potatoes and you'll cut your risk of stroke, cancer, diabetes, and heart disease. Look for boxes or bags of bulgur in your grocery or health food store.

Pearl barley mushroom casserole

Nutritional facts per serving: 185 calories; 29.2g carbohydrates; 0mg cholesterol; 5.7g total fat; 6.1g fiber; 5.4g protein; 265.2mg sodium

Preheat oven to 350 degrees. Spray a 1 1/2- to 2-quart casserole dish with vegetable cooking spray.

Melt butter in a medium saucepan, and sauté onion and mushrooms until lightly cooked. Stir in barley and 2 cups of stock. Pour mixture into the prepared casserole dish. Cover and bake for 1 hour. Add remaining stock, stir well, return to oven, and continue baking for about 30 more minutes, or until stock is absorbed and barley is soft. Toss gently, and top with almonds.

1 cup chopped onion

1 cup sliced fresh mushrooms

1 cup pearl barley (not quick-cooking)

2 tblsp butter or margarine

2 cups low-sodium beef stock

2 tblsp slivered almonds, toasted

5-6 servings

Nutrition **Note** Get 20 to 35 grams of fiber a day, and you can help stop two silent killers — high blood pressure and high cholesterol. Fiber is the part of fruits, vegetables, and grains your body can't digest. Barley contains a form of soluble fiber called beta-glucan, which turns soft and sticky, slowing things down in your stomach and small intestine. This gives your body more time to whisk harmful cholesterol away so it can't gum up your arteries. While barley has been a popular health food for thousands of years, today it's often a secret ingredient in comforting soups, warm-from-the-oven breads, and steaming noodles. Look for barley flour, oil, muesli, and pasta, as well as whole-grain barley.

Spiced couscous

Nutritional facts per serving: 214 calories; 33.6g carbohydrates; 15.6mg cholesterol; 6.1g total fat; 2.2g fiber; 5.6g protein; 65.6mg sodium

In a large saucepan, bring water to a boil. Add butter and salt. When the butter has melted, stir in the couscous. Cover, remove pan from heat, and let sit 5 minutes. Fluff with a fork, and season to taste with the cinnamon and cayenne pepper.

4 servings

1 1/4	cups water
2	tblsp butter
	Salt (optional)
1	cup quick-cooking couscous
1/8	tsp ground cinnamon, or to taste
1/8	tsp cayenne pepper, or to taste

With just a few changes, you can turn this dish into a tangy lemon couscous. Here's how. In a large saucepan, bring the water to a boil. Add grated lemon peel — no white attached — and the juice of four lemons to the water. Omit the butter and salt. Cover, remove pan from the heat, and let sit for five minutes. Although you still add the final flavors just before serving, you don't use cinnamon and cayenne. Instead, add four chopped green onions and 1 tablespoon finely chopped fresh basil. Now, you're ready to serve your lemon couscous.

Nutty couscous salad

Nutritional facts per serving: 286 calories; 37g carbohydrates; 0mg cholesterol; 12.3g total fat; 3.7g fiber; 7.1g protein; 21.6mg sodium

Whisk together vinegar, lime juice, and olive oil. Season to taste with salt and pepper. Place couscous and some salt in a medium heatproof bowl. Add boiling water, stir once, then cover and set aside for 10 minutes. Fluff the couscous with a fork, then add radishes, parsley, mint, celery, walnuts, and scallions, and toss to combine. Add the dressing and toss again.

4 servings

2	tblsp wine vinegar
2	tblsp lime juice
1/4	cup olive oil
	Salt
	Freshly ground black pepper
1	cup instant couscous
1	cup boiling water
2	radishes, finely chopped
3/4	cup finely chopped parsley
1/4	cup finely chopped mint leaves
1/4	cup finely chopped celery
1/4	cup finely chopped toasted walnuts
2	scallions, finely chopped

Nutrition **Note** You may get mood-lifting benefits if you eat complex carbohydrates like whole-grain breads and cereals. Researchers at the University of South Alabama found that complex carbohydrates stimulate serotonin production and have a lasting mood-lifting effect.

Italian-style tuna pasta salad

Nutritional facts per serving: 403 calories; 32.1g carbohydrates; 181.5mg cholesterol; 2.1g total fat; 6.8g fiber; 16.2g protein; 821mg sodium

Mix together tuna, red bell pepper, green onions, olives, capers, olive oil, and vinegar in a bowl. Add the drained pasta and toss. Season to taste with salt and pepper. Serve on a bed of fresh lettuce, if desired.

2 servings

Nutrition Note

Vinegar may help your blood sugar. Because acidic foods are digested slowly, three teaspoons of vinegar can lower your blood sugar after a meal by as much as 30 percent. Adding red wine vinegar or lemon juice to a salad might be enough.

1   6-ounce can tuna, drained

1   red bell pepper, finely chopped

3   green onions, sliced

1/4   cup black olives, pitted and chopped or sliced

1   tblsp capers, drained (optional)

1   tblsp olive oil

1/4   cup red wine vinegar

2   cups small pasta shells, cooked and drained

Salt

Freshly ground black pepper

Fresh lettuce (optional)

Southern stone-ground grits

Nutritional facts per serving: 121 calories; 23.1g carbohydrates; 0mg cholesterol; 1.2g total fat; 1.4g fiber; 5.2g protein; 576.5mg sodium

Spray saucepan with nonstick vegetable spray. Bring stock to a boil over medium-high heat, and gradually stir in grits and salt. (Start with 1/2 teaspoon salt and taste-test.)

As soon as grits begin to simmer, reduce heat to Low, cover, and cook, stirring occasionally, until grits are tender and creamy, 20 to 30 minutes. Add more liquid if necessary during cooking.

4 1/2	cups chicken broth, or half stock and half nonfat milk
1/2-1	tsp salt
1	cup stone-ground grits
	Salt
	Freshly ground black pepper

The exact amount of liquid, and the exact time needed to cook grits varies from bag to bag and pot to pot. Start taste-testing after 20 minutes. Season to taste at the end with salt and freshly ground pepper.

4 servings

Stone-ground grits are available in white, yellow, or a mix of both. Their color comes from the color of the corn that was ground to make them. For even better grits, remember these tips.

- Fresh stone-ground grits must be kept in the freezer because they have no preservatives.

- Use regular chicken broth instead of low-sodium because grits need salt. Always start the pot cooking with some stock. Long cooking with milk alone may cause the bottom to scorch.

- For cheese grits, use real Parmigiano-Reggiano. The grits won't turn yellow, but you'll get a lot more flavor for fewer calories.

Chewy steel-cut oats

Nutritional facts per serving: 315 calories; 50.9g carbohydrates; 4.9mg cholesterol; 4.5g total fat; 4.9g fiber; 18.3g protein; 268.2mg sodium

---

METHOD 1: Soak oats in 3 cups milk or water overnight. Refrigerate the oats if you use milk. Pour the soaked oats and any leftover liquid into a large, heavy-bottomed saucepan sprayed with nonstick vegetable spray. Add enough liquid to cover oats by at least 1 inch. Bring the mixture to a simmer over medium heat, reduce heat to Medium-low, and simmer gently for 25 to 30 minutes. Stir frequently to prevent sticking. The finished texture should be dense and chewy. Stir in salt, cinnamon and sweetener, if used.

1 1/2	cups steel-cut oats
3–4	cups fat-free milk or water, depending on cooking method
1/4	tsp salt
1/2	tsp cinnamon (optional)
3	tblsp molasses, honey, pure maple syrup or 100 percent fruit juice concentrate (optional)

METHOD 2: In a large, heavy-bottomed saucepan sprayed with nonstick vegetable spray, bring 4 cups of milk or water to a boil over medium-high heat. Stir in dry oats, and reduce heat to a simmer. Simmer gently for about 45 minutes. Stir frequently to prevent sticking. The finished texture should be dense and chewy. Stir in salt, cinnamon and sweetener, if used.

Cooking times for both Method 1 and Method 2 can vary slightly. The key is texture. You want your oatmeal soft enough to eat, but still somewhat chewy.

4 servings

Rainbow pasta

Nutritional facts per serving: 258 calories; 20.6g carbohydrates; 49.1mg cholesterol; 11.5g total fat; 2.4g fiber; 18.3g protein; 664.6mg sodium

Bring a large pot of water to a rolling boil. Add pasta and stir. Return to a boil and cook, uncovered, until al dente, according to package directions. Drain well.

While the pasta is cooking, heat olive oil in a medium skillet over medium heat. Add peppers and garlic, and sauté until tender but not browned, about 5 minutes. Set aside.

Cook broccoli in boiling water or in the boiling pasta water for 5 minutes.

1	12-ounce package multi-colored pasta
1/4	cup olive oil
1/2	red bell pepper, sliced into strips or chopped
1/2	yellow bell pepper, sliced into strips or chopped
2	garlic cloves, chopped
1	cup fresh broccoli florets
1	cup grated Parmesan cheese

Drain the pasta and broccoli and transfer to a serving bowl. Mix in the peppers and garlic. Sprinkle generously with Parmesan and serve hot.

6 servings

Nutrition **Note**   A mix of bright colors makes food appealing, but it may do much more for your health. Natural chemicals in plants, called phytochemicals or phytonutrients, can have a powerful effect on the human body. Found in fruits, vegetables, herbs, and spices, these thousands of substances have been used to treat and prevent diseases since ancient times. Many phytonutrients lend their colors to the foods you eat. So, the more colorful your diet becomes, the more nutritious phytonutrients you may get. In fact, the National Cancer Institute recommends you eat lots of colorful fruits and vegetables every day.

Italian vegetable and garlic pasta

Nutritional facts per serving: 258 calories; 52.3g carbohydrates; 0mg cholesterol; 1.5g total fat; 3.7g fiber; 10.1g protein; 29.6mg sodium

---

In a small saucepan, combine chicken broth and garlic. Bring to a boil, then reduce heat and simmer, covered, for 20 minutes. Pour garlic mixture and vinegar into a blender or food processor. Process until smooth. Return to saucepan and keep warm. Steam or microwave zucchini, yellow squash, and red pepper just until crisp-tender. In a large serving bowl, toss cooked pasta with steamed vegetables, green onion, tomatoes, and garlic puree.

6 servings

1 1/4 cups low-sodium chicken broth

10 garlic cloves, minced

2 cups sliced zucchini

1 cup sliced yellow summer squash

1 large red pepper, diced

2 tblsp plus 1 tsp balsamic vinegar

12 ounces angel hair pasta, cooked and drained

1/2 cup chopped green onion

2 cups halved cherry tomatoes

Nutrition **Note**

Dozens of studies have found that clogged arteries virtually disappear when you add garlic to your weekly menu. The sulfur compounds in this amazing herb not only lower cholesterol and triglycerides, but they also go after only the bad LDL cholesterol and leave the good HDL cholesterol alone. In one study, eating a fresh clove of garlic every day for 16 weeks reduced cholesterol by an amazing 20 percent. You may not be that enthusiastic about garlic — yet. So start out working it into two or three recipes a week. Soon you'll learn to love its taste and health benefits.

Lemon-basil-parsley pasta

Nutritional facts per serving: 140 calories; 14.7g carbohydrates; 23.4mg cholesterol; 7.8g total fat; 0.4g fiber; 3g protein; 51.9mg sodium

Bring a large pot of water to a rolling boil. Add the pasta and stir. Return to a boil and cook, uncovered, until al dente, according to package directions. Drain well and transfer to a heated serving bowl.

While the pasta is cooking, toss together lemon peel, garlic, parsley, and basil in a small bowl. Add olive oil to the pasta while it is still hot, and toss well. Add the lemon peel mixture to the pasta, and toss to combine. Season to taste with salt and pepper. Serve warm or at room temperature.

4 servings

1/2 pound pasta, any variety

Grated or chopped peel (no white attached) of 1 lemon

2-3 garlic cloves, finely chopped

1/2 cup finely chopped fresh parsley

2 tblsp chopped basil

2 tblsp extra virgin olive oil

Salt

Freshly ground black pepper

Nutrition **Note**

Use a lemon to put the squeeze on your odds of skin cancer. Research shows that a substance called d-limonene in lemon, grapefruit, and orange peels may ward off this dreaded disease. University of Arizona researchers found that adding citrus peel to your diet reduces your risk of skin cancer. Sip hot black tea with citrus peel, and you'll lower your risk even more. The d-limonene is mostly in the zest, so remember to shave off this outermost, colored section of the peel to get the cancer fighter. Just use the smaller teeth of a hand grater or a sharp knife. You can even buy a tool called a citrus zester that's perfect for the job.

Tangy scallops and tomato pasta

Nutritional facts per serving: 255 calories;31.8g carbohydrates; 18.7mg cholesterol; 8.2g total fat; 3.7g fiber; 14.6g protein; 105.7mg sodium

Sauté onion, pepper, and garlic in olive oil until tender, but not brown. Add tomatoes and seasonings, and simmer for 3 to 5 minutes. Add scallops, and simmer for another 3 minutes or until tender. Don't overcook. Serve sauce over pasta. Top with grated Parmesan cheese, if desired.

4 servings

2	tblsp olive oil
1	medium onion, chopped
1	small bell pepper, chopped
2	garlic cloves, minced
3	large tomatoes, diced
1	tsp oregano
	Salt
	Black pepper
1/2	pound sea scallops
2	cups angel hair pasta, cooked and drained

Nutrition **Note**

If you had to pick just one food as a cancer-fighting superstar, it might be the tomato. It, along with other colorful, flavorful foods — including red grapefruit, guava, watermelon, and papaya — contains the amazing natural chemical lycopene. Because of lycopene, the more tomatoes you eat, the less likely you are to develop stomach, lung, breast, colon, mouth, or throat cancer. And you don't have to eat just raw tomatoes to profit from this health benefit, either. The heat from cooking actually frees up tomato's lycopene. So tomato products — like sauce, paste, etc. — are even better sources for cancer-proofing your body. If there's a little oil paired with your tomatoes, your body can absorb the lycopene even more easily.

Zesty family-style meat sauce for pasta

Nutritional facts per serving: 246 calories; 9.8g carbohydrates; 58.5mg cholesterol; 15.4g total fat; 2.1g fiber; 17.5g protein; 394.7mg sodium

Spray a large frying pan with non-stick vegetable spray. Add ground beef and cook, breaking apart with a spatula, until no longer pink. Season lightly with salt and pepper to taste. Drain beef to eliminate the fat.

Wipe out the pan and spray again. Heat olive oil in the frying pan over medium heat. Add onions and garlic, cover, and cook, stirring occasionally, for 3 minutes. Add the drained meat, tomatoes, tomato sauce, spices, and Worcestershire sauce. Bring the sauce back to a simmer, and simmer for 15 minutes, stirring occasionally. Season to taste with salt and pepper. Serve over hot pasta, or cool, cover, and refrigerate up to 2 days, or freeze up to 3 months.

4 servings

12	ounces lean ground beef
	Salt
	Freshly ground black pepper
1 1/2	tsp olive oil
1	small yellow onion, chopped
2	garlic cloves, chopped
1	14-ounce can low-sodium diced tomatoes
7	ounces tomato sauce
1/4	tsp each dried basil, oregano, and thyme
1/4	tsp Worcestershire sauce

This is a one-pot, quick sauce that is perfect with spaghetti noodles. You can also use it to make lasagna.

Shrimp-tomato pasta sauce with feta

Nutritional facts per serving: 233 calories; 12.1g carbohydrates; 93.4mg cholesterol; 13.9g total fat; 1.3g fiber; 14.5g protein; 420.2mg sodium

Combine the crumbled feta and the tablespoon of fresh oregano. Set aside. Heat olive oil in a large frying pan over medium heat. Add garlic and shallots and cook, stirring occasionally, until they begin to soften, 2 to 3 minutes. Increase heat to Medium-high. Add tomatoes, their juice, tomato clam juice, and wine. Add dried oregano, basil, and dill. Stir to combine well. Cook, stirring frequently, for 10 to 12 minutes, or until the liquid is reduced by half.

Add shrimp and cook for 2 to 3 minutes, or until they turn pink and begin to curl. Remove from heat, and season to taste with salt and pepper. Serve immediately over hot pasta, with feta-oregano topping.

4 servings

- 4 ounces low-fat feta cheese, crumbled
- 1 tblsp chopped fresh oregano
- 2 tblsp olive oil
- 1 garlic clove, finely chopped
- 1/2 cup finely chopped shallots
- 2 cups canned Italian tomatoes, chopped, with juice
- 4 tblsp tomato clam juice
- 1/4 cup dry white wine
- 2 tsp each dried oregano, basil, and dill weed
- 1 pound medium-sized shrimp, peeled and deveined

  Salt

  Freshly ground black pepper

If tomato clam juice isn't readily available, replace it with 4 tablespoons of the homemade shrimp stock recipe on page 286.

Chicken-tomato-broccoli pasta

Nutritional facts per serving: 342 calories; 7.1g carbohydrates; 85.7mg cholesterol; 21.4g total fat; 1.1g fiber; 30.2g protein; 99.7mg sodium

Take meat off the chicken. Remove all skin, fat, and tendons. Chop meat into bite-size pieces.

Blanch broccoli florets in boiling, salted water until just tender, about 2 minutes. Drain. Put on paper towels to dry.

Whisk together oil, vinegar, oregano, basil, and garlic powder. Add salt and pepper to taste. Cook the pasta according to package directions. Drain. Add the dressing and mix gently. Add the chicken, broccoli, tomatoes, and onions. Toss everything together. Cover and chill in the refrigerator. If desired, sprinkle with seasoned croutons and black olives before serving.

4 servings

1	3 1/2- to 4-pound whole roasted chicken
1	small head broccoli, cut into florets
1/4	cup olive oil
1/4	cup red wine vinegar
1	tsp dried oregano
1	tsp dried basil
1/2	tsp garlic powder
	Salt
	Freshly ground black pepper
4	ounces pasta of your choice
2	large ripe tomatoes, cut into large cubes
1	small red onion, chopped
	Seasoned croutons (optional)
	Kalamata olives, pitted (optional)

Using canvas grocery bags may be a better choice for the environment than plastic or paper ones. But they also can fall over, letting bottles and cans roll to the deepest part of the trunk where they're hard to reach. To solve that problem, cut a piece of plywood to fit snugly into the bottom of the canvas bag. Items will sit firmly on the bottom, making it easier to retrieve them when you get your groceries home.

Minty tomato sauce for pasta

Nutritional facts per serving: 129 calories; 21.7g carbohydrates; 9.9mg cholesterol; 4.6g total fat; 6.6g fiber; 4.9g protein; 347.1mg sodium

Heat butter in a skillet. Add onion and cook until soft. Tear tomatoes apart into large chunks, and add to the skillet with the reserved tomato juice. Simmer until sauce is slightly thickened. Add the mint and heat through. Season to taste with salt and pepper. Serve over hot cooked pasta.

2 servings

2 tsp butter

1 small onion, chopped

1 pound tomatoes, canned, juice reserved

Handful coarsely chopped fresh mint leaves and stems

Salt

Freshly ground black pepper

You hate to store that double batch of spaghetti in plastic containers because you know how much damage it will do. In the past, tomato sauce has left stains that just wouldn't come out no matter what you tried. But, with a little clever preparation, you can put an end to that problem once and for all. Just coat the inside of your container with vegetable oil or nonstick cooking spray before you pour in the sauce. You won't miss those stains one bit.

Summer-fresh tomato-basil pasta

Nutritional facts per serving: 294 calories; 12.2g carbohydrates; 0mg cholesterol; 27.9g total fat; 3.1g fiber; 2.3g protein; 26.7mg sodium

---

Put tomatoes, tomato paste, vinegar, and olive oil in a food processor, and process to the desired degree. Depending on the size of your processor, you may need to do this in batches. Add parsley and basil, and process once or twice to mix in. Season to taste with salt and pepper.

Serve hot over cooked pasta. Top with cheese, if desired.

2 servings

2	pounds fresh ripe tomatoes, peeled, seeded, and chopped
1	tsp tomato paste
3/4	cup red wine vinegar
1/4	cup extra-virgin olive oil
2	tblsp chopped fresh parsley
2	tblsp chopped fresh basil
	Salt
	Black pepper
1/4	cup freshly grated Parmigiano-Reggianno cheese (optional)

Use these tips to get even better results from this recipe.

- You need just a little tomato paste to thicken the sauce. Use up the rest of the can by freezing it in tablespoon portions on foil, then storing them in a zip-top bag in the freezer.

- You can puree the sauce until smooth or leave it a little chunky — which is nicer when you use real tomatoes.

- This sauce is at its luscious best in the summer, when big beefsteak tomatoes and fresh basil are available.

Spinach-mushroom-bell pepper pasta sauce

Nutritional facts per serving: 406 calories; 37.5g carbohydrates; 0mg cholesterol; 16g total fat; 15.7g fiber; 21.9g protein; 334.1mg sodium

Remove stems from spinach and wash spinach well. Shake off excess water, tear leaves, and set aside. Wipe mushrooms with a damp paper towel. If using shiitakes, remove stems and discard. Chop the mushroom caps.

Heat olive oil in a large frying pan over medium-high heat. Add red pepper, garlic, and mushrooms, and cook, stirring frequently, until the mushrooms begin to give off their juices, about 5 minutes.

Add wine and chicken broth, and bring to a brisk simmer. Add spinach and toss with the other ingredients. Reduce heat to Medium, cover the pan, and cook until spinach wilts, 4 to 5 minutes. Season to taste with salt and pepper.

Serve over hot cooked pasta, and sprinkle with Parmigiano-Reggiano cheese, if desired.

2 servings

1 1/2	pounds fresh dark curly spinach
1 1/2	pounds shiitake or portobello mushrooms
2	tblsp olive oil
1	red bell pepper, chopped
4	garlic cloves, chopped
1/2	cup white wine
1/2	cup low-sodium chicken broth
	Salt
	Freshly ground black pepper
1/2	cup freshly grated Parmigiano-Reggiano cheese (optional)

Nutrition **Note**

Mushrooms are a potent source of vitamin B2 (riboflavin), vitamin B3 (niacin), and vitamin D as well as minerals like potassium, selenium, and copper.

Rosemary fettucine with basil

Nutritional facts per serving: 186 calories; 18.2g carbohydrates; 55.2mg cholesterol; 10.3g total fat; 0.1g fiber; 5g protein; 140mg sodium

Bring a large pot of water to a rolling boil. Add pasta and stir. Return to a boil and cook, uncovered, until al dente, according to package directions. Drain well and return to the same pot. Add butter, basil, Parmesan, and balsamic vinegar, and toss thoroughly. Season to taste with salt and pepper.

**To make rosemary butter, pulse 3 tablespoons rosemary in a food processor until bruised. Add 1 stick room-temperature butter and 1 peeled garlic clove. Puree until smooth. Form into a cylinder and refrigerate or freeze until needed.

1 pound fettucine

1/4 cup rosemary butter**

2 tblsp chopped fresh basil

2 tblsp grated Parmesan cheese

1 tblsp balsamic vinegar

Salt

Freshly ground black pepper

6 servings

To keep water from boiling over, insert a toothpick between the pot and its lid, treat the pot with nonstick spray before adding the water, or rub a small amount of butter around the inside rim. For an uncovered pot, place a wooden spoon across the top. To boil water quickly, be sure to cover the pot. Uncovered, a gallon of water on a gas range takes approximately 35 minutes to boil, but a covered gallon only takes 23 minutes. Whatever you do, never add pasta before the water boils. If you do, you'll slow down the boiling process, and your pasta will stick together.

Spinach fettucine with clams and tomatoes

Nutritional facts per serving: 245 calories; 15.4g carbohydrates; 65.2mg cholesterol; 9.2g total fat; 1.9g fiber; 22.7g protein; 111mg sodium

Seed and chop the tomato. Steam spinach until wilted. Heat butter in a deep-sided frying pan. Add onion and garlic, and sauté for 1 minute. Add the water and clams. Cover and steam until clams open. When the clams open, add tomato, spinach, and basil. Then season with salt and pepper to taste. Serve over fettucine.

2 servings

1	medium tomato
1	cup fresh spinach
2	tblsp butter
1	tblsp finely chopped onion
1	garlic clove, finely chopped
1/4	cup water
3	dozen small clams
1	cup chopped fresh basil
	Salt
	Freshly ground black pepper
2	ounces refrigerated fresh spinach fettucine

Nutrition **Note** Even if you eat plates of calcium-packed spinach, you may not get much calcium. That's because some calcium-rich foods also contain oxalate — a natural compound that traps most calcium and keeps your body from using it. Spinach is just one oxalate-rich food. Other calcium misers include cranberries, rhubarb, chard, and perhaps sweet potatoes and dried beans as well. These foods still have other nutrients you need, so don't stop eating them. Just don't rely on them for calcium. Instead try dairy products and shellfish if you can tolerate them. You can also eat fortified cereals, sardines, salmon with bones, stewed tomatoes, and broccoli.

Fettucine with basil-pine nut pesto

Nutritional facts per serving: 412 calories; 21g carbohydrates; 9.9mg cholesterol; 33.4g total fat; 4.2g fiber; 10.5g protein; 794.2mg sodium

Puree basil, olive oil, nuts, garlic, and salt in a food processor until smooth. Add cheese and blend. Just before serving, stir in 2 tablespoons of hot water from the pasta pot. Spoon over hot pasta.

4 servings

2	cups packed fresh basil leaves
1/2	cup virgin olive oil
2	tblsp pine nuts
2	garlic cloves, crushed
1	tsp salt
1/2	cup freshly grated Parmesan cheese
2	cups whole-wheat fettucine, cooked and drained

Nutrition **Note** You may be able to ease your backaches or other chronic pain by changing what you drink. Do a test to find out. Try cutting coffee and soft drinks from your diet, and see what happens. You may discover that caffeine has been preventing your body's natural pain fighters from doing their job. Not only does caffeine lower levels of "feel good" chemicals called endorphins, but it also boosts levels of epinephrine, a compound that can make your muscles and nerves more sensitive. Backing off caffeine may not work for everyone, but it's worth a try to find out.

Fresh tomato and mussels spaghetti

Nutritional facts per serving: 297 calories; 33.2g carbohydrates; 67.2mg cholesterol; 9.5g total fat; 2.7g fiber; 21.5g protein; 606.5mg sodium

Bring a large pot of water to a rolling boil. Add pasta and stir. Return to a boil and cook, uncovered, until al dente, according to package directions. Drain well.

In a 5-quart saucepan, heat olive oil over medium-high heat. Add garlic, tomatoes, basil, parsley, hot pepper, and salt and pepper to taste. Sauté 5 minutes, stirring to prevent sticking. Add the cleaned mussels, cover the pot, and cook until the mussels have opened, about 5 to 7 minutes. Discard any mussels that do not open. Pour the sauce and mussels over pasta, toss well, and sprinkle with the chopped parsley or basil.

6 servings

Want perfect, no-clump pasta every time? Add a bit of olive oil to the pot of water, and your pasta won't boil over or stick together.

1	pound spaghetti or other long pasta
2	tblsp olive oil
4	garlic cloves, chopped
1	28-ounce can plum tomatoes, drained and coarsely chopped, or 4 cups cherry or Roma tomatoes, halved
2	tblsp chopped fresh basil
2	tblsp chopped fresh parsley
1	hot red pepper, seeded and chopped (optional)
	Salt
	Freshly ground black pepper
48-60	(about 2 pounds) live mussels, scrubbed and debearded
1	tblsp chopped fresh parsley or basil

Delightful spaghetti frittata

Nutritional facts per serving: 98 calories; 2g carbohydrates; 217.7mg cholesterol; 6.9g total fat; 0g fiber; 6.5g protein; 63.4mg sodium

Preheat oven to 350 degrees.

Beat eggs lightly and add cheese. Season with salt and pepper. Heat butter in a nonstick frying pan with ovenproof handle. Add garlic and sauté briefly, then add the spaghetti and combine. Pour the egg mixture over the spaghetti, and mix well with a fork. Cook about 2 minutes, then transfer to the oven and bake without flipping until the eggs are set, 10 to 15 minutes.

4 servings

1/2	pound spaghetti, cooked and drained
5	eggs
1	cup grated sharp cheddar or mozzarella cheese
3/4	cup grated Parmesan cheese
2	tsp salt
	Freshly ground black pepper
4-6	tblsp butter
1	garlic clove, finely chopped

Nutrition Note

You're plagued with problems with your hair or nails, and the products you bought aren't helping. Perhaps you can build better hair and nails from the inside out. Two protein building blocks — arginine and cysteine — are essential for hair growth. In fact, your hair follicles must have these amino acids to produce strands of hair. Some even think these amino acids may make your nails stronger, too. Although liquid supplements from a health store may be necessary, start by getting your amino acids from food. Find cysteine in cheeses such as mozzarella, cheddar, and Swiss as well as chickpeas (garbanzo beans) and lentils. You can get arginine from peanuts, walnuts, seeds, whole grains, rice, and beans.

Easy-but-good lasagna

Nutritional facts per serving: 448 calories; 14g carbohydrates; 106.6mg cholesterol; 25.6g total fat; 1.8g fiber; 36.7g protein; 986.8mg sodium

Preheat oven to 375 degrees.

Cook noodles in a large quantity of boiling salted water for 9 or 10 minutes. Drain, brown the ground beef, and add onion and garlic to any remaining fat. Cook until soft. Pour off excess fat. Add thyme, oregano, fennel, pepper flakes, salt, pepper to taste, and spaghetti sauce. In a greased 12" x 8" x 1 1/2" baking dish, make layers in this order: lasagna noodles, spaghetti sauce, ricotta, mozzarella. Repeat. Bake for 20 minutes. Sprinkle with Parmesan. Return to oven for 10 minutes.

6 servings

1	6-ounce package lasagna noodles
2	pounds lean ground beef
1	onion, chopped
4	garlic cloves, chopped
1 1/2	tblsp each dried thyme, oregano, and ground fennel seeds
1	tsp dried red pepper flakes
1	tsp salt
	Freshly ground black pepper
3-4	cups spaghetti or marinara sauce (see page 319) or 2 15 1/2-ounce jars spaghetti sauce
5	cups ricotta cheese or cream style cottage cheese
1-2	6-ounce packages sliced mozzarella cheese
2-4	ounces Parmesan cheese

Nutrition **Note**

An amino acid called lysine may help protect against cold sores. According to doctors at Indiana University Medical School, lysine can prevent cold sores from reappearing in chronic sufferers. Good sources of lysine include ricotta cheese, wheat germ, poultry, pork, and cottage cheese.

Roasted tomato-vegetable linguine

Nutritional facts per serving: 165 calories; 32.5g carbohydrates; 23.4mg cholesterol; 1.5g total fat; 5.5g fiber; 5.8g protein; 53.8mg sodium

Preheat oven to 450 degrees.

Roast tomatoes and onions for 20 to 25 minutes, then turn the oven to Broil, and broil the vegetables for 10 minutes to char the tops. Meanwhile, bring a large pot of water to a rolling boil. Add the pasta and stir. Return to a boil and cook, uncovered, until al dente, according to package directions. Drain well.

Transfer the roasted vegetables to the bowl of a food processor, and puree. Add the red peppers, rosemary, and garlic, and puree. Season to taste with salt and pepper. Toss with linguine and serve hot.

4 servings

1/2	pound linguine
3	large tomatoes, cored and halved
2	large onions, sliced 1/2" thick
1	14 1/2-ounce jar roasted red peppers or 3-4 fresh red peppers, roasted
1	tblsp chopped fresh rosemary
1	clove garlic, finely chopped
	Salt
	Freshly ground black pepper

Nutrition **Note**

In the past, audiences threw tomatoes at poor performers. If your blood pressure and cholesterol levels are poor performers, throw tomatoes at them, too — by eating more of these juicy red delights. Tomatoes deliver a treasure box of nutrients that can help. Their lycopene breaks down cholesterol to keep your arteries free-flowing. Valuable folate cleans up homocysteine, an amino acid that teams with cholesterol to trouble your heart. On top of all that, tomatoes are chock-full of potassium, a mineral crucial for lowering blood pressure.

Succulent four-cheese linguini

Nutritional facts per serving: 341 calories; 21.5g carbohydrates; 78.5mg cholesterol; 17.8g total fat; 0g fiber; 23.6g protein; 80mg sodium

Bring a large pot of water to a rolling boil. Add pasta and stir. Return to a boil and cook, uncovered, until al dente, according to package directions. Drain well.

While the pasta is cooking, combine the cheeses, garlic, and milk in a large microwave-safe bowl or heavy pan. Microwave on High in the bowl 2 to 3 minutes, or cook over low heat in the pan for 5 minutes. The cheeses should be soft, but not melted.

Add the drained linguini to the cheese-milk mixture, and toss together. Add butter and Parmesan, and toss again. Season to taste with salt and pepper.

4-6 servings

1	pound linguini
1/4	pound Swiss cheese, cut into 1/2" pieces
1/4	pound sharp cheddar, cut into 1/2" pieces
1/4	pound mozzarella, cut into 1/2" pieces
1	garlic clove, finely chopped
1	cup milk
1/2	stick butter, cut into small pieces
1	cup grated Parmesan cheese
	Salt
	Freshly ground black pepper

Nutrition **Note**

In the United States alone, 2 million men have osteoporosis. Weight-bearing exercises, such as yard work or lifting weights, can help you keep and build strong bones. Ask your doctor about exercises that will strengthen large leg muscles to help prevent falls and fractures.

Vegetables and legumes

Cheese-lover's broccoli potato casserole

Nutritional facts per serving: 163 calories; 18.9g carbohydrates; 17.6mg cholesterol; 6.2g total fat; 1.6g fiber; 8.7g protein; 619.4mg sodium

Preheat oven to 350 degrees.

Melt butter in a medium saucepan. Add flour and salt, stirring constantly until bubbly. Add milk and stir until thick and smooth. Add cream cheese and Swiss cheese. Stir until melted. Add potatoes and heat through.

Pour half this mixture into a small baking dish. Steam broccoli until bright green but still crisp. Layer broccoli over potato mixture and top with remaining potato mixture. Sprinkle seasoned bread crumbs on top.

1	tblsp butter
1	tblsp all-purpose flour
1/2	tsp salt
1	cup low-fat milk
1/4	cup cubed low-fat cream cheese
1/4	cup shredded Swiss cheese
3/4	cup frozen hash brown potatoes
1	cup chopped broccoli
1/4	cup seasoned bread crumbs

Bake for 20 minutes or until bubbly and golden brown.

4 servings

Nutrition **Note**

Learn to love broccoli and your eyes will thank you. By getting a big dose of its natural chemicals — called carotenoids — you lower your risk of developing cataracts and age-related macular degeneration, two vision-related conditions.

For the best nutrition, eat your broccoli raw or lightly steamed. And get adventurous. You can toss this wonder vegetable into almost any dish — salads, casseroles, stir-fries, or omelets.

Spicy pepper and broccoli stir-fry

Nutritional facts per serving: 48 calories; 4.1g carbohydrates; 0mg cholesterol; 3.5g total fat; 1.1g fiber; 0.8g protein; 127mg sodium

Heat the olive oil and chili oil in a wok or skillet until hot. Add the pepper and onion, and stir-fry quickly for about 1 to 2 minutes. Add the broccoli florets and sauté 4 to 5 minutes longer. Sprinkle with soy sauce and vinegar, and add pepper to taste. Toss to combine, and cover to steam lightly until the broccoli is just done, about 3 minutes. Serve immediately.

4 servings

1	tblsp olive oil
1	tsp chili oil (optional)
1	red bell pepper, cut in 2" wedges
1	small onion, cut in 2" wedges
1/2	head broccoli, florets only
1/2	tblsp low-sodium soy sauce
1/2	tblsp rice wine vinegar
	Freshly ground black pepper

Nutrition Note

Onions may not be near and dear to your heart, but they may help your heart stay healthy. This pungent produce delivers a powerful antioxidant called quercetin and also supplies helpful nutritious sulfur compounds. One study suggests that quercetin may help lower your levels of total cholesterol as well as your "bad" low-density lipoprotein (LDL) cholesterol.

In fact, your body absorbs quercetin from onions more quickly than it does from other food sources — and it also retains that quercetin longer. On top of that, onion sulfur compounds may lower your blood pressure and prevent blood clots by keeping the platelets in your blood from clumping together. With all those benefits, maybe onions can become near and dear to your heart after all.

Sautéed mushroom-broccoli medley

Nutritional facts per serving: 100 calories; 10.7g carbohydrates; 10.4mg cholesterol; 5.1g total fat; 4.9g fiber; 5.7g protein; 30.8mg sodium

Heat butter in a large skillet over medium-high heat. Add mushrooms and cook until their liquid has almost evaporated and they're beginning to turn brown, 3 to 5 minutes. Add the cooked broccoli and snowpeas and heat through, 2 to 3 minutes. Season to taste with salt and pepper, and top with sesame seeds if desired.

6 servings

2 tblsp butter

8 ounces button mushrooms, cleaned, stems removed, halved

1 cup cooked broccoli

1 cup fresh snowpeas

Salt

Freshly ground black pepper

1 tblsp sesame seeds (optional)

Nutrition **Note**

Broccoli is a superstar heart protector. It's rich in folate, a B vitamin that fights the artery-damaging amino acid homocysteine. It's also cholesterol-free, low-fat, and packed with natural chemicals called flavonoids. These flavonoids protect your blood and arteries from clotting, oxidation, and inflammation. In fact, a 10-year study of more than 34,000 postmenopausal women found those who ate foods high in flavonoids reduced their risk of fatal heart attack by one-third. You need to eat broccoli or other brightly colored vegetables several times a week to get this heart-saving benefit.

Just-right roasted asparagus

Nutritional facts per serving: 62 calories; 5.6g carbohydrates; 0mg cholesterol; 3.6g total fat; 2.4g fiber; 3.2g protein; 2.4mg sodium

---

Preheat oven to 350 degrees. Line 2 heavy shallow pans with foil.

Toss the asparagus with a small amount of olive oil. Roast the asparagus, turning them over once or twice, until tender, about 20 minutes. Lightly sprinkle with salt, pepper, and herbs, if desired. Serve immediately or cool to room temperature, wrap, and refrigerate for up to 1 day. Reheat or use cold in a salad or as a snack.

4 servings

2   pounds medium-size
     asparagus

2   tblsp olive oil

     Salt

     Freshly ground black pepper

     Herbs of your choice, either
     chopped fresh or dried

Pricey asparagus yields more than you think. Prepare each spear by cutting off and discarding the dried, light-colored end — which is too tough to eat, anyway. Bend the stalk in several places down the stem until the tender part snaps off. Peel the tough green piece below the break with a sharp paring knife, and cook it with the rest of the asparagus for a tender treat.

The length of time needed to roast asparagus depends on the size of the vegetable. A very large asparagus may get too brown before it is done. A pencil-width size works but looks somewhat withered. Your best bet for roasting is a medium-size asparagus, about the size of your finger.

Succulent asparagus and red peppers

Nutritional facts per serving: 96 calories; 7.8g carbohydrates; 0mg cholesterol; 7g total fat; 2.8g fiber; 2.4g protein; 6.2mg sodium

Bring a large frying pan of water to a boil over medium-high heat. Add asparagus and cook until just barely tender, 3 to 5 minutes, depending on the size of the asparagus. Run under cold water to stop further cooking. Drain well.

Heat olive oil in the same pan over medium heat. Add pepper slices, green onions, and garlic. Cover and cook, stirring occasionally, for 3 minutes. Add asparagus, lemon juice, tarragon, and thyme. Sauté, stirring frequently, for 4 to 5 minutes, or until hot through. Season to taste with salt and pepper, and serve.

4 servings

1	pound medium asparagus cut into 2" diagonal pieces
2	tblsp olive oil
1	red bell pepper, sliced
1	cup chopped green onions
3	garlic cloves, chopped
2	tblsp fresh lemon juice
1/2	tsp dried tarragon
1/2	tsp dried thyme
	Salt
	Black pepper

Nutrition **Note**   Asparagus may help spare you from cell damage and disease thanks to antioxidants like glutathione. Glutathione is an ordinary amino acid with super antioxidant power. Research suggests that glutathione may help your body resist cancer, cataracts, and more. Raw asparagus is a good source of glutathione — and so are fresh avocados, potatoes, and raw spinach. Just remember that more highly processed foods, like canned vegetables, contain less glutathione than fresh foods. So choose fresh fruits and vegetables to get the richest sources of this powerful antioxidant.

Easy asparagus with orange zest

Nutritional facts per serving: 71 calories; 3.2g carbohydrates; 0mg cholesterol; 6.8g total fat; 1g fiber; 0.8g protein; 0.8mg sodium

---

Cut off the thick ends of the asparagus. Peel asparagus from the bottom up to the first of the little offshoots. Place in a frying pan, and add enough boiling water to cover. Cook until done, usually 3 to 5 minutes for small spears, 5 to 8 minutes for large spears. Remove. Toss with olive oil and orange rind.

1/2 pound asparagus

1 tblsp olive oil (optional)

Grated rind only of 1 navel orange

To eliminate the fat, leave out the olive oil, and toss with orange rind only.

2 servings

Nutrition **Note**   Folate can help protect your heart, and asparagus is a delicious way to get this important B vitamin. Just four spears of asparagus supply you with 89 micrograms of folate — more than 20 percent of the 400 micrograms you need each day. And here's how it helps. High levels of a chemical called homocysteine in your blood can damage and narrow your arteries. That can increase your risk of heart disease, blood clots, heart attacks and strokes. Fortunately, folate works with two other B vitamins to help lower the level of homocysteine in your blood. And as that drops, your risk of heart trouble drops right along with it.

Heart-healthy baked squash

Nutritional facts per serving: 53 calories; 0.5g carbohydrates; 0mg cholesterol; 3.6g total fat; 2.1g fiber; 1.3g protein; 2.4mg sodium

---

Preheat oven to 350 degrees.

In a large bowl or resealable plastic bag, combine the squash, olive oil, garlic, salt, and pepper to taste. Stir or shake well to coat the squash evenly with oil and seasonings.

Spread the squash on a large baking sheet and cook until crisp-tender, 20 to 25 minutes.

4 servings

4   yellow squash, sliced into 1" rounds

1   tblsp olive oil

1   garlic clove, finely chopped

Salt

Freshly ground black pepper

Nutrition **Note**   Enjoy squash for what it doesn't give you — extra calories. In fact there's only 36 calories in 1 cup of cooked summer squash. And that's a good thing because experts say extra weight hurts your health even more than smoking or heavy drinking. Those extra pounds can increase your risk for diabetes, heart disease, stroke, high blood pressure, gallbladder disease, sleep apnea, osteoarthritis, and some forms of cancer.

But don't lose hope. Just trying to lose weight may add years to your life if you're overweight. In fact, one study found that trying to lose, even if you don't succeed, can help you live longer.

Not everyone should go on a diet, so talk to your doctor first. In the meantime, you can still indulge in low-cal, nutritious foods like yellow squash.

Snappy zucchini stir-fry

Nutritional facts per serving: 88 calories; 2.5g carbohydrates; 23.3mg cholesterol; 8.7g total fat; 0.4g fiber; 0.6g protein; 3.3mg sodium

Salt the grated zucchini in a colander, and let drain to remove excess juice. Rinse, squeeze, and dry zucchini.

Melt butter in a frying pan. Add the shallot, then the zucchini. Toss for 4 to 5 minutes over high heat until tender but crunchy. Add salt and pepper to taste.

1/2	pound zucchini, grated
2	tsp butter
1	shallot, finely chopped
	Salt
	Freshly ground black pepper

The zucchini may be prepared to this point several hours ahead of serving and reheated quickly in a microwave.

You may replace the shallot with green onions, if desired.

2 servings

Nutrition **Note**   Carotenoids are colorful plant nutrients that prevent cell damage and fortify your body against disease. Zucchini supplies at least three important ones — beta carotene, lutein, and zeaxanthin. This may be especially good news for your eyes and joints. Researchers at the University of North Carolina at Chapel Hill discovered that lutein was one of the plant-based nutrients that may lower some people's risk for painful knee osteoarthritis by 30 to 40 percent. What's more, studies seem to suggest you can lower your risk of vision-stealing problems like cataracts and macular degeneration if you eat more lutein and zeaxanthin. So remember, eating more zucchini squash could be a good way to help squash your risk of health problems.

Quick squash sauté

Nutritional facts per serving: 51 calories; 4.5g carbohydrates; 0mg cholesterol; 3.6g total fat; 1.5g fiber; 1.1g protein; 2mg sodium

---

Heat olive oil in a large skillet. Add onion, garlic, jalapeño, yellow squash, and zucchini. Add salt and pepper to taste. Sauté until the vegetables are tender and just beginning to brown, about 10 minutes.

Variation: Sprinkle with feta cheese and black olives or Parmesan cheese and basil.

4 servings

1	tblsp olive oil
1	small onion, sliced thickly
1	garlic clove, chopped
1/2	jalapeño pepper, seeded and chopped (optional)
2	yellow squash, cut in 1/2" slices
2	zucchini, cut in 1/2" slices
	Salt
	Freshly ground black pepper

Have onions to chop? Try these ideas to make the onion smell vanish into thin air.

- Rub your hands with white vinegar before you start, and then do it again after you're done. If you'd rather not smell the vinegar, try rubbing your hands with the end of a stalk of celery, instead.

- Rub your hands with salt before you wash them.

- Rub a spoon on your hands and fingers under running warm water. This trick may work for garlic smell, too.

- Rub a cut lemon on your fingers. This may be the best idea because you replace the onion smell with a clean, fresh scent.

Tuscan zucchini-tomato bake

Nutritional facts per serving: 270 calories; 24.2g carbohydrates; 37.8mg cholesterol; 13.8g total fat; 1.5g fiber; 12.2g protein; 323mg sodium

Preheat oven to 400 degrees. Butter a 9" x 9" baking dish.

Layer half the zucchini and then half the tomatoes in the baking dish. Sprinkle with salt and pepper.

Mix together the bread crumbs, oregano, and Swiss and Parmesan cheeses. Sprinkle half over the zucchini and tomatoes. Repeat layering one more time, ending with cheese mixture. Dot with butter and bake until golden brown and bubbly, 20 to 25 minutes.

4 appetizer servings or 2 main course servings

2   small zucchini, trimmed and sliced lengthwise into 1/4" slices

2   tomatoes, sliced and drained on paper towels

Salt

Freshly ground black pepper

1/2   cup dry bread crumbs

1/2   tblsp chopped oregano

1/2   cup grated Swiss cheese

1/2   cup grated Parmesan cheese

1 1/2   tblsp butter

Nutrition **Note**   The calcium you get from cheeses like Swiss and Parmesan benefits more than just your bones and teeth. Small amounts of this valuable mineral travel into your blood where it helps to steady your blood pressure and clot your blood when necessary. Calcium also helps nerve impulses travel around so your brain and nerve cells can work together. What's more, your muscles, including your heart, need calcium to contract. Without it, your heart couldn't beat regularly. Calcium is one busy little mineral, so it's even more important to make sure you get enough. Dairy products, leafy greens, and fortified orange juice are all good sources.

Cheesy broiled zucchini

Nutritional facts per serving: 74 calories; 2.7g carbohydrates; 11.2mg cholesterol; 4.4g total fat; 0.6g fiber; 6.5g protein; 264.9mg sodium

Heat the broiler. Brush the sliced zucchini and red pepper with oil. Broil about 4 minutes per side. Remove to a large bowl, and toss with vinegar and Parmesan. Season to taste with salt and pepper. Serve warm or at room temperature.

This dish can also be made on the grill using a grill topper or grill basket designed for small food items.

4 servings

3   zucchini, cut lengthwise in 1/4" slices

1/2   red bell pepper, cut lengthwise in 2" wedges

1/2   tblsp olive oil

1/2   tblsp red wine vinegar

1   tblsp shaved Parmesan cheese

Salt

Freshly ground black pepper

Many recipes leave you with bits of leftover vegetables like peppers, celery, and onions. Don't toss them out. Instead, store them for easy use later on. Here's how. Chop up those leftovers, and then pull out an empty ice cube tray. Place a couple of tablespoons of chopped vegetables into each compartment of the ice cube tray. Fill with water and freeze. Shake out the frozen cubes into labeled freezer bags. Next time your favorite hot recipe calls for chopped veggies, just pull out those frozen veggie cubes, and you're ready to go.

Wonderful winter squash gratin

Nutritional facts per serving: 122 calories;27.1g carbohydrates; 5.3mg cholesterol; 1.4g total fat; 0.1g fiber; 3.9g protein; 164.5mg sodium

Preheat oven to 375 degrees. Cover a baking sheet with foil.

Pierce the squash in several places with a knife, and place it on the baking sheet. Bake squash for about 45 minutes, or until knife easily pierces through. Turn the squash at least once while baking.

Let the squash cool enough to handle. Cut open, remove seeds and any strings, and peel off skin. Purée the squash meat in a food processor. Add egg and spices, and process.

Reduce oven temperature to 325 degrees. Spray a baking dish with nonstick vegetable spray. Spoon the squash mixture into the dish. Combine bread crumbs and Parmesan cheese, if using, and sprinkle evenly on top. Place baking dish in oven, and bake for 10 to 15 minutes, or until hot through and topping is golden brown.

2 servings

2	pounds butternut squash
1	egg
1/4	tsp coriander
1/4	tsp cardamom
1/4	tsp salt
1/4	cup bread crumbs (optional)
2 1/2	tblsp grated fresh Parmesan cheese (optional)

The traditional topping for this dish is a mixture of bread crumbs and Parmesan cheese. However, the dish is fine without any topping. If you want to emphasize the sweetness of the squash, sprinkle the top lightly with light brown sugar.

Decadent eggplant "lasagna"

Nutritional facts per serving: 435 calories; 12.5g carbohydrates; 60.3mg cholesterol; 30.6g total fat; 2.3g fiber; 28.9g protein; 832.1mg sodium

Combine oil with oregano, basil, salt, and pepper. Brush it on both sides of the eggplant and zucchini. Lay the eggplant and zucchini in single layers on separate baking sheets. Broil 2" from heat for 4 to 5 minutes, or until cooked. Turn, brush other side with the herbed oil, and broil until done. Remove.

Preheat oven to 350 degrees. Place half the eggplant slices in a wide, shallow 2- or 3-quart baking dish. Top with half the zucchini, then layer on half the mozzarella, ricotta, spaghetti sauce, fennel seed, and Parmesan. Repeat the layers with remaining ingredients. Cover and bake 20 to 25 minutes, or until hot and bubbly.

6 servings

4-6	tblsp olive oil
2	heaping tsp finely chopped fresh oregano
1	heaping tsp finely chopped fresh basil
	Salt
	Freshly ground black pepper
1	12-ounce eggplant, sliced 1/2" thick
1	8-ounce zucchini, sliced 1/2" thick
8	ounces sliced mozzarella cheese
1	cup ricotta cheese, drained
2	cups homemade spaghetti sauce or 2 8-ounce jars
2	tblsp fennel seed, crushed
1	cup freshly grated Parmesan cheese

Don't waste good semi-hard cheese by letting the cut edge harden or get moldy. Give your cheese a light coating of butter, and it will stay fresh.

No-guilt vegetable stir-fry

Nutritional facts per serving: 51 calories; 4.2g carbohydrates; 0mg cholesterol; 3.5g total fat; 1.5g fiber; 1.5g protein; 256.4mg sodium

Heat sesame oil and soy sauce in a large skillet or wok until very hot. Add green onions, garlic, and red pepper flakes, and cook briefly. Add the squash, asparagus, and bell pepper and cook, stirring constantly, for about 3 minutes. Reduce heat, cover, and cook for an additional 1 to 2 minutes or until just done — not too soft, not too crunchy.

4 servings

1	tblsp sesame oil
1	tblsp soy sauce
3	green onions, sliced
1	garlic clove, peeled and chopped
1/2	tsp dried hot red pepper flakes (optional)
2	yellow squash, cut in 1/4" slices
1/4	pound asparagus, cut diagonally into 2" pieces
1	red bell pepper, cut into triangles

Nutrition **Note**

Say "open sesame" to a bottle of sesame oil, and your reward will be a health-helping oil that's high in polyunsaturated fats and lignans. A recent research study suggests cooking with sesame oil instead of other oils may help some people manage their high blood pressure. If you have this condition, ask your doctor whether cooking with sesame seed oil may benefit you.

When shopping for sesame oil, you may find two kinds. The dark-colored unrefined version has a strong flavor, so a little goes a long way in a stir-fry. Yet the milder-tasting refined sesame oil may be best for other dishes because it tolerates high heat without smoking. Once you decide what you'll use it for, your choice will be easier.

243

Quick zucchini and celery sauté

Nutritional facts per serving: 71 calories; 3.5g carbohydrates; 7.8mg cholesterol; 6.4g total fat; 1.3g fiber; 1g protein; 57.4mg sodium

Heat olive oil and butter in a large frying pan. Add celery slices and sauté for 2 minutes. Add zucchini sticks, and sauté with the celery 2 minutes longer or until crisp-tender. Reduce heat to medium, add garlic and parsley, and sauté 1 minute longer. Season to taste with salt and pepper.

4 servings

1	tblsp olive or vegetable oil
1	tblsp butter
4	celery stalks, sliced into 1/2" diagonal slices
3	small zucchini, cut into 1 1/2" long sticks
2	garlic cloves, chopped
1	tblsp parsley, chopped
	Salt
	Freshly ground black pepper

Don't let your celery go limp in the refrigerator. Wrap it in aluminum foil as soon as you get it home, and it will keep for weeks. Or place it in a paper bag with the outside stalks and leaves on it for best storage. If you do accidentally let that celery go limp, you can still do something about it. Trim the ends, and let it soak in some water for up to half an hour. Don't use hot water — only water that is tepid or downright cold will do the trick. Your celery will regain its snap in no time flat.

Lightly spiced turnips and red peppers

Nutritional facts per serving: 69 calories; 4.1g carbohydrates; 15.6mg cholesterol; 5.9g total fat; 1.2g fiber; 0.6g protein; 11.8mg sodium

Add turnips to a pan of boiling salted water for 2 to 3 minutes if they are small or 8 to 10 minutes if they are large. Drain. Melt a little of the butter in a large, heavy skillet. Add the red peppers, turnips, and garlic, and stir-fry over moderate heat, adding more butter if necessary. Cook until turnips are tender when pierced with a knife, but peppers are still crunchy. Season with salt and pepper.

4 servings

1	pound small white turnips, peeled and sliced
2	tblsp butter
1	pound red bell peppers, sliced
1	garlic clove, finely chopped
1	tsp salt
	Freshly ground black pepper

Nutrition **Note** Turn to turnip greens for nutrients that can charge up your immune system, help protect your eyesight, and keep your bones strong.

Turnip greens are a good source of vitamin C, which gives your immune system a boost and may help you recover faster during cold and flu season. Turnip greens also give you lutein and zeaxanthin. These healthy nutrients help fortify your eyes against the cataracts and macular degeneration that can cause vision loss.

But that's not all. Experts say women may need as much as 1,200 milligrams of calcium daily to help keep bones strong and hold off osteoporosis. At 249 milligrams per cup, turnip greens are a super start. As a nutritional bonus, turnips can also help you get a little extra iron and omega-3 fatty acids in your diet. That's five nutritious reasons to make turnip greens one of your "five a day."

Oriental cabbage stir-fry

Nutritional facts per serving: 39 calories; 4.5g carbohydrates; 0mg cholesterol; 2g total fat; 1.4g fiber; 1.3g protein; 201.2mg sodium

Heat oil in a wok or large skillet. Add remaining ingredients. Cook over high heat, stirring constantly, until cabbage is crisp-tender.

4 servings

1/2	tblsp canola oil
1/2	onion, thinly sliced
2	cups coarsely shredded cabbage
1/2	cup thinly sliced celery
1/4	cup chicken broth
1	tblsp low-sodium soy sauce

Nutrition **Note**

Cabbage is part of the brassica family — a group of vegetables that also includes broccoli and cauliflower. They are all famous for their cancer-fighting abilities. While cabbage is inexpensive and low in calories, it's rich in some specific natural chemicals that increase your body's ability to ward off cancer. In fact, research shows it helps protect you from cancer of the colon, brain, breast, stomach, bladder, and lung.

Pick a head of cabbage that is firm, not soft or spongy. You may have a little trouble digesting cabbage if your body isn't used to brassica vegetables. But that's normal. Just add it to your diet a little at a time.

Quick and simple spinach quiche

Nutritional facts per serving: 247 calories; 21.9g carbohydrates; 104.3mg cholesterol; 10.3g total fat; 2.6g fiber; 17g protein; 360mg sodium

Preheat oven to 350 degrees. Melt margarine or butter in a 13" x 9" x 2" baking dish. Tilt pan to coat bottom. Set aside.

In a large mixing bowl, beat eggs with milk. Stir in flour, baking powder, and shredded cheese. Stir in spinach. Pour into baking dish and sprinkle with Parmesan cheese.

Bake for 50 to 60 minutes or until top is golden brown. Cool for at least 10 minutes. Cut into squares and serve. May be served hot or at room temperature.

1	pound fresh, chopped spinach
2	tblsp butter or margarine
3	eggs
1	cup low-fat milk
1	cup all-purpose flour
1	tsp baking powder
1 1/2	cups low-fat shredded cheese
1/4	cup grated Parmesan cheese

6 servings

Nutrition **Note**

There's nothing better for you — head to toe — than yummy, nutrient-packed spinach. Make a salad or side dish out of this garden-fresh delight and you'll strengthen your bones, protect your heart, stop strokes, boost your immune system, and fight cancer.

But if you want to say "no" to macular degeneration and have eagle-eye vision for years to come, then really pile on the spinach. It contains carotenoids — special antioxidants that protect your eyes from light damage and support the blood vessels to your retina. Boosting the amount of carotenoids in your body can keep your retina strong and efficient — and has proven to cut risk of developing age-related macular degeneration by 43 percent.

Speedy stir-fried spinach

Nutritional facts per serving: 41 calories; 1.5g carbohydrates; 0mg cholesterol; 3.7g total fat; 0.8g fiber; 1.2g protein; 48.2mg sodium

If using frozen spinach, thaw and squeeze dry. If using fresh spinach, wash it well, remove the stems, and tear into bite-size pieces.

Heat a wok or skillet and add the oil. Add the garlic and stir-fry until light brown, about 2 minutes. Add the spinach and stir-fry 1 minute. Stir in the chicken broth and salt and cook 1 minute longer. Season to taste with salt and pepper.

2 servings

1/2 pound fresh spinach or 1 10-ounce package frozen

2 tsp canola oil

1 garlic clove, peeled and chopped

1 tblsp low-sodium chicken broth

Salt

Freshly ground black pepper

Nutrition **Note**
Have you ever washed spinach carefully only to have your family complain that it's gritty? Don't worry. Just start washing that spinach with salt water. You'll say goodbye to the grit and hello to better health. After all, spinach fortifies you with plenty of disease-battling antioxidants. Studies even find that spinach may help prevent colorectal, stomach, breast, prostate, bladder, and lung cancers. So get rid of the grit, but keep feeding your family that nutritious spinach.

Sautéed spinach and shiitake mushrooms

Nutritional facts per serving: 47 calories; 17.6g carbohydrates; 0mg cholesterol; 7.7g total fat; 7.4g fiber; 7.7g protein; 182.6mg sodium

Wash spinach, place in a medium-size frying pan, cover, and cook over medium heat until spinach wilts, 3 to 4 minutes. The water on the leaves should provide enough moisture for cooking. Drain, cool, and squeeze out any remaining moisture.

Heat olive oil in the same pan over medium heat. Add garlic and sauté for 2 minutes, stirring constantly. Add mushrooms, toss with oil and garlic, and sauté until just tender, 8 to 10 minutes. Add the spinach and toss until hot through. Season to taste with salt. (You will need less salt if you add the cheese.)

1 pound fresh spinach, stems removed

1 tblsp olive oil

3 garlic cloves, finely chopped

1/4 pound shiitake mushrooms, cleaned and stems removed

Salt

Freshly ground pepper

3 tblsp freshly grated Parmigiano-Reggiano cheese (optional)

Lemon (optional)

Sprinkle with pepper. Add either the Parmigiano-Reggiano cheese or a squeeze of lemon juice. Serve immediately.

2 servings

Nutrition **Note**   Eat a meal of ginger-seasoned salmon filet, a glass of fortified milk, and sautéed spinach with mushrooms, and you may help yourself fight off migraines. That's because spinach and fish both contain magnesium, which may be lacking in your system. Nearly 80 percent of 3,000 migraine sufferers reported relief after getting 200 milligrams of magnesium per day.

Fresh collard greens with pepper vinegar

Nutritional facts per serving: 70 calories; 20.5g carbohydrates; 0mg cholesterol; 8.7g total fat; 12.6g fiber; 8.7g protein; 70mg sodium

1 1/2 large bunches collard greens (about 3 pounds)

Salt

1 ham hock (optional)

2 tblsp olive oil

3/4 cup finely chopped yellow onion

1/2 tsp pepper

2 tblsp hot pepper vinegar

Wash the collards twice and remove the stems. Stack the leaves and cut them into 1/8" strips. Cutting the leaves thin will break down the fibers sooner, so the collards won't have to be cooked as long and will retain their green color.

Put 1 gallon of water, salt, and ham hock, if desired, in a large nonreactive pot, and bring to a boil over high heat. Add the collards and let them cook for 3 minutes. Drain and run under cold water to stop further cooking. Remove and squeeze dry.

Heat the ham hock or olive oil in a large frying pan over medium-high heat. Add the onion and simmer for 2 minutes. Add the collards and cook just long enough to heat them through. Toss with the pepper and hot pepper vinegar. Serve with a slotted spoon to remove any excess liquid.

4 servings

Nutrition **Note**

Collard greens give you bone-building calcium, protective vitamin C, eye-helping antioxidants, and even a little of the omega-3 fatty acids everyone raves about. Although cleaning collards may take time, their extra nutrition may help you keep a sparkling clean bill of health.

Tangy green beans

Nutritional facts per serving: 179 calories; 12.8g carbohydrates; 0mg cholesterol; 13.9g total fat; 5g fiber; 3.5g protein; 20.2mg sodium

Bring a saucepan of water to a boil over medium-high heat. Add green beans, reduce the heat to medium, and simmer until just soft, about 4 to 5 minutes, depending on the size of the green bean. Run under cold water to stop further cooking. When cool, drain well.

Heat olive oil in a large frying pan over medium-high heat. Add onion slices, reduce the heat to medium, cover the pan, and cook for 3 minutes, stirring once or twice, to bring out the juices. Add the stock and cook over medium, stirring occasionally, until the liquid has almost evaporated and the onion slices are becoming tender. Add the bell pepper, cover and simmer, stirring occasionally to prevent scorching, until just tender, 4 to 5 minutes. Add the green beans. Stir until beans are hot, about 3 minutes. Season to taste with salt and pepper, and serve.

2 servings

1/2 pound young, tender green beans, ends removed

2 tblsp olive oil

1/2 medium sweet yellow onion, thinly sliced

1/3 cup chicken stock, home made or low-sodium

1/2 large red bell pepper, sliced

Salt

Freshly ground black pepper

Snow peas, asparagus, or broccoli could be substituted for the green beans. Adjust the cooking time accordingly.

Herbed peas with onions

Nutritional facts per serving: 70 calories; 3g carbohydrates; 15.6mg cholesterol; 6g total fat; 1.4g fiber; 1.5g protein; 101.3mg sodium

Heat butter in a pan. Add the peas, herb, lettuce, and onions. Add the chicken broth. Bring to a boil and continue cooking, covered, adding more water if necessary, until the peas are done yet slightly crunchy, about 6 to 8 minutes. Taste for seasoning, and add salt and pepper as desired.

2 servings

1   tblsp butter

1/2   cup shelled green peas

1   tblsp chopped fresh mint or thyme

1   leaf iceberg or romaine lettuce

2   green onions, trimmed of roots and outside layers

1/4   cup low-sodium chicken broth

Salt

Freshly ground black pepper

Nutrition **Note**

Did you know that a cup of green peas has more protein than a large egg? Plus it has no cholesterol and just a tiny amount of fat. Getting more of your protein from plant sources instead of from animals is a good idea. A study by the American Cancer Society found that people who ate more than three servings of meat a week added extra fat around their mid-section. This increases the risk of heart disease, diabetes, and some cancers.

In addition, a cup of green peas provides healthy amounts of folate, vitamin C, and vitamin K as well as iron, magnesium, potassium and several important B vitamins. So if you'd like to get a good variety of nutrition in one food, say "please pass the peas."

Tomato-spangled green peas

Nutritional facts per serving: 73 calories; 7g carbohydrates; 10.4mg cholesterol; 4g total fat; 2.5g fiber; 2.7g protein; 3mg sodium

Heat butter in a large skillet over medium heat. Add the peas, tomato, and basil, and toss just until warmed through. Do not cook too long or the tomatoes will wilt and give up their juices, making the dish too soggy. Season to taste with salt and pepper.

2-3 servings

1 tblsp butter

1 8-ounce package frozen green peas, defrosted

1 tomato, cut into small cubes

1 tblsp finely chopped fresh basil

Salt

Freshly ground black pepper

Even if you love tomatoes, you can only eat so many from your garden. Leave what you can use in a few days on the counter for everyone to admire, but don't put any in the refrigerator. Tomatoes don't take kindly to cool temperatures and quickly lose their flavor. Yet, they freeze just fine. Spread them out on a cookie sheet, and put it in the freezer overnight. Once frozen, store them in your freezer in freezer bags. When you need tomatoes for cooking, simply thaw a few.

Southern-style black-eyed peas

Nutritional facts per serving: 340 calories; 55.2g carbohydrates; 0mg cholesterol; 2.6g total fat; 8.9g fiber; 27.3g protein; 121.6mg sodium

Soak peas in a pot of water overnight. Or cover with water, bring to a boil, boil for 2 minutes, cover, and let set for 30 minutes. Drain and rinse.

Place the peas, 2 cups of chicken broth, the ham hock, garlic, red pepper flakes, and bay leaf in a pot, and stir to combine. Bring to boil over high heat.

Reduce heat to medium-low and simmer the peas, stirring occasionally until tender, about 20 minutes. Add the remaining chicken stock as necessary to keep the peas covered. Drain peas, remove bay leaf, and season with salt and pepper to taste. Serve, or cool, cover and refrigerate for up to 2 days.

1	cup dried black-eyed peas
2-3	cups low-sodium chicken broth
1	ham hock (optional)
1	garlic clove, finely chopped
1/8	tsp red pepper flakes
1	bay leaf
	Salt
	Freshly ground black pepper

2 servings

Nutrition **Note** You could stop a killer, and black-eyed peas could help do the job. High blood pressure is called the silent killer because it doesn't have any symptoms. Many people don't even know they have it. Left untreated, it can lead to heart attack, stroke, congestive heart failure, kidney damage, and atherosclerosis. But you can manage this dangerous condition. Start by keeping your weight down and making sure you get plenty of magnesium, calcium, and potassium. Eat foods like dairy products, leafy greens, baked potatoes, citrus fruits, bananas, avocados, and of course, black-eyed peas.

Traditional hoppin' john

Nutritional facts per serving: 199 calories; 42.4g carbohydrates; 0mg cholesterol; 1.4g total fat; 6.7g fiber; 5.6g protein; 318.1mg sodium

Soak the beans in water overnight. Drain, rinse, and cover with fresh water. Cook over medium heat until tender, about 30 minutes to 1 hour.

In a separate saucepan, cook the onions in a little water until they are caramelized, about 15 minutes. Add the garlic, carrots, and celery and cook until tender. Stir in the vinegar, seasonings, and the drained, cooked peas (reserve liquid). Add enough water from the bean pot to make a thick sauce. Heat through.

Serve over rice and top with the tomato and green onions. Add hot sauce, if desired.

4 servings

1/2	pound dried black-eyed peas
3 1/2	cups water
1	cup chopped onion
4	garlic cloves, chopped
1/2	cup sliced carrots
1/2	cup diced celery
4	tsp balsamic vinegar
1/4	tsp cayenne pepper, or to taste
1/2	tsp salt, or to taste
1	tomato, diced
2	green onions, chopped
	Hot sauce
2	cups cooked brown rice

Nutrition **Note**

It's a New Year's Day tradition for many families — eat black-eyed peas and you'll have good luck (some say riches) throughout the coming year. It's a good theory, because you just may be lucky in health if you eat these nutritious legumes. Remember beans, peas, lentils, peanuts, and soybeans all offer flavorful, unbeatable nutrition. They're low in saturated fat but high in healthy fiber, protein, magnesium, and the B vitamin biotin. Try this zesty recipe that will make you hop with good health.

Texas-style black beans

Nutritional facts per serving: 214 calories; 26.1g carbohydrates; 0mg cholesterol; 1.1g total fat; 5.9g fiber; 11g protein; 96mg sodium

---

Rinse black beans and pick them over for stones. Soak black beans in a pot of water overnight, or cover with water, bring to a boil, boil for 2 minutes, cover, and let set for 30 minutes. Drain and rinse.

Heat olive oil in a heavy-bottomed large pot over medium heat. Add garlic, onion, celery, carrot, and poblano pepper. If poblano pepper isn't available, substitute a small bell pepper and small jalapeño. Cook, stirring occasionally, just until soft.

Add the beans, bay leaf, chili powder, cumin, black pepper, and chicken broth and mix well. Bring the beans to a simmer, cover, reduce heat to low, and cook, stirring occasionally, until beans are soft, 1 1/2 to 2 hours. Check occasionally to be sure there is still enough liquid in the pot. If liquid is needed, add hot chicken stock or hot water to prevent scorching. When beans are soft, remove from heat and remove bay leaf. Season to taste with salt and Tabasco, and serve.

1/4	pound dried black beans
1	tblsp olive oil
1	garlic clove, finely chopped
1/2	small yellow onion, chopped
1	rib celery, chopped
1	small peeled carrot, chopped
1	small, fresh poblano pepper, cored, seeded, and finely chopped
1	small bay leaf
1/2	tsp chili powder, or to taste
3/4	tsp ground cumin
3/4	tsp freshly ground black pepper
1 3/4	cups low-sodium chicken broth
	Salt
	Tabasco

2 servings

Nutritious herbed green lentils

Nutritional facts per serving: 304 calories; 49.4g carbohydrates; 0mg cholesterol; 2.7g total fat; 8.9g fiber; 23.5g protein; 97.3mg sodium

Rinse the lentils and check them over for stones. Heat the butter in a heavy-bottomed pot over medium heat. Add onion, carrots, and celery, and cover. Cook, stirring occasionally, until just tender, about 3 minutes. Add the stock and bring to a boil.

Add the lentils, stir to mix well, and bring back to a simmer. Reduce the heat to low, and simmer gently, stirring occasionally. After 20 minutes, add the thyme and tarragon. If the lentils need more liquid, add hot water. Continue to simmer until the lentils are tender, about 45 minutes. Drain. Season to taste with salt and pepper, toss with parsley, and serve.

4 servings

1 1/2	cups green lentils
2	tblsp butter
1	small sweet onion, finely chopped
1/2	cup finely chopped peeled carrots
1/2	cup finely chopped celery
4	cups low-sodium chicken stock
3/4	tsp dried thyme
3/4	tsp dried tarragon
2	tblsp chopped fresh parsley
	Salt
	Black pepper

Lentils come in a color range of green, yellow, red-orange, brown, and black. Green lentils, especially the expensive French green lentilles du Puy, are to the lentil family as Lady Peas are to the field pea family — small with a decidedly more delicate taste. Lentils do not need to be soaked before cooking. In fact, take care that you don't overcook them or they will become mushy.

Minty butter-glazed carrots

Nutritional facts per serving: 63 calories; 5.8g carbohydrates; 11.7mg cholesterol; 4.4g total fat; 1.8g fiber; 0.6g protein; 20.7mg sodium

Place the carrots in a heavy saucepan and barely cover with water. Add the butter and cover. Bring to a boil, reduce the heat, and cook 15 minutes or until still firm but easy to pierce with a fork.

1/2   pound baby carrots

1   tsp butter

2   tsp chopped mint

Salt

Freshly ground black pepper

Remove the cover and boil down until the liquid has evaporated and the carrots are coated with butter. Watch them carefully or they will burn.

Add the chopped mint and season with salt and pepper.

2 servings

Nutrition **Note**   Crunch down on more carrots, and you may protect yourself from secondhand smoke, air pollution, and ultimately, lung cancer. Doctors at the Harvard School of Public Health found that if you don't smoke, a nutrient called alpha carotene may lower your risk of lung cancer. Like beta carotene, alpha carotene is a disease-thwarting antioxidant found in carrots. Just one regular-sized carrot will give you a daily dose of alpha carotene that can help protect your lungs. So take a tip from that famous bunny. You may find a carrot a day keeps the doctor away.

Gingered celery and carrots

Nutritional facts per serving: 133 calories; 19.2g carbohydrates; 15.6mg cholesterol; 6.1g total fat; 6g fiber; 2.1g protein; 100.1mg sodium

Melt butter in a sauce pan. Add celery and carrots. Cover and cook over low heat until crisp but tender.

Sprinkle the sugar and ginger over the celery and carrots. Stir slowly and gently until the vegetables are well-glazed and slightly golden brown. Season with salt and pepper to taste.

If the mint leaves aren't small and pretty, chop coarsely; otherwise stir them in whole. Serve hot.

4 servings

3	tblsp butter
4	ribs celery, sliced on the diagonal
4	large carrots, sliced on the diagonal
1/4	cup sugar (or less)
1 1/2	tsp fresh chopped ginger
2	tsp chopped mint leaves
	Salt
	Freshly ground black pepper

Nutrition Note

A little spice could make your stomach "play nice." Not only does ginger have antioxidants that are good for your health, but it also may prevent or stop nausea — especially that queasy feeling from motion sickness. In fact, one study suggests that ginger is as effective as drugstore medicines. Yet, it won't make you drowsy like many motion sickness drugs.

When you're not adding ginger to a favorite recipe, steep some in a pot of tea or sample sugary candied ginger. Just know that ginger might not work for everyone. Although most people can enjoy fresh or powdered ginger without side effects, be sure to talk to your doctor before taking ginger supplements.

Orange-glazed vegetables

Nutritional facts per serving: 213 calories; 38.9g carbohydrates; 15.6mg cholesterol; 6.3g total fat; 6.4g fiber; 2.6g protein; 70.1mg sodium

Peel carrots and cut them into 2" sticks. Heat the butter in a frying pan until it foams. Add the onion, ginger, and carrots. Cover and simmer for 5 minutes to bring out juices and begin to soften carrots. Uncover and add the peppers, orange juice, and sugar. Stir-fry for 5 minutes, or until vegetables are tender and the liquid has evaporated into a glaze.

4 servings

1	pound carrots
2	tblsp butter
1	small yellow onion, chopped
1/2	cup finely chopped fresh ginger
1	large red pepper, cored, seeded, and sliced
1/2	cup fresh orange juice
1/4	cup brown sugar

Nutrition **Note** Eat like a rabbit and you might ward off cancer, heart disease, and vision problems. According to one study, cooked carrots twice a week reduced breast cancer risk by nearly 40 percent. What's more, a single carrot can give you 2 grams of fiber. That's a tasty first step towards your daily fiber goal. If you eat 25 to 40 grams of fiber a day, you may lower your heart disease risk by up to 30 percent. But that's not all. Natural chemicals called carotenes help protect your eyes from disease. Add in the fact that carrot fiber keeps you regular, and every carrot you eat becomes a 24-karat value for your health.

Easy gingered vegetable medley

Nutritional facts per serving: 36 calories; 2.2g carbohydrates; 7.8mg cholesterol; 3g total fat; 0.7g fiber; 0.5g protein; 20mg sodium

---

Peel and julienne the carrot and turnip. Wash and julienne the zucchini.

Heat the butter or oil in a large frying pan until hot. Add the ginger and cook 1 to 2 minutes. Add the carrots and turnips to the ginger and cook 2 to 3 minutes, until just beginning to soften. Add the zucchini and cook 2 to 3 minutes more. Stir to mix well. Season to taste with salt and pepper.

4 servings

1	large carrot
1	white turnip (about 1/4 pound)
2	zucchini (about 1/2 pound)
1 1/2	tblsp butter or oil
1/2-1	tblsp finely chopped fresh ginger
	Salt
	Freshly ground black pepper

Nutrition **Note**

Ginger may taste spicy hot, but it could also beat the heat of arthritis pain. A group of osteoarthritis sufferers in Denmark ate 5 grams of fresh ginger a day, and 75 percent of them reported significant relief from the achy pain and swelling of arthritis. In fact, the more ginger they ate, the better they felt. Researchers think ginger may work as a natural anti-inflammatory, reducing the redness, pain, and swelling that often accompanies arthritis. Just remember that ginger may not be for everyone and be sure to talk to your doctor before trying it in large amounts.

Festive celery-pimento bundles

Nutritional facts per serving: 121 calories; 4.9g carbohydrates; 31.1mg cholesterol; 11.7g total fat; 1.7g fiber; 1.4g protein; 60.3mg sodium

Rinse the pimentos and tear into long strips. Cut each stalk of celery into 3 3 1/2" lengths, 1/4" thick. Melt the butter. Add celery and cook over low heat 5 minutes. Divide into 4 bundles of 4 or 5 pieces of celery and put a ring of pimento around each bundle. When ready to eat, reheat the bundles in a microwave. Season with salt and pepper.

1	small can whole pimentos
1	bunch celery
1/4	cup butter
	Salt
	Freshly ground black pepper

4 servings

Nutrition **Note**

A single crunchy stalk of medium-sized celery can give you around 10 percent of your body's daily requirement for vitamin K — and that's great news for both your bones and your blood. First of all, your blood needs vitamin K to clot properly. In fact, doctors sometimes give people vitamin K before surgery to help reduce bleeding during the operation.

In addition, vitamin K helps your body produce a protein necessary for building bone. It works along with vitamin D to make sure your bones are strong and healthy. For rich sources of vitamin K, pick the greenest vegetables you can find. Kale, broccoli, and spinach are good ones to try. Don't freeze these foods because it may destroy their vitamin K content.

Zesty brussels sprouts

Nutritional facts per serving: 111 calories; 11.4g carbohydrates; 15.6mg cholesterol; 6.9g total fat; 4.7g fiber; 4.3g protein; 30.5mg sodium

Preheat oven to 350 degrees.

Slice brussels sprouts into 1/4" slices. Bring water to a boil over medium-high heat in a large frying pan or skillet. Add the sprouts and simmer until tender, 5 to 7 minutes. Cook the brussels sprouts in 2 batches if necessary. Drain well.

Toast sesame seeds for about 8 minutes or until golden brown. Return the frying pan to the stove on medium heat. Add the butter and coriander and stir until the butter starts to sizzle. Add the sprouts and heat through. Add the lemon juice, zest, sesame seeds, and parsley. Season to taste with salt and pepper, and serve.

4 servings

1   pound small brussels sprouts, brown bottoms trimmed off

2   tsp sesame seeds

2   tblsp butter

1   tsp coriander

1   tblsp fresh lemon juice

Zest of 1 lemon

1   tblsp chopped fresh parsley

Salt

Freshly ground black pepper

Look for solid, bright green brussels sprouts. If they feel light or have yellow leaves, they are not your best buy. If you buy different sizes, cook them sliced so they will be done before they lose their green color.

Minted hot cucumbers

Nutritional facts per serving: 44 calories; 3.9g carbohydrates; 7.8mg cholesterol; 3.1g total fat; 1.1g fiber; 0.8g protein; 3.6mg sodium

---

Peel cucumbers and cut in half lengthwise. Scoop out the seeds with a spoon and discard. Cut into thin slices.

Melt butter in a skillet over medium heat. Add onion and sauté until soft. Add cucumber slices and toss just until tender, about 2 minutes. Do not overcook or they will become mushy.

2	large English cucumbers
1	tblsp butter
1	medium onion, chopped
3	tblsp chopped fresh mint
	Salt
	Freshly ground black pepper

Remove your pan from the heat, and stir in the mint. Season to taste with salt and pepper, and serve immediately.

4 servings

Nutrition **Note**

A bruise that seems to appear from nowhere may be a sign of a vitamin K deficiency. Oddly enough, cucumbers can help. Women over 50 need 90 micrograms (mcg) of vitamin K every day and men need 120 mcg. A single unpeeled cucumber has almost 50 mcg. Without the peel you get about 20. That's a good start on the amount you need to help your blood clot and prevent those mystery bruises.

You can also get vitamin K from spinach, cabbage, carrots, avocados, tomatoes, dairy products, and olive and canola oil. But remember to avoid freezing these foods because that may destroy the vitamin K. And avoid adding too much vitamin K to your diet if you're on blood thinning medicines like Warfarin, since vitamin K may counter this kind of drug.

Herb-baked tomatoes

Nutritional facts per serving: 255 calories; 7.3g carbohydrates; 24.6mg cholesterol; 20.7g total fat; 1.5g fiber; 11.5g protein; 210.5mg sodium

---

Preheat oven to 450 degrees. Grease an ovenproof casserole.

Slice the stem ends off the tomatoes, scoop out the inside pulp and seeds, and discard. Drain completely upside down on a rack. Mix the parsley, basil, garlic, and oil. Season to taste with salt and pepper.

Put the tomatoes, open side up, in the casserole. Divide the herb mixture among the drained tomatoes. Bake for about 5 minutes, then top each tomato with a slice of cheese, and return to the oven for another 10 minutes.

4	tomatoes
2	tblsp chopped fresh parsley
2	tblsp chopped fresh basil
1	garlic clove, chopped
1/4	cup olive oil
	Salt
	Freshly ground black pepper
4	slices Fontina or mozzarella cheese
	Basil leaves
	Parsley sprigs

Serve hot, garnished with basil leaves and parsley sprigs.

4 servings

Nutrition **Note** A golden stream of olive oil could be a delicious defense against rheumatoid arthritis — a painful disease where your immune system attacks your joints. In a clinical study, those who ate the least olive oil were more than twice as likely to develop rheumatoid arthritis. Perhaps monounsaturated fats in olive oil rally to help fight joint inflammation, or maybe the antioxidants in olive oil jump in to fend off free radicals. Either way, olive oil seems to give you an edge against arthritis. So slide a little olive oil into your meals. It may help keep your joints well-oiled and arthritis-free.

Sautéed cherry tomatoes and onions

Nutritional facts per serving: 100 calories; 17.9g carbohydrates; 0mg cholesterol; 7.3g total fat; 2.3g fiber; 1.9g protein; 39mg sodium

Heat olive oil in a large frying pan or skillet over medium heat. Add green onions and garlic, cover, and cook for 2 minutes, stirring once or twice.

Reduce heat to low, add tomatoes, and stir to combine. Cover and cook for 5 minutes, stirring occasionally. Stop cooking sooner if any of the tomatoes begin to split open. Season with salt and pepper to taste. Toss with parsley and serve.

2 servings

1	tblsp olive oil
1/2	cup chopped green onions
1	garlic clove, chopped
1	pint cherry tomatoes
	Kosher salt
	Freshly ground black pepper
2	tblsp chopped fresh parsley

This is what you cook when it's the dead of winter, and you're craving a real fresh-tasting tomato instead of the much less vibrant taste of "tomato product." Bright red, thick-skinned cherry tomatoes can deliver real tomato flavor year round. So choose those instead of the thin-skinned, pinkish-red ones, which are less flavorful.

Prepare cherry tomatoes simply, without adding too many flavors. Cook them just enough to tell they're done, but don't let them even start to split, or you may lose that flavor you've been craving. For added variety, try the new "sweet" grape cherry tomatoes.

European-style sautéed apples

Nutritional facts per serving: 200 calories; 35.8g carbohydrates; 0mg cholesterol; 7.6g total fat; 6.4g fiber; 0.9g protein; 1.3mg sodium

---

Heat olive oil in a frying pan over medium heat and add onions. Add the apples and cook, stirring occasionally, until they just begin to get tender. Add the chopped garlic and cook, stirring, until soft. Season with salt and pepper to taste.

4 servings

2	tblsp olive oil
2	red onions, sliced thickly
4	Granny Smith apples, sliced thickly
2	garlic cloves, chopped
	Salt
	Black pepper

Nutrition **Note**

Apples are good heart food. Not only are they high in fiber, vitamins, minerals, and antioxidants, but they're also fat-free, cholesterol free, and low in sodium. But there's more. The magnesium and potassium in apples help regulate your blood pressure and keep your heart beating steadily. Apples also have the flavonoid quercetin, a naturally occurring antioxidant, that protects your artery walls from damage and keeps your blood flowing smoothly. In fact, adding flavonoid-rich foods like apples to your diet has been scientifically confirmed to lower your risk of heart disease. So an apple a day really might keep a doctor away.

Tasty cranberry-vegetable pie

Nutritional facts per serving: 311 calories; 43.5g carbohydrates; 109.1mg cholesterol; 11g total fat; 3.3g fiber; 10.1g protein; 348.8mg sodium

Preheat oven to 375 degrees.

Peel and grate the sweet potatoes and carrots. Fill a large saucepan with salted water and bring to a boil. Carefully transfer the grated vegetables to the pot and allow to boil for 5 minutes. Drain and set aside.

Wash and sort the cranberries. Place in a medium saucepan with the sugar, cover, and cook over low heat for 10 minutes. Stir occasionally. Remove the lid and cook for 5 more minutes, stirring constantly.

1/2	pound sweet potatoes
1/2	pound carrots
1/2	pound fresh raw cranberries
2/3	cup sugar
1/2	cup low-fat milk
4	eggs
8	ounces light cream cheese, cubed
	Dash nutmeg
	Dash salt
1	9" pre-baked quiche shell

Nutrition **Note**

With powerful flavonoids, vitamin C, potassium, and fiber, cranberries can protect you from urinary tract infections, heart disease, and cancer. They might even fight ulcers and gum disease.

Add the cooked vegetable mixture to the cranberries and cook for 3 to 4 minutes, stirring constantly.

In a separate bowl, beat the milk, eggs, cream cheese, nutmeg, and salt until well blended. Stir in the cranberry vegetable mixture. Pour this filling carefully into the prepared shell. Bake for 40 minutes or until firm and golden brown.

8 servings

Cranberried sweet potatoes

Nutritional facts per serving: 264 calories; 47.2g carbohydrates; 0mg cholesterol; 7.1g total fat; 5.7g fiber; 4.1g protein; 18.3mg sodium

Preheat oven to 350 degrees. Spray a 1-quart baking dish with nonstick cooking spray.

Mash sweet potatoes in a large bowl. Stir in orange rind and cranberries. In a separate bowl, blend flour, brown sugar, oats, cinnamon, and butter until crumbly. Add half the crumb mixture to the sweet potatoes and spoon into the prepared baking dish. Top with the remaining crumb mixture.

Bake 15 to 20 minutes, or until heated through.

4 servings

1	pound sweet potatoes, baked, cooled, and peeled
1/2	tsp grated orange rind
1	cup fresh whole cranberries
2	tblsp flour
2	tblsp brown sugar
1/4	cup oats
1/2	tsp ground cinnamon
2	tblsp butter

Nutrition **Note**

Want a jazzed up side dish with few calories, virtually no fat, absolutely no cholesterol, yet loaded with vitamins, minerals, and fiber? Then you want a sweet potato.

This colorful tuber has the potassium, beta carotene, folate, and vitamin C to fight cancer, lower your blood pressure, and keep your arteries clear. Besides that, you'll protect your stomach lining from ulcers and your eyes from cataracts.

Some people call sweet potatoes "yams," but they're actually two separate vegetables. The sweet potato you're familiar with comes from the root of the morning glory vine.

Zesty lemon-ginger sweet potatoes

Nutritional facts per serving: 352 calories; 70.9g carbohydrates; 15.6mg cholesterol; 6.5g total fat; 7.1g fiber; 4g protein; 315.3mg sodium

Preheat oven to 350 degrees.

Cover a baking sheet with foil to catch drips from the potatoes. Wash sweet potatoes, and stick them several times with a knife to let steam escape. Place on baking sheet, and bake until soft, 1 1/2 to 2 hours, depending on size.

Peel potatoes when cool enough to handle, and place in bowl. Mix in the butter, beating with the flat beater on an electric mixer. Add the brown sugar, salt, cinnamon, ginger, lemon zest, and orange juice, and beat well. Place in a greased baking dish. Sprinkle the top lightly with brown sugar and dot with butter, if desired. Bake for 30 minutes.

4 servings

2	pounds sweet potatoes
2	tblsp butter, softened
1/4	cup packed dark brown sugar
1/2	tsp salt
1/2	tsp cinnamon
1	tsp finely chopped fresh ginger
1	tsp finely chopped lemon zest
1/4	cup fresh orange juice
	Extra brown sugar and butter (optional)

Whatever you do, don't store your sweet potatoes in the refrigerator. It breaks down the starch in them. Instead, remember that the sweet potato is a root vegetable, and put it where a root would feel at home. While that doesn't mean you have to bury the poor vegetable, try to keep it in places that mimic what it's like to be underground. In other words, store raw sweet potatoes somewhere cool and dark. If you store them properly, they will keep for months.

Buttermilk mashed potatoes

Nutritional facts per serving: 51 calories; 9g carbohydrates; 1.8mg cholesterol; 0.5g total fat; 3.2g fiber; 3.6g protein; 612mg sodium

Cut the potatoes into equal-sized chunks. Cover with cold water in a large saucepan, add the salt, and bring to a boil. Cover and cook for 12 minutes or until the potatoes are just tender. Drain.

Mash with a potato masher or ricer. Add the buttermilk until the potatoes are of the desired consistency. Season to taste with salt and pepper. Stir in chives.

1	pound red-skinned potatoes
1	tsp salt
3/4	cup buttermilk
2	tblsp chopped chives
	Salt
	Black pepper

4 servings

Experts offer these tips for preparing the best mashed potatoes:

- Idaho and russet potatoes yield the smoothest mashed potatoes.

- Add a quarter of a lemon or a few drops of vinegar to the cooking water to keep the potatoes white and prevent them from breaking up.

- Drain the potatoes but put them back on the stove for a minute or two to dry off all the remaining moisture.

- For best flavor, heat milk in the microwave until it's warm before adding to the potatoes.

- Add a pinch of baking soda with the milk or buttermilk for extra fluffiness.

Twice-baked potatoes deluxe

Nutritional facts per serving: 255 calories; 49.7g carbohydrates; 51.4mg cholesterol; 2g total fat; 4.1g fiber; 10g protein; 446.5mg sodium

Cut the hot baked potatoes in half lengthwise. Scoop the potato flesh into a bowl, leaving the skins intact for stuffing.

Add the cream cheese, sour cream, chives, salt, nutmeg, and pepper to the bowl of potatoes. Mix with electric mixer or whisk until smooth. Add egg and beat until well blended.

Place the potato shells on an ungreased cookie sheet and fill, dividing the potato mixture equally. Sprinkle with paprika and bake at 375 degrees until puffed and golden brown.

4	medium potatoes, baked
1	3-ounce package low-fat cream cheese
1/2	cup fat-free sour cream
1	tblsp chopped chives
1/2	tsp salt
	Dash nutmeg
	Dash pepper
1	egg
	Paprika

4 servings

Enjoy a delicious baked potato in half the time. Simply choose a medium-size potato and place it on end in a muffin pan. Bake as usual, but remember, it'll be done before you can say spud.

Potato ribbons

Nutritional facts per serving: 166 calories; 26.5g carbohydrates; 15.6mg cholesterol; 6g total fat; 1.9g fiber; 2.5g protein; 295.8mg sodium

---

To make ribbons, pare strips from the potatoes with a vegetable peeler. Drain in a colander.

Heat the butter in a large skillet over medium-high heat. Add potatoes and cook until tender, about 5 minutes, stirring constantly. Add the chopped parsley, season to taste with salt and pepper, and serve hot.

4 servings

4   baking potatoes, peeled

2   tblsp butter

2   tblsp chopped fresh parsley

Salt

Freshly ground black pepper

It's no surprise that peeling potatoes is considered a punishment in the Army. It might be considered a punishment in a lot of other places, too. But potatoes can easily be coaxed to remove their jackets without all that elbow grease. Give them a good scrub, pierce with a fork in several places, microwave for 10 minutes, and let cool. The skins will become wrinkled. Run each potato under cold water, and you'll be able to pull that skin off more easily.

And the next time you buy potatoes, remember to weigh pre-bagged items like that 5-pound bag of potatoes. Even though they may be labeled 5 pounds, some will weigh more than others. Test a few on the scale, and purchase the one that weighs the most. The savings will add up.

Roasted rosemary-garlic new potatoes

Nutritional facts per serving: 184 calories; 32g carbohydrates; 0mg cholesterol; 7.5g total fat; 1.5g fiber; 0.6g protein; 2mg sodium

---

Preheat oven to 350 degrees.

Wash new potatoes, cut in half, and put in a baker or casserole dish, preferably one that can go straight from oven to table.

Add the garlic and rosemary and toss. Add the olive oil and toss. Sprinkle with salt and pepper and toss. Bake for 30 minutes, or until potatoes are tender, stirring occasionally. Serve.

4 servings

16	small new potatoes
8	garlic cloves
1	tblsp finely chopped fresh rosemary
1/4	cup olive oil
	Kosher salt
	Black pepper

America's favorite vegetable, the potato, didn't originate in Ireland, as many people think. In the 16th century, Spanish explorers found Indians growing potatoes in South America and brought the food back to Europe. Farmers in Europe began growing the well-traveled tuber, and it soon became the main crop of Ireland. Historians believe Irish immigrants are responsible for bringing the potato to America, where it now enjoys great popularity.

If you have any leftover potatoes after making this recipe, remember this. Red round potatoes hold their shape well, so they're best suited for salads, soups, and stews. If you want baked potatoes, mashed potatoes, or spuds you can fry, stick with brown oblong potatoes.

Peppy potato pancakes

Nutritional facts per serving: 356 calories; 32.8g carbohydrates; 80.2mg cholesterol; 3.9g total fat; 3.6g fiber; 7.2g protein; 201.3mg sodium

Squeeze any excess liquid out of the freshly grated potatoes and pat dry. Mix the potatoes with onion, bell pepper, egg, and flour, and season to taste with salt and pepper. Blend well.

Pour enough oil into a large skillet to cover the surface, and place over medium-high heat until very hot. Drop the potato batter into the skillet by heaping tablespoonfuls, and flatten with the back of the spoon.

Cook until the bottoms are golden brown, about 5 minutes. Turn and cook the other side until golden brown, about 3 minutes. Keep warm in a 200-degree oven while you cook the remaining batter. Season with additional salt before serving.

4 servings

2	large baking potatoes, peeled and grated
1	small onion, chopped
3	tblsp finely chopped red bell pepper (optional)
3	tblsp canola oil
1	large egg, lightly beaten
2	tblsp all-purpose flour
	Salt
	Freshly ground black pepper

If you want to cut back on the amount of fat, salt, or sugar you eat, try adjusting your recipes. First, cook any dish the way the recipe is given — to get a sense of the full taste. Then, cut any less-than-healthy ingredients in half. If it still tastes good, make those changes a part of the recipe. If the taste or texture falls too short of the original, try again, cutting back one-fourth. More often than not, with just a few attempts, you will get the recipe to fit your health needs.

Seasoned homefries

Nutritional facts per serving: 189 calories; 14.4g carbohydrates; 0mg cholesterol; 14.2g total fat; 4.6g fiber; 2.5g protein; 149.8mg sodium

Preheat oven to 400 degrees.

Toss potatoes in 3 tablespoons of oil. Transfer to a baking sheet, and place in the oven. Roast, tossing to cook evenly, until the potatoes begin to brown and crust like homefries.

Reduce heat to 325 degrees. Toss the onion, peppers, and seasonings in the remaining tablespoon of oil. Toss with the potatoes. Continue to roast, turning occasionally, until the potatoes and vegetables are tender, 10 to 15 minutes. Serve hot.

4 servings

1	pound white potatoes, cut in 1/4" pieces
4	tblsp canola oil
1	medium yellow onion, cut into 1/4" pieces
1	red bell pepper, cut into 1/4" pieces
1	green bell pepper, cut into 1/4" pieces
1/4	tsp each paprika, cayenne pepper, and salt
1/2	tsp garlic powder
1/2	tsp black pepper

Nutrition **Note** Bright red and green bell peppers may be a good way to "feed a cold." Like orange juice, these sweet peppers are a leading source of vitamin C — a vigorous vitamin that revs up your body's immune system to help you fend off germs and illness. Although experts say vitamin C does not reduce the number of colds you get, it does cut down on how long and how serious an illness you have. You can also get extra vitamin C from citrus fruits, kiwifruit, broccoli, brussels sprouts, cabbage, and strawberries. And you may be surprised to discover that potatoes provide a bit of vitamin C, too.

Warm-you-up beef barley stew

Nutritional facts per serving: 374 calories; 45.9g carbohydrates; 38.6mg cholesterol; 11.5g total fat; 9.7g fiber; 23.1g protein; 436.5mg sodium

Coat a large pot with nonstick cooking spray.

Over medium heat, brown stew meat. Add onion and cook until soft. Drain fat. Add salt, pepper, and garlic, and cook 1 minute. Add rest of the ingredients and stir to blend. Bring to a boil, reduce heat, and simmer 30 minutes or until meat is tender.

4 servings

Save money by buying less expensive cuts of meat, then tenderizing them in tea. The tannins, naturally occurring chemicals in tea, work to break down the fibers for "cut with a fork" tenderness.

1/2	pound beef stew meat, cubed
1/2	small onion, chopped
	Pinch salt
1/8	tsp pepper
2	garlic cloves, minced
1	14-ounce can low-sodium beef broth
1 3/4	cups water
1/2	cup diced tomatoes
1	medium potato, peeled and cubed
1	large carrot, chopped
2	cups shredded cabbage
2	tblsp and 2 tsp quick-cooking barley
1	14 1/2-ounce can great northern beans, rinsed and drained
1/8	tsp dried oregano
1/8	tsp dried basil
1/8	tsp dried rosemary
1/8	tsp caraway seeds

Spicy vegetable stew

Nutritional facts per serving: 454 calories; 90.5g carbohydrates; 0mg cholesterol; 6.7g total fat; 13g fiber; 13g protein; 583.9mg sodium

Cut leaves from the stalks of the Swiss chard, and chop stalks into bite-size pieces. Heat oil in a large saucepan. Sauté the Swiss chard stalks, onion, and garlic until soft. Chop and add the greens. Slice sweet potatoes into thick rounds. Add sweet potatoes, chickpeas, raisins, tomatoes, and water to the pot. Add salt and pepper to taste. Cook for 2 to 3 minutes. Turn the heat to simmer, and add rice. Stir, cover, and cook about 30 minutes or until rice is done. Add Tabasco to taste.

4 servings

1   large onion, chopped

2   garlic cloves, minced (or more to taste)

1   bunch Swiss chard, with stalks

1   tblsp vegetable oil

2   sweet potatoes, peeled

1   16-ounce can chickpeas, undrained

1/2   cup raisins

4   cups diced tomatoes

2   cups water (less for a thicker stew)

1/2   cup uncooked brown rice

   Salt

   Freshly ground black pepper

   Tabasco

Nutrition Note

Mama mia! There's too much garlic in your stew. Don't throw it out. Just put a few parsley flakes in a tea infuser, and place it in the pot for a few minutes. The parsley will attract and absorb the garlic while boosting the nutritional value. Parsley is packed with vitamins and minerals — beta carotene, folate, vitamins C and K, and iron, to name a few. Plus, it's brimming with flavonoids that may prevent cancer and fight heart disease.

Deep South okra-tomato stew

Nutritional facts per serving: 168 calories; 22.6g carbohydrates; 25.5mg cholesterol; 6.4g total fat; 6.8g fiber; 9g protein; 434.5mg sodium

Spray a soup pot with nonstick vegetable spray. Add bacon and cook over medium heat until it begins to brown. Add onion, toss with the bacon, cover the pot, and cook for 3 minutes, stirring occasionally.

Add tomatoes, okra, bay leaves, salt, and Worcestershire sauce, and bring to a simmer. Reduce heat and cook over low for 1 1/2 hours, or until the okra is tender, stirring occasionally to prevent scorching.

Season to taste with salt and pepper. Remove bay leaves. Serve, or cool to room temperature, cover, and refrigerate for up to 2 days.

4 servings

4   slices turkey bacon, chopped

1   cup chopped yellow onion

2   pounds fresh summer tomatoes, peeled, seeded, and chopped

1   pound okra, sliced

2   bay leaves

2   tsp Worcestershire sauce

Salt

Freshly ground black pepper

Although pork bacon is usually part of this Southern favorite, a switch to turkey bacon retains the texture and meaty taste, but with far less fat. You can also substitute a 28-ounce can of diced tomatoes and juice or frozen okra for the fresh vegetables.

Savory goulash

Nutritional facts per serving: 401 calories; 11.3g carbohydrates; 77.2mg cholesterol; 27.7g total fat; 3.4g fiber; 26.7g protein; 859mg sodium

Heat butter or margarine in a Dutch oven, and sauté onion until golden brown. Stir in paprika and vinegar. Add beef, broth, marjoram, caraway seeds, and tomato paste. Add salt and pepper to taste. Mix well.

Cover and simmer for 1 to 1 1/2 hours or until meat is tender. Combine flour and a little liquid from the pot, stirring until dissolved. Stir this mixture into the goulash. Add potatoes, and cook until tender.

4 servings

2   tblsp butter or margarine

1   large onion, chopped

1   tblsp paprika

2/3 tsp vinegar

1   pound beef stew meat, cut into 1" cubes

4   cups beef broth

1/3 tsp marjoram

2   tsp caraway seed

2   tsp tomato paste

1 1/3 tblsp flour

2/3 pound potatoes, cubed

Salt

Freshly ground black pepper

Don't cross beef off your menu because you can't afford the expensive cuts. You still need the nutrients you get in meat — like vitamin B12, iron, selenium, zinc, and protein. So go ahead and buy those cheaper cuts but tenderize them with vinegar. Add a tablespoon to the cooking water, and that tough stew meat will melt in your mouth.

Chicken bouillabaisse

Nutritional facts per serving: 354 calories; 11.7g carbohydrates; 101.7mg cholesterol; 16.7g total fat; 2.5g fiber; 39.6g protein; 195.7mg sodium

Take meat off the chicken, and chop into generous bite-size pieces.

Heat olive oil. Add onion, celery, fennel, garlic, oregano, and fennel seed. Stir. Cook 2 to 3 minutes, or until vegetables are tender. Add chicken broth, tomatoes, tarragon, and basil. Stir well, and bring to a simmer. Add chicken, stir, bring to a simmer again, and cook until chicken is hot through. Season to taste with salt and pepper. Sprinkle with chopped fennel fronds and serve.

1	3 1/2- to 4-pound whole roasted chicken
2	tblsp olive oil
2	cups chopped onion
1 1/2	cups diced celery
1	cup chopped fresh fennel bulb, fronds reserved
4	garlic cloves, finely chopped
1	tblsp chopped fresh oregano
1/2	tsp fennel seed
4	cups low-sodium chicken broth
1	16-ounce can diced tomatoes with juice
1	tblsp chopped fresh tarragon
1/4	cup chopped fresh basil
	Salt
	Freshly ground black pepper
2	tblsp finely chopped fennel fronds

4 servings

Nutrition **Note**

Walk 30 to 45 minutes three times a week, and you could halve your heart attack risk. Here's what else exercise can do for heart health.

- Reduce the risk of a second heart attack.

- Cut triglycerides and total cholesterol.

- Lower the odds of high blood pressure.

Tantalizing tomato bouillon

Nutritional facts per serving: 59 calories; 10.2g carbohydrates; 0mg cholesterol; 1.1g total fat; 2.3g fiber; 4.1g protein; 1165.5mg sodium

Puree tomatoes and onions in blender or food processor. Place in soup pot. Add all ingredients except pepper. Bring to a boil, and simmer for 10 minutes. Add pepper to taste. Serve hot, or chill and serve cold.

2 servings

1	pound ripe tomatoes, peeled and chopped
1/4	cup chopped yellow onion
1	cup low-sodium chicken broth
1	tsp salt
1/2	tsp thyme
1/2	tsp curry powder
12	fresh basil leaves, chopped
	Freshly ground black pepper

Nutrition **Note**

Your waist and hip measurements can help you figure your odds for heart trouble — and perhaps even help you prevent it. Researchers calculated waist-to-hip ratios (WHR) and found that a ratio greater than .85 in women and .95 in men was associated with higher blood pressure and other heart disease risk factors. Another study found that a high WHR increased heart disease risk factors like blood pressure and cholesterol levels even in folks who weren't obese.

To figure out your waist-to-hip ratio, measure your waist and hips, and divide your waist measurement by your hip measurement. For example, if your waist is 28 inches, and your hips are 40 inches, your WHR would be 28 divided by 40, which is .70. With that number, you'd be in good shape for avoiding heart disease.

Extra-flavorful brown chicken stock

Nutritional facts per cup: 346 calories; 7.5g carbohydrates; 182.9mg cholesterol; 10.4g total fat; 0.8g fiber; 53.9g protein; 315.4mg sodium

Preheat oven to 400 degrees.

Place chopped bones or meat in a single layer on a heavy baking sheet with sides. Roast until evenly browned, about 20 minutes.

In a large stockpot, cover the browned bones with the broth, and bring to a simmer over medium heat. Simmer for 1 hour, skimming off rising foam and fat. Add onion, celery, carrot, peppercorns, thyme, and parsley. Simmer for an additional 1 1/2 hours, skimming as necessary, and adding additional hot chicken stock to keep bones and vegetables covered. Strain stock, cool to room temperature, cover, and refrigerate. Lift off any fat that rises to the surface while it chills.

2	pounds chicken bones (backs, necks, wings roughly chopped into 2" to 3" pieces)*
6	cups canned low-sodium chicken broth
3/4	cup chopped onion
1/4	cup chopped celery
1/4	cup chopped carrot
1/2	tsp whole black peppercorns
3	sprigs fresh thyme
3	sprigs fresh parsley

*Whole chicken thighs or legs may be substituted, chopped into 2" to 3" pieces. Have the butcher chop the chicken bones or thighs and legs.

Keep a good stock in the freezer to give an extra boost of protein to soups, stews, and sauces. Just use it in place of water.

To make a strong, easy-to-store chicken stock, return stock to the stove after straining, and rapidly simmer until it is reduced by two-thirds. Freeze in ice cube trays, then bag. Reconstitute with water (like bouillon cubes) when ready to use.

4 cups

Hearty beef stock

Nutritional facts per cup: 300 calories; 4.5g carbohydrates; 80.4mg cholesterol; 22.1g total fat; 1.1g fiber; 20.3g protein; 152.7mg sodium

Preheat oven to 400 degrees.

Place bones or meat in a large heavy roasting pan, and roast until well-browned, about 25 minutes, turning occasionally. Remove bones or meat from the roasting pan. Put onion, celery, and carrot in the pan, and roast the vegetables, turning once, until lightly browned, about 10 minutes.

In a large stockpot, cover bones with cold water, and bring to a simmer over medium heat. Simmer for 1 1/2 hours while skimming off rising foam and fat. Add roasted vegetables, tomato paste, peppercorns, thyme, and parsley, and simmer for an additional 1 1/2 to 2 hours, skimming as necessary. Add extra hot water if necessary to keep bones and vegetables covered. Strain stock. Cool to room temperature, cover, and refrigerate. Lift off any fat that rises to the surface while it chills.

To make a strong, easy-to-store beef stock, see instructions for chicken stock on the previous page.

4 cups

2	pounds beef bones, cubed stew meat, or chopped beef roast
1 1/2	quarts cold water
3/4	cup chopped onion
1/4	cup chopped celery
1/4	cup chopped carrot
2	rounded tblsp tomato paste
1/2	tsp whole black peppercorns
3	sprigs fresh thyme
3	sprigs fresh parsley

You can substitute an inexpensive roast or cubed stew beef for the bones. Cut the roast into 2" pieces before browning in the oven. Use stew beef as is.

Speedy shrimp stock

Nutritional facts per cup: 10 calories; 2.3g carbohydrates; 0mg cholesterol; 0.1g total fat; 0.7g fiber; 0.4g protein; 204mg sodium

In a nonreactive saucepan, combine shrimp shells, onion, celery, bay leaves, salt, peppercorns, and water. Bring to a boil over high heat. Reduce heat to Medium-low, and simmer the stock uncovered for 20 minutes. Add extra hot water if necessary to keep shells and vegetables covered. Strain stock. Remove bay leaves.

Shells from 1 pound shrimp

1/2   cup roughly chopped onion

1/2   cup roughly chopped celery

2   bay leaves

1/4   tsp salt

1   tsp whole black peppercorns

4   cups water

Cool to room temperature, cover, and refrigerate. Lift off any fat that rises to the surface while it chills.

To make a strong, easy-to-store shrimp stock, see instructions for chicken stock on page 284.

Save your shrimp shells, and store them in the freezer until you have enough to make this high-calcium stock. Use it in gumbos, sauces, and seafood stews — or any time clam juice or fish stock is called for.

3 cups

Coastal crab stew

Nutritional facts per serving: 234 calories; 17.5g carbohydrates; 85.4mg cholesterol; 9.2g total fat; 3.7g fiber; 20.4g protein; 323.9mg sodium

Melt butter in a large pan. Add onion, green onions, and celery. Cook until soft. Add water, bring to a boil, add potatoes, and continue to cook until potatoes are soft. Add crabmeat and milk, and heat through without boiling.

Season with salt, pepper, and hot sauce.

4 servings

2	tblsp butter
1	large onion, chopped
1	bunch green onions, chopped
2	ribs celery, chopped
1	cup water
1 1/2	cups peeled and diced potatoes
2	cups lump crabmeat
2	cups milk
	Salt
	Freshly ground black pepper
	Hot sauce

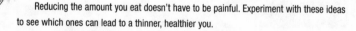

Reducing the amount you eat doesn't have to be painful. Experiment with these ideas to see which ones can lead to a thinner, healthier you.

• Make less food look like more by serving your meal on a salad or breakfast plate.

• Drink a glass of water or other "no-calorie" beverage 10 minutes before your meal to take the edge off your appetite.

• Teaspoons, salad forks, or child-size utensils may help you take smaller bites and eat less.

• Keep meat, poultry and fish servings to about 3 ounces — about the size of a deck of cards.

Choose-your-shellfish chowder

Nutritional facts per serving: 86 calories; 11.2g carbohydrates; 6.4mg cholesterol; 2.2g total fat; 2.4g fiber; 5.5g protein; 151.6mg sodium

Fry bacon in a large saucepan until crisp. Remove and set aside, reserving 2 tablespoons of fat.

Add onion to the pan, and cook until soft. Add broth and potatoes, cover, and bring to a boil. Reduce heat and simmer until potatoes are done. Add shellfish and their juices, thyme, and milk. Return bacon to the pan. Bring to a boil, reduce heat, and simmer until shellfish are plump and heated through, about 1 to 3 minutes. Add salt and pepper to taste. Garnish with thyme sprigs or paprika.

6 servings

2	strips bacon
1	onion, chopped
4	ounces chicken broth or stock
3	medium potatoes, cut into 1" cubes
2	cups clams, oysters, or scallops, shelled, juice reserved
2	tsp thyme
2	cups milk
	Salt
	Freshly ground black pepper
	Thyme sprigs
	Paprika

Nutrition **Note** Just 3 ounces of scallops contain 48 milligrams of magnesium. That's more than 10 percent of the daily recommended amount. This mineral relaxes blood vessels and balances the potassium and sodium in your blood cells. A four-year study of more than 30,000 men found that getting more magnesium into your diet was significantly associated with a lower risk of high blood pressure. For extra magnesium, eat whole-wheat breads and cereals, broccoli, spinach, okra, sea bass, mackerel, beans, nuts, and seeds.

Gulf Coast seafood gumbo

Nutritional facts per serving: 253 calories; 14.8g carbohydrates; 69.4mg cholesterol; 16g total fat; 2.3g fiber; 13.6g protein; 270.7mg sodium

Heat oil in a heavy-bottomed soup pot over medium heat. Gradually whisk in flour. Reduce heat to Low, and cook "roux" mixture, stirring often, until it reaches a rich brown color, 20 to 30 minutes.

Meanwhile, slice sausage into 1/2" pieces and cook until brown. Remove and drain on paper towels.

Add onion, celery, bell pepper, and garlic to the pot sausage was cooked in. Cook, stirring occasionally, until just tender, about 3 minutes. Drain on paper towels. Discard fat.

When roux has browned, add cold shrimp stock all at once, and whisk until smooth. Increase heat to Medium-high, and add cooked vegetables, tomatoes, tomato paste, thyme, oregano, black pepper, bay leaf, and Tabasco. Stir well. Simmer for 30 minutes, or until it thickens. Add sausage and shrimp, and cook until shrimp turn pink and begin to curl. Season to taste with salt, pepper, and Tabasco. Remove bay leaf, and serve immediately.

4 servings

- 1/4 pound low-fat spicy sausage
- 4 tblsp canola oil
- 4 tblsp all-purpose flour
- 1 medium yellow onion, chopped
- 2/3 cup chopped celery
- 2/3 cup chopped green bell pepper
- 1 garlic clove, finely chopped
- 2 cups shrimp stock (see page 286) or clam juice
- 2/3 cup ripe tomatoes, chopped
- 4 tblsp tomato paste
- 1/8 generous tsp each dried thyme, oregano, and black pepper
- 1 small bay leaf
- 1 generous dash Tabasco
- 1 pound medium (26-30 count) shrimp
- Salt

Steaming fresh catfish chowder

Nutritional facts per serving: 174 calories; 8.2g carbohydrates; 69mg cholesterol; 6.8g total fat; 2.5g fiber; 20.4g protein; 347.6mg sodium

Fry bacon until crisp, and drain. Discard all but about 1/2 tablespoon of the fat, add bell pepper and onion, and cook until almost soft, about 5 minutes. Add garlic, and cook 1 to 2 minutes more. Add carrots, potatoes, bay leaf, milk, lemon juice, clam juice, and reserved bacon. Bring to a boil, stirring occasionally. Reduce heat, and simmer until potatoes and carrots are tender, about 20 to 25 minutes.

Add fish, stir lightly, and cook until fish is tender, about 5 minutes. Season to taste with salt, pepper, and parsley. Remove bay leaf. Serve hot.

4 servings

1	slice turkey bacon, chopped
1/2	bell pepper, cut into 1/2" pieces
1	onion, chopped
1	large garlic clove, finely chopped
1	medium carrot, peeled and chopped
1/2	pound potatoes, peeled and cut into 1/2" pieces
1	bay leaf
1/2	cup milk
1	tblsp fresh lemon juice
1/2	cup bottled clam juice
3/4	pound fresh catfish filets, cut into 1" pieces
	Salt
	Freshly ground black pepper
1	tblsp finely chopped fresh parsley

Nutrition Note

Cracks at the corners of your mouth, dry scaly skin, depression, and red, itchy, burning eyes may mean you need more vitamin B2. To reduce the loss of vitamin B2 from milk, buy it or store it in opaque containers — and use some of that milk with fortified cereals to help get extra vitamin B2.

290

Texas mild-to-wild chili

Nutritional facts per serving: 216 calories; 18.2g carbohydrates; 53.1mg cholesterol; 4.7g total fat; 4.7g fiber; 25.9g protein; 283.5mg sodium

Spray a large heavy-bottomed frying pan with nonstick vegetable spray. Add olive oil, and heat over Medium.

Add onion, garlic, bell pepper, and banana pepper. Cover, and cook over medium heat, stirring occasionally, until just tender, about 3 minutes. Add ground turkey, and cook until no longer pink. Season lightly with salt and pepper to taste.

Add chili powder, cumin, and bay leaf, and stir to mix well. Cook for 2 minutes, stirring constantly. Add tomatoes and kidney beans. Reduce heat to Low, and simmer for 30 minutes, stirring occasionally. Season to taste with salt, pepper, and Tabasco. Remove bay leaf before serving. Serve, or cool, cover, and refrigerate for up to 2 days. The chili may also be frozen for up to 3 months.

1	tblsp olive oil
1/2	large yellow onion, chopped
2	garlic cloves, chopped
3/4	cups chopped green bell pepper
1	small banana pepper, chopped
3/4	pound ground turkey
	Salt
	Freshly ground black pepper
1 1/2	tsp chili powder
1/4	tsp cumin
1	bay leaf
1	14-ounce can diced tomatoes and juice
1	8-ounce can kidney beans and liquid
	Tabasco

Variation: For a spicier chili, try adding jalepeños, hot sauce, or additional chili powder.

4 servings

Robust bulgur and black bean chili

Nutritional facts per serving: 434 calories; 49.2g carbohydrates; 31.6mg cholesterol; 18.3g total fat; 14.2g fiber; 22g protein; 762.3mg sodium

Soak bulgur in 2 cups boiling water for 20-30 minutes.

Heat oil in a Dutch oven. Add onions, carrots, and bell peppers, and cook for 5 to 8 minutes. Add black beans, bulgur, tomatoes, chicken stock, chili powder, cumin, and coriander. Bring to a boil, reduce heat, and simmer for 30 to 45 minutes, until thickened. Season to taste with salt and pepper.

Serve in bowls with yogurt, green onions, and grated cheese topping, as desired.

4 servings

Nutrition Note

A fascinating new study suggests black beans may have a pretty hefty stockpile of antioxidants. What's more, these antioxidants include health-building plant pigments like anthocyanins, the same family of heavy-hitter nutrients found in blueberries and blackberries.

2   tblsp vegetable oil

1   onion, chopped

2   carrots, chopped

1   red bell pepper, chopped

1   green bell pepper, chopped

1   16-ounce can black beans, drained and rinsed

1/2   cup bulgur

1   16-ounce can whole tomatoes with juice

1   cup canned chicken stock or broth

1   tblsp chili powder

1/2   tblsp ground cumin

1/2   tblsp ground coriander

Salt

Freshly ground black pepper

1/2   cup plain yogurt

3   green onions, sliced

1/4   pound cheddar cheese, shredded

Homemade lentil soup with basil

Nutritional facts per serving: 177 calories; 23g carbohydrates; 3.4mg cholesterol; 2.8g total fat; 10.6g fiber; 15.3g protein; 896.1mg sodium

---

Fry bacon until crisp. Remove and let drain on paper towels. Spoon out all but 2 tablespoons of the fat, and add onion, garlic, and carrot. Cook over medium heat until soft, about 5 minutes. Add 4 cups of the chicken stock and the lentils, and cook, covered, over medium heat until lentils are soft, about 40 to 60 minutes, adding liquid if needed. Stir in tomato, spinach, and turkey bacon, and cook until just heated through, about 5 minutes. Add basil, and season to taste with salt and pepper. Serve garnished with a dollop of yogurt or sour cream, if desired.

6 servings

1   cup dried green lentils

3   slices turkey bacon

1   onion, chopped

2   garlic cloves, chopped

1   carrot, shredded

6   cups chicken broth or stock

1   tomato, seeded and cut into small cubes

1   10-ounce package frozen spinach, thawed and drained

2   tblsp chopped fresh basil

   Salt

   Freshly ground black pepper

2   tblsp plain low-fat yogurt (optional)

There's no need to throw your soup out if you accidentally added too much salt. Simply cut a raw potato or apple into medium-size chunks and toss them into the pot for about 10 minutes. These will soak up much of the salt. Remove them when they start to soften, and your soup will be saved.

Boston white bean soup

Nutritional facts per serving: 272 calories; 41.4g carbohydrates; 0mg cholesterol; 7.8g total fat; 7g fiber; 11.1g protein; 378.5mg sodium

Sauté vegetables in olive oil. Stir in spices and the rest of the ingredients. Simmer for 1 hour. Sprinkle with grated Romano cheese.

6 servings

1/2	cup chopped celery
1	large onion, chopped
1	carrot, chopped
1	garlic clove, minced
3	tblsp olive oil
1/4	tsp oregano
1/4	tsp basil
1/4	tsp thyme
1/4	tsp parsley
1/4	tsp crushed red pepper
1	16-ounce can white kidney beans, drained
1	cup tube pasta, cooked and drained
1	14 1/2-ounce can crushed tomatoes
2	cups beef consommé
1 1/2	quarts boiling water
	Romano cheese

Nutrition Note

Fiber is a natural substance found in a variety of fruits, vegetables, and whole grains. Not only does it help prevent disease, lower cholesterol, and keep you regular, it also helps you lose weight. In fact, you can eat as much fiber as your body can handle and add absolutely no calories to your diet. Also, your body has a harder time converting high-fiber foods into fat. That makes beans — a simple, inexpensive, fiber-rich food — one super good-for-you choice.

Hearty lamb and navy bean soup

Nutritional facts per serving: 117 calories; 21.2g carbohydrates; 0mg cholesterol; 0.5g total fat; 8.5g fiber; 7.8g protein; 4.9mg sodium

Chop up the lamb bone and refrigerate. If using trimmings, refrigerate and set aside. Soak navy beans overnight in water to cover, or bring to boil, cover, and let sit 1 hour. Drain.

Simmer the leg of lamb bone, beans, water, and onion on medium-high heat for 2 hours, covered. If using trimmings, add at this point. Simmer another hour. Just before serving, add Tabasco, and season to taste with salt and pepper.

1　leg of lamb bone, or 1 cup trimmings

1　cup dried navy beans

6　cups water

1　onion, finely chopped

　Dash Tabasco (optional)

　Salt

　Freshly ground black pepper

Variation: Add 2 tablespoons chopped cilantro to the finished soup when serving.

6 servings

Nutrition **Note**　　Get a notion to get in motion, and you may get more than just a fitter and healthier body. Your brain may benefit, too.

A study out of Case Western Reserve University School of Medicine in Ohio supports the theory that regular exercise — especially between the ages of 20 and 60 — may lower your chances of getting Alzheimer's disease. Experts emphasize that the exercise must be done over the long term to have any effect.

Granny's potato and green bean soup

Nutritional facts per serving: 46 calories; 6.1g carbohydrates; 0mg cholesterol; 0.8g total fat; 2.6g fiber; 4.2g protein; 393.7mg sodium

---

Bring potatoes and chicken broth to a boil over high heat, cover, and reduce heat. Simmer gently until potatoes are nearly cooked through, but not mushy, about 15 minutes. Add green beans and cook, uncovered, until tender about 15 minutes.

Meanwhile, heat olive oil in a small saucepan. Add garlic, and cook, stirring, until golden brown, about 5 to 8 minutes. When ready to serve, bring the soup base back to a boil, add the garlic and olive oil, and stir. Season to taste with salt and pepper.

6 servings

1/2	pound potatoes, peeled and cut into 1" chunks
3	cups chicken broth or stock
1/2	pound green beans, ends removed
2	tblsp olive oil
3	large garlic cloves, thinly sliced
	Salt
	Freshly ground black pepper

Freeze soup and other liquids in a plastic bag inside a coffee can. This makes a shape that's easier to store. Once the food is frozen, you can remove the can and use it again.

Whenever you have just a little leftover soup or stew, you can pour it into an ice cube tray and freeze. It will keep longer than it would in the refrigerator, and the next time you make soup, you can just add the extra cubes to the pot.

Delicious carrot-potato soup

Nutritional facts per serving: 198 calories; 23.4g carbohydrates; 0mg cholesterol; 8.4g total fat; 5.5g fiber; 8.1g protein; 822.7mg sodium

Melt oil in a heavy pan. Add onions. Microwave the head of garlic 1 to 2 minutes until tender; peel. Or break up the head, add the unpeeled cloves to boiling water to cover, and cook for 30 minutes. Let cool enough to peel. Add peeled cloves to the pan with onions, heat, and cook until golden brown. Heat the carrots, potatoes, and broth in another pan until hot.

When garlic and onions are golden, add the broth-vegetable mixture, and bring to a boil. Cover. Cook 30 minutes or until potatoes are cooked and carrots are crisp-cooked. Add salt and pepper to taste. Serve hot with the Parmesan, if desired.

4 servings

2	tblsp olive oil
2	onions, sliced
1	large head garlic (2 ounces)
3	carrots, cut diagonally into 1/2" slices
1/2	pound potatoes, peeled and cut into 2" chunks
2	14 1/2-ounce cans chicken or beef broth
	Salt
	Freshly ground black pepper
4	ounces freshly grated Parmesan cheese (optional)

Nutrition **Note**   You don't need to eat pennies, but you do need the edible kind of copper to help you stay healthy. Copper is a trace mineral that can be found in all the tissues in your body. It helps your body absorb iron and assists in building healthy blood. You don't need very much copper, so eat tasty foods to get it. Good sources of copper include oysters, lobster, crab, shiitake mushrooms, and sunflower seeds.

Farmer's best sweet potato-apple soup

Nutritional facts per serving: 313 calories; 58.8g carbohydrates; 1.7mg cholesterol; 5.9g total fat; 7.8g fiber; 8.5g protein; 634.5mg sodium

Preheat oven to 400 degrees.

Pierce potatoes with a fork, and bake for 1 hour. Let potatoes cool to room temperature, halve them, and scoop out the pulp, discarding the skins. Set aside.

Heat oil in a stock pot. Add leeks and apples, and sauté over moderate heat until soft, about 10 minutes. Add chicken stock and potato pulp, and simmer 20 minutes. Remove the solids from the stock, and puree until smooth. Add the puree back into the stock, and season to taste with salt and pepper. Stir in yogurt, and refrigerate until cool. Serve chilled, or heat without boiling, and ladle into warm bowls. Place a dollop of yogurt in each bowl, and garnish with chives and orange peel.

4 servings

1	pound sweet potatoes
1	tblsp olive oil
2	chopped leeks, white part only
2	Granny Smith apples, peeled, cored, and cubed
3	cups chicken stock or broth
	Salt
	Freshly ground black pepper
1/2	cup low-fat yogurt
	Chopped fresh chives
	Orange peel

If you buy fresh produce in bulk, separate out what you can eat in a week and blanch, then freeze, the rest. It will store better and stay fresh-tasting longer.

Creamy zucchini soup with pecans

Nutritional facts per serving: 58 calories; 6.8g carbohydrates; 1.8mg cholesterol; 1.3g total fat; 1.2g fiber; 5.1g protein; 551.6mg sodium

Bring zucchini, onions, garlic, and chicken broth to a boil in a large saucepan or flameproof casserole. Lower the heat and simmer, covered, for 10 minutes until zucchini is tender. Remove the solids, saving the liquid, and puree the solids in a blender or food processor. Return the pureed mixture to the liquid and stir. Blend in yogurt, add salt and pepper to taste, and cool until ready to serve. If serving hot, reheat without boiling.

For the optional garnish, add pecans to a small pan, and toast over medium heat, 2 to 3 minutes, until browned. When ready to serve, top the soup with the pecans.

4 servings

1	pound zucchini, unpeeled, sliced
1	medium onion, sliced
1	garlic clove, crushed or chopped
2	cups low-sodium chicken broth
1/2	cup plain yogurt
	Salt
	Freshly ground black pepper
1/2	cup pecan halves or chopped pecans (optional)

Nutrition **Note** Fabulous-tasting pecans helped reduce total cholesterol by 6.7 percent and LDL cholesterol by 10.4 percent, according to research findings. These nuts are rich in heart-healthy monounsaturated fat, but don't forget that this high fat content can also invite rancidity. Store shelled pecans in the refrigerator for up to three months — or the freezer for up to six months.

Zucchini and zest of lemon soup

Nutritional facts per serving: 79 calories; 2.6g carbohydrates; 15.6mg cholesterol; 6.5g total fat; 0.3g fiber; 2.9g protein; 389.5mg sodium

Melt butter over medium heat. Add onion and garlic, and cook until soft but not browned, about 6 minutes. Add zucchini slices, cover, and cook until soft, about 10 to 15 minutes, stirring frequently. Puree the zucchini mixture until smooth. Return mixture to the pan, and add chicken stock and lemon peel. Season to taste with lemon juice, salt, and pepper. Serve hot.

4 servings

2	tblsp butter
1	onion, sliced
1	garlic clove, mashed to a paste with salt
4-5	medium zucchini (about 2 1/2 pounds), cut into 1/4" thick slices
2	cups chicken stock or broth
	Grated peel of 1 lemon
	Juice of 2 lemons
	Salt
	Freshly ground black pepper

Save big bucks on groceries with these tips.

- Use the per unit pricing information found on the shelf labels to compare products. Sometimes the larger size is a better bargain — sometimes not. Take a calculator to figure out price comparisons that aren't labeled.

- Use coupons and rebates. And don't forget to shop on double coupon day or senior day. These are usually in the middle of the week. So are "special" sale days.

- Buy store brand or generic — but only if the quality and nutrition are truly acceptable.

- Slice, shred, dice, and chop yourself. You pay extra for the convenience packaging.

- Pick through dented, damaged, and day-old products. Choose items that are good buys but still safe.

Butternut squash soup with red peppers

Nutritional facts per serving: 135 calories; 18.7g carbohydrates; 0mg cholesterol; 4.9g total fat; 1.2g fiber; 6.4g protein; 759mg sodium

Heat oil in a soup pot. Add onion, garlic, and chili powder, and cook until onion is soft, about 6 minutes. Stir in tomatoes, and cook for 5 minutes. Add cubed squash, roasted peppers, reserved tomato juice, and 3 cups of the stock. Simmer, uncovered, until squash is tender, about 30 to 50 minutes. Thin with more stock if needed, and season with salt and pepper. Serve soup hot, garnished with parsley and mint.

4 servings

1	pound butternut squash, halved, seeded, and cut in 1" pieces
1	tblsp olive oil
1	onion, finely chopped
1	garlic clove, chopped
1	tblsp chili powder
1/2	pound fresh Italian tomatoes, peeled, seeded, and chopped, juice reserved
1	red bell pepper, roasted and peeled, or 2 pimentos, cut in 1/2" squares
3 1/2	cups chicken stock or broth
	Salt
	Freshly ground black pepper
1	tblsp chopped fresh parsley
1	tblsp chopped fresh mint

Food labels can be confusing — or even misleading. A serving size may be much smaller or larger than what you consider a single serving. Light (or lite) means one-third fewer calories or half the fat of the higher-calorie, higher-fat food. Or half the sodium of a low-calorie, low-fat food. And fat-free is less than 0.5 grams of fat per serving.

Smooth smoked eggplant soup

Nutritional facts per serving: 78 calories; 1g carbohydrates; 2.2mg cholesterol; 2.4g total fat; 2.2g fiber; 7.1g protein; 832.7mg sodium

Cut eggplants in half and score the flesh. Brush cut sides lightly with a little olive oil, and grill or broil until browned and soft, about 10 minutes. Scoop out the flesh and coarsely chop it. Set aside.

Heat the remaining olive oil in a large, heavy pot. Add onion and garlic, and sauté over medium heat until golden, 7 to 8 minutes. Add tomato and cook until lightly wilted, about 5 minutes. Add eggplant flesh and chicken stock, and bring to a boil. Reduce heat to a simmer and cook 10 minutes.

2	eggplants
2	tblsp olive oil
1	onion sliced
2	garlic cloves, chopped
1	tomato, chopped
4	cups chicken broth or stock
	Salt
	Freshly ground black pepper
	Tabasco
1/2	cup freshly grated Parmesan cheese (optional)

Strain the solids, and puree in a food processor or blender until smooth and creamy. Return the puree to the pot, and reheat to just below simmer. Season to taste with salt, pepper, and Tabasco, and garnish with Parmesan cheese.

4 servings

Add barley, tapioca, or oatmeal to thicken any vegetable soup or broth.

Old-fashioned vegetable soup

Nutritional facts per serving: 210 calories; 19.1g carbohydrates; 40.8mg cholesterol; 47.5g total fat; 4.6g fiber; 19g protein; 206.2mg sodium

Place meat and stock or broth in a large soup pot, and bring to a simmer over medium-high heat. Reduce heat to Low, cover, and simmer until meat falls off the bone, 1 1/2 to 2 hours. Remove the bone and any fat.

Add onion, okra, tomatoes, and juice. Add Worcestershire sauce to taste. Increase heat to Medium, and bring soup back to a simmer. Simmer soup until onion and okra are tender, 15 to 20 minutes. Season to taste with Tabasco, salt, and pepper.

If not serving soup immediately, remove from stove, cool to room temperature, cover, and refrigerate. Remove any fat that comes to the top before reheating. Tightly sealed, the soup will keep for up to 3 days in the refrigerator or 2 months in the freezer. Reheat on medium-high heat, stirring occasionally.

4 servings

3/4	pound beef chuck roast, bone in, fat trimmed
1/2	cup beef stock or canned broth
1/2	small yellow onion, chopped
1/2	pound sliced okra, fresh or frozen
1	14-ounce can crushed tomatoes
12	ounces low-sodium V8® juice
	Worcestershire sauce
	Tabasco
	Salt
	Freshly ground black pepper

Nutrition **Note**

Experts who looked at a variety of research suggest that a diet high in vitamin C may slow down the development of osteoarthritis.

Rich and tasty broccoli-cheese soup

Nutritional facts per serving: 181 calories; 9.2g carbohydrates; 32.9mg cholesterol; 11.9g total fat; 8g fiber; 9.1g protein; 522.6mg sodium

Bring broth, onion, celery, carrot, broccoli, and garlic to a boil. Reduce heat, and simmer 10 minutes. Meanwhile, melt butter in a heavy saucepan, stir in the flour, then the milk. Bring to a boil, stirring, and add the cheese. Pour the cheese mixture into the simmering vegetable mixture, stirring. Before serving, season to taste with salt, pepper, and hot sauce, if desired.

4 servings

2	cups chicken broth or stock
1/3	tblsp onion, chopped
1	stalk celery, sliced
1	small carrot, shredded
1	cup broccoli florets and sliced stems
2	garlic cloves, chopped
2	tblsp butter
2	tblsp flour
1	cup milk
2	ounces shredded sharp cheddar cheese
	Freshly ground black pepper
	Hot sauce (optional)

Nutrition **Note** Get the right amount of magnesium to keep your body healthy. If you don't get enough magnesium, your levels of other minerals like calcium and potassium will also drop. Magnesium is easily lost during washing, peeling, and processing, so choose fresh or minimally processed foods whenever possible. Get your magnesium from foods like halibut, spinach, pumpkin seeds, Brazil nuts, and black beans.

Garlic soup with grapes and croutons

Nutritional facts per serving: 136 calories; 15g carbohydrates; 15.4mg cholesterol; 7.1g total fat; 0.9g fiber; 3.7g protein; 98.2mg sodium

Heat oil until hot. Add leeks and garlic, and cook until soft, about 10 minutes. Add chicken stock, and simmer for 20 minutes. Remove from heat, and stir in vinegar. Meanwhile, soak bread in the milk until all the liquid is absorbed. Transfer the soaked bread and the soup solids to a food processor or blender, and puree until smooth. Add to the hot broth and blend gently. Season to taste with salt and pepper. Top each bowl of soup with croutons, if desired, and a spoonful of chopped grapes.

6 servings

2	tblsp olive oil
1	cup chopped leeks, white part only
12	garlic cloves, chopped
4	cups chicken broth or stock
2	tblsp red wine vinegar
3	slices white bread
1	cup milk
	Salt
	Freshly ground black pepper
	Croutons (optional)
1/2	cup seedless white grapes, chopped

Nutrition **Note**   You can fight diabetes with your feet. Moderate exercise — such as walking an hour a day — may slash your risk of type 2 diabetes in half. What's more, this type of activity also lowers blood glucose, pushing it closer to normal. So if you enjoy a brisk walk or do other moderate activities for fun, these hobbies can help you battle diabetes. Just remember, if you already have diabetes, check with your doctor before starting any exercise program.

Unique fennel and turkey bacon soup

Nutritional facts per serving: 93 calories; 10.5g carbohydrates; 12.8mg cholesterol; 3.4g total fat; 3.1g fiber; 5.7g protein; 471.1mg sodium

---

Fry bacon until crisp, drain on paper towels, reserving the drippings. When cool, crumble into small pieces and set aside.

Add 3 tablespoons bacon drippings to a Dutch oven. Add onions, garlic, and fennel and cook until soft, 20 minutes, stirring as needed. Add potatoes and chicken stock, and bring to a boil. Reduce heat, cover, and simmer until potatoes are done, about 15 to 20 minutes.

3	ounces turkey bacon
2	onions, finely chopped
2	garlic cloves, chopped
1	large fennel bulb, coarsely chopped
2	cups potatoes, peeled and coarsely chopped
2	cups chicken stock or broth
	Salt
	Freshly ground black pepper

Remove the solids, and puree them in a blender or food processor. Return to the pan, and season with salt and pepper. Serve hot, topped with the crumbled bacon.

6 servings

Nutrition **Note**
A powerful, all-natural solution could help you manage arthritis even more effectively. Exercise can increase your strength and flexibility and reduce the amount of medication needed to control pain. It may even delay or prevent arthritis from developing in other joints. Walk, swim, and cycle to help increase your mobility and decrease joint pain and stiffness. Just be sure to clear your exercise plan with your doctor first.

Vegetable-sausage soup dinner

Nutritional facts per serving: 336 calories; 16.3g carbohydrates; 58.9mg cholesterol; 19.8g total fat; 2.2g fiber; 23.7g protein; 1291.1mg sodium

Heat oil in a large pan, add onions and 1 clove garlic, and cook until translucent. Add celery, carrots, green pepper, zucchini, and mushrooms, and cook for 3 minutes. Cover and cook 5 minutes over medium heat. Add boiling broth to the vegetables. Return to a boil, then reduce heat and simmer, uncovered, for 10 minutes until vegetables are tender.

Sauté sausage until cooked through, drain, and add to soup. Add salt and pepper to taste. When ready to serve, reheat to boiling, add pasta, tomatoes, and spinach, and simmer until pasta is done. Add 1/4 cup parsley.

Combine remaining parsley and garlic, basil, and cheese to make garnish. Top soup with garnish, and serve with the bread.

8 servings

2	quarts low-sodium chicken broth
3	tblsp olive oil
2	small onions, chopped
3	garlic cloves, chopped, divided
1	stalk celery, chopped
2	medium carrots, sliced on an angle
1/2	green bell pepper, chopped
2	medium zucchini, sliced
1/2	cup mushrooms, sliced
1/2	pound Italian turkey sausage
	Salt
	Freshly ground black pepper
1/3	pound thin spaghetti
3	fresh tomatoes, peeled, seeded, and coarsely chopped
1	cup coarsely shredded fresh spinach
1/2	cup chopped fresh parsley, divided
1/4	cup chopped fresh basil
1	cup grated Parmesan cheese
	French or Italian bread, sliced thick

Oriental pork and cabbage soup

Nutritional facts per serving: 174 calories; 1.5g carbohydrates; 35.5mg cholesterol; 11.6g total fat; 0.3g fiber; 14.8g protein; 805.6mg sodium

Heat oil in a large pan. Add pork and ginger, and stir-fry briefly until pork is white. Heat broth to boiling, and add to pork with soy sauce. Reduce to medium heat, and simmer, covered, 15 minutes. Add cabbage, and simmer until wilted, 3 to 4 minutes. Add salt, pepper, sugar, and Tabasco to taste.

To serve, garnish with fresh tomatoes. This recipe may be made ahead a couple of days and reheated.

6 servings

1 tblsp dark sesame oil

8 ounces lean pork, chopped, ground, or shredded

2 tblsp chopped fresh ginger

6 cups chicken broth or stock

1 tblsp soy sauce

8 ounces Chinese cabbage, sliced thinly

Salt

Freshly ground black pepper

Sugar (optional)

Dash Tabasco

2 fresh ripe tomatoes, roughly chopped (optional)

Nutrition **Note**

Irritability, tiredness, and sleep disturbances may be mild symptoms of a thiamin deficiency. Thiamin, like all B vitamins, is water-soluble — and that means your body doesn't store it on a long-term basis. Elderly people who don't eat a well-balanced diet are particularly at risk for a deficiency of thiamin. Unfortunately, their symptoms may be mistaken for normal changes associated with aging and may go untreated. But, since you don't need large amounts of thiamin, just eat the right foods and you'll eat away at deficiency. Good thiamin sources include fortified cereals, enriched white rice, enriched flours, pork chops, and tropical trail mix.

American Oriental chicken soup

Nutritional facts per serving: 125 calories; 8.3g carbohydrates; 26.3mg cholesterol; 3.6g total fat; 2.1g fiber; 14.7g protein; 1150.2mg sodium

Put chicken broth in a soup pot. Add ginger, green onions, and celery. Bring to a boil over high heat, reduce heat, and simmer 10 minutes. Add chicken, soy sauce, and hoisin sauce, and simmer 5 minutes. Add water chestnuts, if desired. Add salt and pepper to taste.

4 servings

3 cups chicken broth or stock

1 2" slice fresh ginger, cut into strips

2 bunches green onions, sliced on the diagonal into 1/2" pieces

1 stalk celery, cut into thin diagonal slices

1 cup cooked chicken, slivered or torn into bite-sized pieces

2 tblsp soy sauce

1 tsp hoisin sauce

4 ounces sliced canned water chestnuts (optional)

Salt

Freshly ground black pepper

Make soups easier and even more appetizing with these tips.

- Keep two containers in your freezer for soup fixings. Use one for meat scraps and bones. Put vegetable leftovers, like celery leaves and carrot tops, in the other. Use for meat broth and vegetable stock.

- To remove grease from soup or chili while it's cooking, drop in a lettuce leaf to attract the grease. When you're done, just toss the lettuce and serve the soup!

- Stir dry instant potatoes into your soup or stew for instant thickening.

Chilled curried zucchini soup

Nutritional facts per serving: 176 calories; 12.4g carbohydrates; 2.4mg cholesterol; 12.4g total fat; 2.8g fiber; 7g protein; 110.8mg sodium

Heat oil in a large saucepan over medium-high heat. Add zucchini and cook, stirring frequently, until it begins to soften, about 5 minutes. Add garlic, cumin, curry powder, and white pepper and mix well. Add chicken stock, reduce heat to medium, and simmer the mixture until zucchini is very soft, about 10 minutes.

Cool the mixture to room temperature. Pour it into a blender or food processor, and puree until smooth. Cover and refrigerate until well chilled, or up to 6 hours.

Studies show that families who keep fruits and vegetables around and "in sight" eat more of them. So put a bowl of fruit on the table, and keep cut-up carrot and celery sticks in a clear container in the refrigerator.

When ready to serve, add buttermilk and green onions to the chilled zucchini mixture, and stir to combine well. Sprinkle each serving with chopped parsley.

3   tblsp canola oil

2   pounds zucchini, chopped

4   garlic cloves, finely chopped

1   tblsp ground cumin

1   tsp curry powder, or to taste

1   tsp white pepper

2   cups low-sodium chicken stock

1   cup buttermilk

1   cup sliced green onion

2   tblsp chopped parsley

4 servings

Beat-the-heat fruit and veggie soup

Nutritional facts per serving: 163 calories; 18.3g carbohydrates; 3.7mg cholesterol; 8.2g total fat; 2.3g fiber; 5.1g protein; 161.7mg sodium

Heat olive oil in a large saucepan. Add onion, garlic, and carrots, and cook over medium heat until soft, about 5 minutes. Stir in coriander, chicken broth, orange juice, and apricots, and bring to a boil. Cover, and cook over a low heat until apricots are soft, 15-20 minutes.

Strain the solids, reserving the liquid in a mixing bowl. Puree the solids in a blender or food processor until smooth, then stir back into the reserved cooking liquid. This can be done in advance and refrigerated or frozen. Stir in the yogurt. Season to taste with salt and pepper. Refrigerate until well chilled. Serve cold.

4 servings

2	tblsp olive oil
1	green onion, chopped
1	garlic clove, mashed to a paste
1/2	pound carrots, peeled and thinly sliced
1/2	tsp ground coriander
1/2	cup chicken broth or stock
1	cup fresh orange juice
1/2	cup finely chopped dried apricots
1	cup plain low-fat yogurt
	Salt
	Freshly ground black pepper

Nutrition **Note**   Believe it or not, some people claim apricots are the secret to living to age 120. They get this idea from the Hunzas, a tribe living in the Himalayan Mountains of Asia. Common health problems like cancer, heart disease, high blood pressure, and high cholesterol do not exist in Hunza. And researchers are wondering if apricots, a main part of their diet, are partly responsible. The Hunzas eat fresh apricots in season and dry the rest to eat during their long, cold winter.

Cool-as-a-cucumber soup

Nutritional facts per serving: 127 calories; 12.2g carbohydrates; 7.4mg cholesterol; 5.6g total fat; 0.8g fiber; 7.7g protein; 185.2mg sodium

---

Whisk together yogurt and stock until smooth. Add cucumbers, vinegar, olive oil, garlic, mint, and sugar. Add salt and pepper to taste. Mix well, and chill until ready to serve. Garnish each bowl with a cucumber slice and a mint sprig.

4 servings

2   cups plain low-fat yogurt

1/2   cup chicken broth or stock

2   cucumbers, peeled, seeded, and grated

1   tblsp olive oil

2   tblsp lemon juice

1   garlic clove, finely chopped

2   tblsp finely chopped fresh mint

1   tsp sugar (optional)

   Salt

   Freshly ground black pepper

4   thin slices cucumber

4   sprigs mint

Cut back on salt to control your blood pressure, and you may also pave the way to better-tasting soups and stews. The secret is to know which spices can help you add flavor. Experiment with these ideas from the American Heart Association. For soups, try chives, dill, garlic, onions, paprika, thyme, basil, caraway seeds, or parsley. In stews, allspice, basil, caraway seeds, and sage are fine choices. Bay leaves are good for both soups and stews, but always remember to remove them before serving or eating your dishes. Their sharp edges can make them dangerous to swallow.

Delightful low-fat maple-yogurt sauce

Nutritional facts per serving: 90 calories; 17.5g carbohydrates; 3.7mg cholesterol; 1g total fat; 0g fiber; 3.2g protein; 44.6mg sodium

In a medium-size bowl, combine yogurt, syrup, and vanilla, and stir until smooth and well-blended. Refrigerate until ready to serve.

1	cup plain low-fat yogurt
1/4	cup maple syrup
1	tsp vanilla extract

This sauce can be made ahead of time. It will last until the original expiration date on the yogurt container.

4 servings

Quick, simple, and perfect for many desserts, maple-infused yogurt is a low-fat way to enhance apple cobbler, brownies, pies, waffles, pancakes, and crepes. For example, you can use this sauce with Lazy-day apple cobbler on page 358. But why stop with this low-fat sauce? Cut fat or calories in other recipes with these tips.

- Replace heavy cream in a recipe with evaporated milk, and you'll cut the calories by 75 percent.

- Cook with egg whites or egg substitutes instead of eggs or egg yolks.

- Substitute a little unsaturated olive oil or canola oil for solid fats like shortening, butter, lard, or margarine.

Tart yogurt-honey sauce

Nutritional facts per serving: 86 calories; 12.6g carbohydrates; 8.1mg cholesterol; 2.5g total fat; 0.6g fiber; 4g protein; 115.5mg sodium

Combine yogurt, sour cream, green onions, mustard, honey, lemon juice, and herbs. Season to taste with salt and pepper. Refrigerate, covered, 2 hours or more.

4 servings

1	cup plain low-fat yogurt
3	tblsp low-fat sour cream
2	green onions, finely chopped
1 1/2	tblsp Dijon mustard
1/3	cup honey
2	tblsp lemon juice
2	cups finely chopped fresh basil, thyme, or parsley
	Salt
	Freshly ground black pepper

Nutrition **Note**

In ancient times honey was so highly prized that merchants and landowners accepted it as a form of money.

Today, people are still buzzing about honey's importance. Experts say this sweet treat is a valuable medicine — one that can destroy dangerous infections, clean dirty wounds, revive dry skin, and soothe an upset tummy. Honey even pours on antioxidants that defeat cancer-causing free radicals.

In recent years honey has taken a back seat to man-made antibiotics and to processed sweeteners. But modern science shows honey kills bacteria that even the most powerful antibiotics can't handle. And since it contains traces of vitamins, minerals, proteins, and other nutrients — which sugar doesn't have — it is the sweetener of choice again for many people.

Creamy spinach-yogurt sauce

Nutritional facts per serving: 18 calories; 0.9g carbohydrates; 3.9mg cholesterol; 1.5g total fat; 0.4g fiber; 0.4g protein; 0.9mg sodium

Squeeze spinach to remove excess moisture. Melt butter on low heat. Add onion and cook until soft and translucent, 3 to 4 minutes. Add spinach and nutmeg, and simmer for 5 minutes. Transfer the solids to a food processor, and puree until smooth. Return the puree to the skillet, and stir in the yogurt. Bring to a gentle boil, add salt and pepper to taste, and serve hot.

3 servings

2	10-ounce boxes frozen chopped spinach, thawed
1	tblsp butter
1	medium onion, finely chopped
1/2	tsp freshly grated nutmeg
1	cup plain yogurt
	Salt
	Freshly ground black pepper

Nutrition **Note**

Cleverly hidden in the cool smoothness of yogurt are surprising substances that may jump-start your immune system. A healthy immune system means you're better able to fight off a multitude of diseases, including cancer. A University of California study found that eating two cups of yogurt daily increased an important immune system substance called gamma-interferon. Researchers have tested other specific probiotics in yogurt and found many of them cause your body's defense system to kick in. To get this benefit, check the yogurt container's label to make sure your yogurt contains live and active cultures.

Chunky tomato-avocado salsa

Nutritional facts per serving: 74 calories; 7g carbohydrates; 0mg cholesterol; 5.3g total fat; 2.8g fiber; 1.6g protein; 78.9mg sodium

Lightly combine tomatoes, garlic, lemon juice, green onions, oil, parsley, and avocado. Season to taste with salt and pepper.

4 servings

1   14 1/2-ounce can salsa-style chunky tomatoes

2   garlic cloves, finely chopped

Juice of 2 lemons

3   green onions, sliced 1/8" thick

1   tblsp olive oil

2   tblsp chopped fresh parsley

1   avocado, pitted, peeled and cut into 1/2" pieces

Salt

Freshly ground black pepper

Nutrition **Note**   Avocados may have high fat content, but you can still call on them to help cut fat, to add healthy vitamin E to your diet, and to replace saturated fat. Here's how. If you use avocado to replace mayonnaise or butter, you may actually reduce your fat intake. But be careful. If you are on a low-fat diet and you slash your fat intake too much, you run the risk of not getting enough vitamin E. Fortunately, avocados can provide a natural source of vitamin E and a healthier type of fat. Most of the fat in avocados is monounsaturated fat — which is better for you than saturated fat. Studies find that replacing saturated fats with unsaturated fats in your diet can reduce your risk of heart disease. What's more, here's a useful bonus tip. Choose a Florida avocado over a California avocado, and you'll get less fat per ounce, but more vitamin E.

Go-bananas salsa

Nutritional facts per serving: 410.2 calories; 29.2g carbohydrates; 0mg cholesterol; 2.1g total fat; 8.9g fiber; 1.2g protein; 124.2mg sodium

Lightly combine the bananas, red bell pepper, green bell pepper, jalapeño, onions, ginger, lime or lemon juice, mint leaves, cardamom, and sugar. Add salt and pepper to taste.

4 servings

Try these surprisingly clever tricks for more tempting and flavorful veggies.

- Top corn or black beans with salsa or a dash of hot sauce.

- Add garlic to mashed potatoes.

- Make a grated carrot salad.

- Add a dash of nutmeg to spinach dishes.

2   large bananas, peeled and chopped into 1/4" pieces

1   red bell pepper, chopped into 1/4" pieces

1   green bell pepper, chopped into 1/4" pieces

1   jalapeño pepper, finely chopped

3   green onions, finely chopped

1   tblsp chopped fresh ginger

3   tblsp fresh lime or lemon juice

1/4   cup chopped fresh mint leaves

1/4   tsp ground cardamom

2   tblsp packed light brown sugar (optional)

Salt

Freshly ground black pepper

Tangy marinara sauce

Nutritional facts per serving: 232 calories; 51.1g carbohydrates; 0mg cholesterol; 3.1g total fat; 10.7g fiber; 9.7g protein; 230.8mg sodium

---

Heat oil in a heavy pan over medium heat. Add garlic and cook until soft. Add canned tomatoes, basil, and optional fennel seed to the pan, and cook for 25 minutes, stirring often. Remove solids to a blender or food processor, and puree. Return sauce to the pan, season with salt and pepper to taste, and simmer over medium heat for 10 minutes to reduce slightly.

4 servings

4	ounces olive oil
2	large garlic cloves, chopped
2	pounds canned tomatoes, drained and broken up
5	tblsp basil or parsley
1	tsp fennel seed (optional)
	Salt
	Freshly ground black pepper

Nutrition **Note**

Know which foods lead the list of repeat offenders for heartburn because avoiding them might cool the blaze. Top villains include ketchup and other tomato products, citrus fruits, chocolate, mustard, pepper, onions, garlic, spearmint, peppermint, vinegar, and high-fat foods. Not everyone is bothered by the same foods. Yet, if you have frequent heartburn or if you've been diagnosed with gastroesophageal reflux disease (GERD), try eliminating these flame-feeding foods. You may feel much better.

Also, be sure to ask your doctor whether any medications you take may be causing your heartburn. For example, aspirin or blood pressure medications can cause problems for some people. Switching to a new medicine might help.

Fresh vine-ripened tomato sauce

Nutritional facts per serving: 144 calories; 6g carbohydrates; 0mg cholesterol; 13.8g total fat; 1.2g fiber; 0.9g protein; 11.2mg sodium

---

Peel the tomatoes, cut them in half, and remove the seeds. Place tomatoes, tomato paste, and vinegar in a food processor. With the processor running, slowly pour in the oil. Season to taste with salt and pepper. Add parsley when ready to serve.

This is great hot on a side dish of pasta, or completely pureed as dressing for a pasta salad.

4 servings

1	pound vine-ripened summer tomatoes
1	tsp tomato paste
6	tblsp red wine vinegar
4	tblsp olive oil
3	tblsp chopped fresh parsley
	Salt
	Freshly ground black pepper

Nutrition **Note** This mouth-watering recipe may tempt you to make tomatoes one of your "five a day" every day. But here's one case where you should take a few days off. Plants in the nightshade family — which include potatoes, tomatoes, and eggplant — contain compounds called solanaceous glycoalkaloids (SGAs). These substances act as natural insecticides, protecting the plants from attack by animals, insects, and fungi. Unfortunately, even small amounts of these compounds can cause your body to break down anesthetics and muscle relaxants more slowly — causing the anesthetic to remain in your body longer than it should. Until more is known about this, it might be a good idea to eliminate nightshades from your diet for at least a few days prior to surgery.

Make-ahead turkey gravy

Nutritional facts per serving: 281 calories; 6.1g carbohydrates; 72.8mg cholesterol; 16.4g total fat; 1g fiber; 26.6g protein; 125.9mg sodium

Preheat oven to 350 degrees.

Place wings on a baking sheet. Cover another baking sheet with foil, and place the garlic and onion on it. Roast both, turning occasionally, for 20 to 30 minutes, or until brown. The garlic and onions will brown first.

Put wings and any juices in a large heavy-bottomed pot. Pour 1/4 cup of the chicken broth onto the baking sheet so you can scrape up any flavorful brown bits left there. Pour into the pot. Add garlic, onion, remaining chicken broth, carrot, celery, parsley, peppercorns, bay leaf, and oregano. Bring mixture to a boil, and simmer for 2 hours, adding hot water or more chicken stock if needed to keep the wings covered.

1 pound turkey wings, roughly chopped into 2" to 3" pieces*

2 large garlic cloves, peeled

1 small onion, thickly sliced

3 cups low-sodium chicken broth

1 carrot, thickly sliced

1 rib celery, thickly sliced

6 stems parsley

12 black peppercorns

1 bay leaf

1/8 tsp dried oregano

*Ask the butcher in your grocery store to chop the wings for you.

Strain the stock, pressing down on the wings and vegetables to release all juices. Discard the solids. Cool the stock to room temperature, cover, and refrigerate overnight. Spoon off any fat that rises to the top. Return to the stove, and simmer until reduced to 2 cups. Remove bay leaf.

Cool and freeze in a zip-top freezer bag lying flat on a baking sheet. When ready to use, thaw at room temperature in a saucepan, or defrost in a microwave.

4 servings

Apricot honey-mustard sauce

Nutritional facts per serving: 178 calories; 46.1g carbohydrates; 0mg cholesterol; 1g total fat; 0g fiber; 2.2g protein; 68.4mg sodium

Combine honey, mustard, and water in a heavy-bottomed saucepan, and bring to a boil over medium heat. Add apricots and return to a simmer. Cover and simmer, stirring occasionally, for 20 minutes, or until apricots are very tender. Cool and puree. Reheat when ready to serve.

2	tblsp honey
2	tsp Dijon mustard
1 1/4	cups water
1/2	pound dried apricots, chopped

4 servings

Use this versatile sauce to accompany Easy roasted Cornish hens on page 138 or to fancy up store-bought rotisserie chicken. You can even make it ahead of time. If you do, be sure to let it cool, cover it tightly, and refrigerate. It will keep for up to 3 days.

Although this recipe shouldn't give you any problems, here's a bonus tip for those days when you end up with food that sticks to your saucepan. Simply pour in a little fabric softener, and let it sit overnight. Next morning, just wash and rinse.

Quick homemade cocktail sauce

Nutritional facts per serving: 79 calories; 20.2g carbohydrates; 0mg cholesterol; 0.5g total fat; 1.3g fiber; 1g protein; 142.7mg sodium

Combine ketchup, lemon juice, Worcestershire sauce, and horseradish and mix well. Season to taste with salt and pepper. Cover tightly and refrigerate. Tightly covered, the cocktail sauce will keep in the refrigerator for up to 2 days.

4 servings

1 cup low-sodium ketchup

2 tblsp fresh lemon juice

2 tblsp Worcestershire sauce

2 tblsp prepared horseradish

Salt

Freshly ground black pepper

Nutrition **Note**

Even though a pomegranate may look a bit like old leather, it could be the right remedy to reach for when a nasty cold strikes. Cut open a pomegranate, and you'll find a bright red, yummy fruit that's high in vitamin C — just what you need for a cold. Start slurping sweet pomegranate juice at the first sign of a cold, and you'll start treating your sore throat, cough, and congestion. It's also a delicious way to keep up your fluids.

But this juice has more than just vitamin C going for it. Loaded with antioxidants, this tangy beverage can prevent LDL cholesterol oxidation, a step in the development of hardened arteries. That means you'll be fighting heart disease and your cold at the same time.

Spicy and creamy horseradish sauce

Nutritional facts per serving: 76 calories; 4.8g carbohydrates; 13.7mg cholesterol; 6.1g total fat; 0.3g fiber; 1.1g protein; 94.1mg sodium

Mix sour cream, mayonnaise, lemon juice, and horseradish. The amount of horseradish to use depends on whether the horseradish is fresh or is a particularly hot brand — and how hot you want the sauce to be. Refrigerated in a covered container, the sauce will keep for about 1 week.

This sauce is good with seafood, turkey, or beef.

4 servings

1/2 cup low-fat sour cream

2 tblsp mayonnaise

2 tblsp fresh lemon juice

2-3 tblsp prepared horseradish

Salt

Freshly ground black pepper

Nutrition Note

This dip could be a great way to help clear your sinuses. Foods like cayenne and horseradish may help you say say-onara to the sinus pain and headaches that can accompany blocked sinuses. But don't confuse regular horseradish with Japanese horseradish — a popular sushi condiment. Japanese horseradish is actually wasabi, a plant that belongs to the same cruciferous family as broccoli and cabbage. Wasabi contains compounds called isothiocyanates that stop your platelets from clumping — a benefit that may help prevent stroke. Wasabi may also be useful in fighting tooth decay. According to a study, isothiocyanates also stop bacteria from sticking to your teeth. Just remember — a little of this fiery topping goes a long way.

Smooth red bell pepper sauce

Nutritional facts per serving: 123 calories; 12g carbohydrates; 0mg cholesterol; 7.3g total fat; 3.7g fiber; 2.6g protein; 101.3mg sodium

---

Heat olive oil in a large sauté pan over medium heat. Add red peppers and shallots and sauté, stirring frequently, until softened, about 5 minutes. Add chicken broth, and simmer until peppers are soft and the liquid is reduced by half.

Place the mixture in a blender or food processor, and puree. Press sauce through a very fine sieve with a rubber spatula to remove any bits of skin. Add salt and pepper to taste. Serve warm.

4 servings

2	tblsp olive oil
4	cups diced red bell pepper
2	tblsp chopped shallots
1/2	cup low-sodium chicken broth
	Salt
	Freshly ground black pepper

This is a tasty sauce for grilled or broiled veal chops. It also adds great color to the plate.

Sesame-garlic-ginger marinade

Nutritional facts per cup: 180 calories; 3.2g carbohydrates; 0mg cholesterol; 6.1g total fat; 3.2g fiber; 0g protein; 982.6mg sodium

Mix together garlic, ginger, sugar, canola oil, green onions, red pepper flakes, wine vinegar, sesame seeds, soy sauce, and dark sesame oil. Stir until blended.

1 cup

6	garlic cloves, chopped
1	tblsp freshly grated ginger
2	tblsp sugar (optional)
2	tblsp canola oil (optional)
5	green onions, chopped
1	tsp red pepper flakes
4	tsp rice wine or white wine vinegar
2	tblsp sesame seeds
2	tblsp soy sauce
1	tsp dark sesame oil

Nutrition Note

According to dental experts, the following conditions — not tooth decay — could be causing your "toothache."

- Sinus infection. If you feel pain bending over, suffer from chronic allergies, had a recent cold, or just flew on a plane, your ache could signal an infection called acute maxillary sinusitis (AMS). The right prescription medicines might cure you.

- Neurological disorder. Nerve problems — like Atypical Facial Pain (AFP) and Trigeminal Neuralgia — may be causing your discomfort. Your dentist can recommend a good neurologist.

- Bruxism. Grinding your teeth can become a painful habit. Talk with your dentist about how to kick it.

Susan's wonderful apple walnut cake

Nutritional facts per serving: 423 calories; 49.7g carbohydrates; 39.8mg cholesterol; 23.6g total fat; 1.9g fiber; 4.8g protein; 241mg sodium

Preheat oven to 350 degrees. Grease a tube pan.

Beat together brown sugar and eggs. Add vanilla and oil. Combine flour, salt, baking soda, and spices, and fold into egg mixture. Fold in apples and nuts. Bake for 1 hour and 15 minutes, or until a cake tester tests clean. Cool in pan for 10 minutes before unmolding on a wire cake rack.

16 servings

2	cups packed light brown sugar
3	large eggs
2	tsp vanilla extract
1 1/4	cups canola oil
3	cups all-purpose flour
1	tsp salt
1	tsp baking soda
2	tsp cinnamon
1/4	tsp ground cloves
1/2	tsp ground ginger
3	cups finely chopped Granny Smith apples, unpeeled
1	cup chopped walnuts

Nutrition **Note** For hundreds of years, the ancient Greeks and Romans used cinnamon for better digestion. Although scientists aren't sure how it works, it may have to do with the way cinnamon heats up your stomach. Whatever the reason, adding some aromatic cinnamon to your meal could help relieve your discomfort if you have trouble with frequent indigestion. Be creative with this delightful spice. Try adding it to cooked carrots, winter squash, or sweet potatoes. But be careful not to eat cinnamon oil. It can be toxic even in small amounts.

Spiced angel food cake with apple glaze

Nutritional facts per serving: 248 calories; 60.1g carbohydrates; 0mg cholesterol; 0.2g total fat; 0.7g fiber; 2g protein; 243.7mg sodium

Preheat oven to 375 degrees.

Sift flour, mace, and 3/4 cup of the sugar together 3 times. Set aside.

Beat egg whites in an electric mixer on high until soft peaks form. Gradually add the remaining cup of sugar, and beat on high until stiff, glossy peaks hold their shape.

Sift 1/4 of the flour and sugar mixture over the egg white mixture. Gently fold it into the mixture with a rubber spatula. Repeat with remaining flour and sugar mixture, adding 1/4 at a time.

Scoop the batter into a tube pan, preferably with a removable bottom. Gently run a knife through the batter to remove air pockets. Bake the cake in the lower third of the oven for 30 to 40 minutes, or until a thin wooden skewer inserted in the center comes out clean. Remove from the oven, and invert over the neck of a bottle until completely cool.

Loosen the cake around the edges and center with a knife. Invert onto a cake platter. Melt the jelly. Add the spices and stir well. Drizzle over the cake.

16 servings

1 1/4	cups sifted self-rising flour
1/2	tsp ground mace
1 3/4	cups sugar
1 3/4	cups egg whites (12-14 eggs)
1/2	cup pure apple jelly
1/4	tsp apple juice
1/8	tsp ground ginger
1/8	tsp ground mace
1/8	tsp ground cinnamon

Egg white is high in protein, riboflavin, and lysine, and it does almost everything whole eggs do — but without the tiniest hint of fat or cholesterol.

Carrot cake with pecan cream cheese icing

Nutritional facts per serving: 556 calories; 74.8g carbohydrates; 63.2mg cholesterol; 27.6g total fat; 1.4g fiber; 4.7g protein; 340.1mg sodium

Preheat oven to 350 degrees.

Combine flour, baking soda, salt, cinnamon, and sugar in the bowl of an electric mixer. Combine eggs and oil, add them to the dry ingredients, and mix well. Fold in the carrots. Divide batter between 2 greased and floured 9" cake pans. Bake for 30 to 40 minutes, or until a cake tester or thin wooden skewer inserted in the middle comes out clean. Let cool in pans for 10 minutes, then let finish cooling on cake racks.

Don't let your beautiful cake stick to your knife and fall apart when you try to cut it. Serve perfect pieces for your friends and family by dipping your knife in a glass of cold water between slices.

To make icing, beat cream cheese until fluffy. Beat in butter and vanilla until completely incorporated. Gradually beat in the confectioner's sugar. Use this for the filling between the two layers and to ice the outside. Pat nuts around the sides.

Chill before cutting.

2	cups all-purpose flour
2	tsp baking soda
1	tsp salt
2	tsp cinnamon
2	cups sugar
1 1/2	cups canola oil
4	large eggs, lightly beaten
3	cups grated carrots
8	ounces low-fat cream cheese, cold
4	tblsp butter, softened
2	tsp pure vanilla extract
3 1/2	cups confectioner's sugar
1/2	cup toasted chopped pecans

16 servings

Dutch apple crumb cakes

Nutritional facts per serving: 428 calories; 53.3g carbohydrates; 46.9mg cholesterol; 23.1g total fat; 3.1g fiber; 4.8g protein; 7.7mg sodium

Preheat oven to 350 degrees. Grease and flour a 12-cup muffin pan, and set aside.

Combine butter, flour, oats, sugar, and cinnamon with your fingers until the mixture forms crumbs. Set aside.

Sift together the flours, sugar, baking powder, and cinnamon in a bowl. Add melted butter, milk, eggs, and vanilla, and beat with a wooden spoon just until the batter is blended; do not overbeat. Gently fold in the apples, raisins, and pecans.

Spoon batter into the prepared muffin pan, and sprinkle crumbs over the tops, pressing gently. Bake until the tops are golden and springy to the touch and the crumbs are crisp, about 30 minutes. Cool on a wire rack for 5 minutes. Carefully unmold, and serve warm or at room temperature.

12 servings

1	stick butter
1	cup all-purpose flour
1/2	cup rolled oats
3/4	cup sugar
2	tsp ground cinnamon
1 1/2	cups all-purpose flour
3/4	cup whole-wheat flour
1	cup sugar
1	tblsp baking powder
1	tsp ground cinnamon
1 1/2	sticks butter, melted
1/3	cup milk
3	eggs, lightly beaten
1	tsp vanilla extract
2	Granny Smith apples, peeled and coarsely chopped
1/2	cup raisins
1/2	cup chopped pecans

Low-cal ricotta cheesecake

Nutritional facts per serving: 355 calories; 30.8g carbohydrates; 11.8mg cholesterol; 19.7g total fat; 0.4g fiber; 14.4g protein; 286mg sodium

Preheat oven to 375 degrees. Grease a 9" springform pan, or spray with nonstick spray.

To make the crust, place graham crackers, butter, brown sugar, and ginger in the bowl of a food processor, and process until well combined. Press into the bottom of the springform pan. Place the pan in the oven and bake 5 to 8 minutes. Remove from the oven, and set aside to cool.

To make the filling, place ricotta, eggs, egg white, buttermilk, sugar, vanilla, orange peel, and juice in the bowl of a food processor or electric mixer, and process or mix until smooth. Pour the mixture into the cooled crust, put on a baking sheet, place in the oven, and place a pan of water in the bottom of the oven. Bake 45 to 60 minutes, or until set.

10 servings

1	5 1/2-ounce package graham crackers
3	tblsp butter
2	tblsp packed dark brown sugar
1 1/2	tsp ground ginger
2	15-ounce containers part-skim ricotta cheese
3	eggs
1	egg white
1	cup buttermilk
1/2	cup granulated sugar
1	tblsp vanilla extract
	Grated peel of 1 orange
2	tblsp orange juice

Nutrition Note

Creamy ricotta cheese serves up both calcium and phosphorous. Although phosphorous is widely available in foods, seniors are less likely to get enough from their diets. Ricotta helps add extra phosphorous, and it's a treat to eat.

Autumn apple-cranberry cake

Nutritional facts per serving: 323 calories; 51.5g carbohydrates; 69.2mg cholesterol; 11.7g total fat; 2.4g fiber; 4.6g protein; 251.1mg sodium

Preheat oven to 350 degrees.
Grease and flour a 9" baking pan.

Cream butter and sugar. Add eggs and cream well. Add applesauce and blend thoroughly. Sift flour, baking soda, salt, and spices together in a separate bowl. Add to creamed mixture and blend well. Stir in oatmeal and cranberry sauce. Pour into pan, and bake for 45 minutes.

Cool, and sprinkle with confectioner's sugar, if desired.

9 servings

1/2	cup butter
3/4	cup sugar
2	eggs
1	cup applesauce
1 1/2	cups flour
3/4	tsp baking soda
1/2	tsp salt
1	tsp cinnamon
1/2	tsp ground cloves
1/4	tsp grated nutmeg
1	cup quick-cooking oatmeal
3/4	cup whole berry cranberry sauce
	Confectioner's sugar (optional)

Nutrition **Note**   A pinch of spicy-sweet cinnamon can make insulin work better, according to test tube studies. While scientists try to figure out how cinnamon does this, you might reap rewards from this ancient spice. If you have adult-onset diabetes, talk with your doctor about using cinnamon in your diet. If he gives you a green light, start using it in baked goods, sprinkling it on meats and vegetables, or adding it to fruit drinks.

Chocolate cake royale

Nutritional facts per serving: 421 calories; 46g carbohydrates; 40.8mg cholesterol; 25.8g total fat; 2g fiber; 3.9g protein; 12.9mg sodium

Preheat oven to 375 degrees.

Sift together sugar, flour, cocoa, baking soda, and salt. Add vanilla, oil, water, and vinegar. Stir well to combine. Pour into 9" square baking pan, and bake until the center is slightly puffed, 20 to 25 minutes. A toothpick inserted into the center should come out clean. Remove to a rack to cool. Turn out the cake, cut into squares, and serve topped with the sweetened whipped cream.

8 servings

1	cup sugar
1 1/2	cups all-purpose flour
1/3	cup cocoa
1	tsp baking soda
1/2	tsp salt
2	tsp vanilla extract
1/2	cup vegetable oil
1	cup cold water
2	tblsp white vinegar
1	cup heavy cream, whipped with 1 tblsp confectioner's sugar (optional)

You baked it to perfection, but now your masterpiece of a cake is stuck to the bottom of the pan. Don't panic. You need to heat the bottom of the pan to soften the hardened sugar and oil that are making it stick. You can do this by filling a large bowl with hot water and dipping the bottom of the pan in it. Or, if you have an electric stove, heat a burner, then turn it off. Wait until it's warm but not hot, and place the cake pan on it for a few minutes. Either way, your cake should willingly exit the pan.

Fast and fabulous chocolate cake

Nutritional facts per serving: 301 calories; 22.6g carbohydrates; 137.3mg cholesterol; 23.5g total fat; 1.9g fiber; 4.7g protein; 36.9mg sodium

Preheat oven to 300 degrees. Grease and flour an 8" x 12" pan.

Melt water and chocolate chips together in a medium-size saucepan over low heat. Remove from heat, and beat in the butter piece by piece. Stir in egg yolks. Add flour, sugar, and vanilla.

In a separate bowl, beat egg whites and cream of tartar to form stiff peaks. Whisk a bit of the egg whites into the batter, then fold the chocolate into the whites. Pour batter into prepared pan, and bake for 20 minutes; the cake will seem slightly undercooked. Cool on a wire rack, then invert onto a cake plate, and cut into squares. Serve each square with a dollop of whipped cream and a sprinkle of chocolate shavings, if desired.

1/4	cup water
1	12-ounce package semisweet chocolate chips
1	stick butter, cut into cubes and softened
4	eggs, separated
1	tblsp all-purpose flour
1	tblsp sugar
1	tsp vanilla
	Pinch cream of tartar
	Whipped cream (optional)
	Chocolate shavings (optional)

8 servings

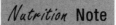 **Note**

Long infamous for its status as a nutritional arch villain and health horror, chocolate may not be quite so bad after all. It does have harmful saturated fat and oodles of calories, but chocolate also comes crammed with antioxidants called polyphenols. These polyphenols can help your heart by preventing LDL cholesterol from teaming up with oxygen to harm your arteries. While that doesn't mean you can go hog wild eating chocolate, some experts think a little chocolate may not be a bad thing.

Ginger brownies in a jiffy

Nutritional facts per serving: 416 calories; 38.6g carbohydrates; 46.1mg cholesterol; 29g total fat; 3.9g fiber; 4.7g protein; 129.5mg sodium

Preheat oven to 325 degrees. Grease and flour a 9" square baking pan.

Beat together butter, sugar, egg, rum, vanilla, and almond extract until light, about 5 minutes. Sift together cocoa, flour, and salt, and combine with the butter mixture, stirring just until mixed. Fold in the pecans, chocolate chips, and ginger.

Pour batter into the pan, and bake 25 to 30 minutes. Do not overbake. Cool in the pan on a wire rack, then cut into squares.

10 brownies

1/2	cup butter
1	cup packed light brown sugar
1	egg, lightly beaten
1	tblsp rum
1	tsp vanilla extract
1/2	tsp almond extract
1/3	cup cocoa
2/3	cup all-purpose flour
1/2	tsp salt
1/2	cup chopped pecans
1/2	cup semisweet chocolate chips
1	tblsp chopped candied ginger

Decorate cakes or brownies like a pastry chef. Place half a plain chocolate bar in a small, microwavable plastic bag. Heat in the microwave until the chocolate melts. Then snip a tiny bit off a corner of the bag, and squeeze as you drizzle a design on your creation.

When you're done, you may need to preserve your newly iced creations. Try this tip for freshly frosted brownies and more. If you're going to wrap a cake or other food item with plastic wrap, but you don't want the wrap to touch the surface of the food, poke toothpicks into strategic areas to form a "tent" that keeps the plastic elevated.

Quick-and-luscious cake brownies

Nutritional facts per serving: 255 calories; 39.3g carbohydrates; 25mg cholesterol; 10g total fat; 0.7g fiber; 2.4g protein; 42.2mg sodium

Preheat oven to 350 degrees.

Sift together flour, sugar, cocoa, baking powder, and salt into a 9" square baking pan. Add butter, vanilla extract, vinegar, and water to dry ingredients, and stir well until blended. Bake until a knife comes out clean, 30 to 35 minutes. Invert onto a rack to cool, then cut into squares.

8-10 brownies

1 1/2	cups all-purpose flour
1	cup sugar
1/4	cup cocoa
1	tblsp baking powder
	Pinch salt
1	stick butter, melted
1	tblsp vanilla extract
1	tblsp apple cider vinegar
1	cup cold water

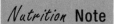 **Nutrition Note**
You adore the silky richness of sweet chocolate treats, but are afraid of what it does to your cholesterol levels.

Fortunately, you don't have to give up chocolate forever. Here's the scoop. Chocolate and cocoa both contain fats from cocoa butter, but these fats are mostly stearic triglycerides. Such fats are harder to absorb than other fats, so they pass right through your body and have almost no effect on your cholesterol. This doesn't mean you need an all-chocolate diet, but the occasional treat won't drive up your cholesterol. And that's a pretty sweet deal.

Gingerbread cakes with lemon yogurt sauce

Nutritional facts per serving: 298 calories; 50.5g carbohydrates; 57.4mg cholesterol; 9.2g total fat; 1.5g fiber; 5.5g protein; 359.5mg sodium

---

Preheat oven to 375 degrees. Grease and flour a 12-cup muffin tin, and set aside.

Toss rum with the candied ginger and raisins. Sift together flour, ginger, cinnamon, and coriander separately. Beat brown sugar, molasses, and butter with an electric mixer until light, about 2 minutes. Add eggs and vanilla, and beat 1 minute more. Stir in the flour mixture, and mix until just blended. Fold in the candied ginger, raisins, and rum.

Fill muffin tins 2/3 full. Bake about 25 minutes. Remove from the oven, and cool for 5 minutes in the pan. Remove from the pan, and cool completely on wire racks.

Mix the yogurt cheese, confectioner's sugar, lemon juice, lemon peel, and vanilla until smooth.

Serve the cooled cakes with a dollop of lemon yogurt sauce.

12 servings

2	tblsp rum, light or dark
1	tblsp chopped candied ginger
1	cup raisins
2 1/2	cups self-rising flour
2	tsp ground ginger
1	tsp ground cinnamon
1	tsp ground coriander
1/2	cup packed light brown sugar
1/2	cup molasses
1	stick butter, softened
2	eggs
1	tsp vanilla extract
1	cup yogurt cheese (see page 70)
1/2	cup confectioner's sugar
2	tblsp lemon juice
1	tblsp grated lemon peel (no white attached)
1	tsp vanilla extract

Nutty spice bar cookies

Nutritional facts per serving: 85 calories; 12.5g carbohydrates; 11.8mg cholesterol; 3.5g total fat; 1.2g fiber; 2g protein; 3.9mg sodium

Preheat oven to 350 degrees. Grease and flour a 9" square cake pan.

Sift together sugar, flour, baking powder, cinnamon, nutmeg, cloves, and ginger. Stir in the chopped dates and almonds, and beat in the eggs and rum extract quickly. Pour batter into the prepared pan, and bake for 25 to 30 minutes. Remove to a rack to cool slightly. Cut into 1 1/2" squares and serve warm.

36 bars

1	cup sugar
3/4	cup all-purpose flour
1	tsp baking powder
1	tsp cinnamon
1/2	tsp freshly grated nutmeg
1/4	tsp ground cloves
1/4	tsp ground ginger
1	cup dates, chopped
1	cup almonds, chopped
2	eggs, lightly beaten
1	tsp rum extract

Most people get far more sugar than they need in a day. Try these tips to help satisfy your sweet cravings with less sugar.

- Sneak a peak at the Nutrition Facts label. Compare the total sugars in similar products, and choose those with the least amount.

- Add flavor not sugar. Cook with sweet-tasting spices like allspice, cinnamon, nutmeg, or cloves.

- Make low-sugar dishes, and serve them warm. This makes many foods taste sweeter.

- Watch out for surprise sugars in odd places like soups and salty foods.

Chocolate-pecan bar cookies

Nutritional facts per serving: 304 calories; 31g carbohydrates; 59.1mg cholesterol; 20.2g total fat; 1.7g fiber; 2.8g protein; 14.7mg sodium

---

Preheat oven to 350 degrees. Grease a 9" x 13" baking pan.

Beat butter and sugar in a mixer bowl until light. Add egg and vanilla. On low speed, add oats, pecans, whole-wheat flour, and all-purpose flour. Stir in the chocolate chips. Spread dough in the prepared pan. Bake until light golden brown, 20 to 25 minutes. Cool on a wire rack and cut into squares.

24 bars

1	cup butter, softened
3/4	cup packed dark brown sugar
1	egg, lightly beaten
1 1/2	tsp vanilla extract
1	cup rolled oats
1	cup pecans, finely chopped
1/2	cup whole-wheat flour
1/2	cup all-purpose flour
1	cup semisweet chocolate chips

Nutrition **Note** Sudden grouchiness, hunger, or tiredness could be a sign of hypoglycemia if you're diabetic. Hypoglycemia occurs when your blood sugar dips too low. Other symptoms include weakness, confusion, sweating, headache, and shakiness. If you experience any of these symptoms, check your blood sugar level. A reading of 70 or lower means you are hypoglycemic. Raise your blood sugar back to a safe level with one of these speedy remedies:

- half a cup of fruit juice or regular (not diet) soda

- a piece of fruit or small box of raisins

- 5 or 6 pieces of hard candy

- 1-2 teaspoons of sugar or honey

- 2-3 store-bought glucose tablets

Delectable Danish cookies

Nutritional facts per serving: 85 calories; 9.3g carbohydrates; 17.4mg cholesterol; 4.9g total fat; 0.2g fiber; 0.9g protein; 3.5mg sodium

Preheat oven to 350 degrees.

Beat shortening, butter, sugar, and vanilla until light. Beat in the egg. Sift together flour, soda, and cream of tartar, and add to the butter mixture. Mix until well blended.

Drop dough by the teaspoonful about 2" apart on an ungreased cookie sheet. Dip the bottom of a small glass into the confectioner's sugar, and use it to flatten the tops of the cookies. Bake until the edges are light brown, 8 to 10 minutes.

3 1/2 dozen cookies

1/2	cup shortening
1	stick butter
1	cup sugar
1	tsp vanilla extract
1	egg, lightly beaten
2	cups all-purpose flour
1/2	tsp baking soda
1/2	tsp cream of tartar
2	tblsp confectioner's sugar

For best results, bake cookies on a shiny flat cookie sheet that has no edge on one to three sides. It should be at least two inches narrower and shorter than the oven rack. And you don't need an insulated cookie sheet to keep cookies from burning. Just turn an old cookie sheet upside down, and place the one you are using on top. It works just as well.

Sugar-topped ginger-cinnamon chews

Nutritional facts per serving: 52 calories; 8g carbohydrates; 11.1mg cholesterol; 2.1g total fat; 0.1g fiber; 0.6g protein; 72.4mg sodium

Preheat oven to 325 degrees.

Cream butter and sugar. Beat in egg and molasses. Set aside. Combine flour, baking soda, ginger, cinnamon, and salt. Stir into molasses mixture. Drop from a teaspoon onto an ungreased cookie sheet, three cookies across. Sprinkle with granulated sugar, if desired. Bake 12 to 15 minutes.

3 dozen cookies

3/4	stick butter
1/2	cup light brown sugar
1	large egg
6	tblsp molasses
1	cup all-purpose flour
1	tsp baking soda
1 1/2	tsp ground ginger
1/2	tsp cinnamon
1/4	tsp salt
	Granulated sugar (optional)

You can just open a packet and shake pure white sugar into your coffee, but it hasn't always been that easy. Before the days of commercial refineries, a housewife had to refine sugar in her own kitchen. The sugar she purchased was black with molasses. To make it white, she would mix it with beaten egg whites and water, then boil it, skimming dark scum off the surface. When at last it looked clear, she would strain it and boil it again. She had to work for hours with four pounds of unrefined sugar to get one pound of the white stuff we take for granted today.

Mixed melons with raspberry sauce

Nutritional facts per serving: 166 calories; 41.6g carbohydrates; 0mg cholesterol; 1g total fat; 6.8g fiber; 2.9g protein; 37.4mg sodium

---

Puree raspberries in a food processor or blender until smooth. Pour through a fine strainer to remove seeds. Mix in sugar to taste, and chill.

2   cups fresh raspberries

Sugar

1   medium cantaloupe

1   medium honeydew melon

Cut melons in half and remove seeds. Cut into thin slices and peel. To serve, alternate slices of cantaloupe and honeydew on individual small plates. Drizzle raspberry puree on top, and garnish with fresh raspberries.

4 servings

Nutrition Note

Cantaloupes are full of beta carotene, a carotenoid your body converts into vitamin A. This natural chemical not only gives the melon its brilliant orange color but also acts as an antioxidant in your body, protecting your eyes from cataracts and macular degeneration. These two serious eye problems most often strike seniors. Cataracts blind over 1 million people worldwide every year, and age-related macular degeneration (AMD) is the leading cause of blindness in people over 65. But you can guard against both these sight-stealers just by treating yourself to these sweet melons.

Tangy winter fruit compote

Nutritional facts per serving: 399 calories; 105g carbohydrates; 0mg cholesterol; 0.8g total fat; 7g fiber; 1.3g protein; 6.9mg sodium

Combine juice and honey in a large, heavy-bottomed frying pan, and stir over medium-high heat until the honey dissolves. Add ginger and cranberries and bring to a boil. Reduce heat to medium, and briskly simmer the mixture, stirring frequently, until thickened, about 20 minutes. The juice should reduce to about 2 cups.

Slice apples and pears about 1/4" thick, and toss them in the lemon juice. Do not peel them. Add the apples to the cranberry mixture, and simmer for 5 minutes, stirring occasionally. Add the pears, any lemon juice that is left, and the lemon zest, and simmer for 5 minutes, stirring occasionally. Remove from stove. The fruit should be tender but will continue to cook off the stove for a few minutes more in the hot syrup. Serve immediately, or cool to room temperature, cover, and refrigerate for up to 2 days.

4 servings

2	cups cranapple juice
1/2	cup honey
2	tblsp finely chopped fresh ginger
1/2	cup fresh cranberries
	Juice and zest of 1 lemon
1	medium Granny Smith apple
1	medium Fuji or Gala apple
1	Anjou pear

Use the Anjou variety of pear in this recipe because its skin is delicate enough to avoid turning grainy when cooked. For an even sweeter treat, try this dish with frozen nonfat vanilla yogurt.

Peach-blueberry compote with orange zest

Nutritional facts per serving: 157 calories; 40.3g carbohydrates; 0mg cholesterol; 0.4g total fat; 5.2g fiber; 1.8g protein; 4.8mg sodium

---

Zest a large orange, wrap the zest in plastic wrap, and set aside.

Squeeze the orange, and combine the orange juice, lemon juice, honey, and almond extract in a small saucepan. Bring the mixture to a full boil. Turn off the heat, but leave the saucepan on the stove.

1	tsp orange zest
1/4	cup fresh orange juice
1	tblsp fresh lemon juice
3	tblsp honey
1/4	tsp almond extract
4	ripe firm peaches
1	pint blueberries

Peel and slice the peaches. Pour the juice mixture over them, and let them steep for 5 minutes, or until cool. Add the orange zest and blueberries, toss gently to combine, and serve.

4 servings

That honey-sweet mix of peaches and blueberries is just the beginning. You can try many tantalizing fruit combinations using this recipe as a base. Trade the peaches for nectarines. Try blackberries or raspberries instead of blueberries. Oranges and blueberries work great together, too. You could even drop strawberries into the mix — if you don't mind the way cut strawberries leech their red color. Experiment to see what you like best. For an extra change of taste, try replacing the almond extract with a tablespoon of Amaretto extract.

Roasted pineapple with honey glaze

Nutritional facts per serving: 184 calories; 32g carbohydrates; 0mg cholesterol; 7.5g total fat; 1.5g fiber; 0.6g protein; 2mg sodium

Preheat oven to 450 degrees.

Heat oil in a large frying pan. Add pineapple slices, leaving some space in between. Put the pan into the oven and roast the pineapple, turning occasionally, until it begins to soften and caramelize around the edges, about 10 minutes.

Combine honey, thyme, pepper, and balsamic vinegar. Spread it on top of the pineapple, return frying pan to the oven, and roast for about 4 minutes more, or until the edges of the pineapple have turned golden brown. You may have to do this step in 2 batches.

If you want to add vin santo or port, remove the pineapple to a heatproof serving dish, and place the frying pan, with the juices in it, over medium heat. Add the vin santo or port, mix well with the juices in the pan, and simmer briskly until thick and syrupy. Pour over the pineapple. Top with a scoop of nonfat vanilla yogurt, if desired, and serve.

4 servings

1	tblsp canola oil
1	ripe golden pineapple, peeled, cored, and cut into 1" thick slices
1/4	cup honey
1	tsp chopped fresh thyme or 1/4 tsp dried thyme
	Dash of freshly ground black pepper
1/4	tsp balsamic vinegar
1/4	cup vin santo or light port (optional)
	Nonfat vanilla yogurt (optional)

If you do not want to add the vin santo (a light Italian after-dinner fortified wine) or port, follow this recipe through the first roasting and stop.

Sweet caramelized pears and apples

Nutritional facts per serving: 256 calories; 22.7g carbohydrates; 58mg cholesterol; 19.2g total fat; 3.4g fiber; 7g protein; 9.1mg sodium

Slice unpeeled pear or apple into 6 or 8 wedges, and remove the core and seeds. Melt butter in a heavy frying pan until hot. Add fruit wedges and cook on one side for a minute. Sprinkle with sugar and turn. Repeat several times until fruit is lightly caramelized. Add cream to the pan, if using, and continue to cook until the fruit is soft and the cream has boiled down to half, about 5 minutes. (If the pears or apples are already soft when the cream is added, remove them before preparing the sauce, and then pour the warm sauce over when ready to serve.)

1-2	ripe firm pears or apples, or a combination
2-4	tblsp unsalted butter
2-4	tblsp sugar
1/3	cup heavy cream (optional)

2-4 servings

Remember these tips to make this sweet dish even more delicious.

- Add a little cream for extra decadence.

- A good pear to use would be Bosc; a good apple, Granny Smith.

- This recipe is good by itself, but a fabulous cookie, like a palmier, could make this dessert really stand out.

- When a variation is in order, add a bit of candied ginger for zip.

Quick-bake pineapple-banana treat

Nutritional facts per serving: 182 calories; 34.9g carbohydrates; 0mg cholesterol; 5.5g total fat; 4.4g fiber; 2.7g protein; 3.1mg sodium

Preheat the broiler.

Toss pineapple, bananas, coconut, sliced almonds, brown sugar, cinnamon, orange peel, rum, and orange juice together, coating completely. Pour into a shallow broilerproof dish, and broil 4" to 6" from the heat until the sugar and juices begin to caramelize, about 3 to 4 minutes. Serve hot or at room temperature.

4 servings

1	pineapple, peeled, cored, and cut into 1" chunks
2	bananas, peeled and cut into 1" chunks
1/4	cup flaked unsweetened coconut
1/4	cup sliced almonds
1/4	cup packed brown sugar
1/2	tsp ground cinnamon
	Grated peel of 1 orange
1	tsp rum extract
2	tblsp orange juice

Try these clever ideas for fruit.

- Thread chunks of pineapple, strawberries, bananas, peaches, or nectarines on wooden skewers, and grill.

- Toss cubed fruits with a tropical juice blend and flaked coconut for easy ambrosia.

- Whirl 1 cup of frozen blueberries or strawberries with vanilla yogurt and serve in tall glasses.

- Top wedges of cantaloupes with vanilla yogurt and fresh blueberries.

- Sprinkle peach halves with brown sugar, and broil until golden brown.

Elegant low-fat fruit brûlée

Nutritional facts per serving: 309 calories; 62.1g carbohydrates; 17.3mg cholesterol; 5.2g total fat; 2.6g fiber; 6.6g protein; 92.8mg sodium

1 1/2	pounds peaches, pears, or plums
1/2-3/4	cup packed light brown sugar
1 1/2	cups plain yogurt
1/2	cup low-fat sour cream

Preheat the broiler.

Halve the fruit and remove the pits, seeds, or stones. Place the fruit cut-side down in a 9" shallow gratin dish. Sprinkle with 2 tablespoons of the sugar. Beat together the yogurt and sour cream. Spread over the fruit and sprinkle with enough of the remaining sugar to coat the top of the fruit. Place under the broiler until the sugar has caramelized, about 5 minutes. Serve hot or cold.

4 servings

Nutrition **Note** You may be surprised to find that the color of a nectarine or peach can affect the nutrition you get from it. The fuzzy peach and its clean-shaven brother, the nectarine, come in three flesh colors — red, white, and yellow. The yellow ones are highest in vitamin A, although all are good sources of vitamins A and C. And both can give you a boost of health-protecting antioxidants, including beta carotene, lutein, zeaxanthin, and beta cryptoxanthin. Whether you prefer peaches or nectarines, though, you can't go wrong with these sweet, delicious, 40-calorie treats.

Taste of the Tropics ambrosia

Nutritional facts per serving: 152 calories; 31g carbohydrates; 0mg cholesterol; 3.9g total fat; 5.5g fiber; 2.1g protein; 2.8mg sodium

Peel oranges, taking care to remove all the white pith. Slice oranges over a bowl to catch the juices. Circular slices hold together best and are less work than sections.

Gently toss orange slices, pineapple, and coconut. Cover and refrigerate for up to one day. When ready to serve, slice the banana and toss it with the other fruit. Add cherries last, if using.

4 servings

3   navel oranges

1/2   ripe golden pineapple, peeled, cored, and cut into 1" thick chunks

1/2   cup grated or shredded coconut

1   small banana

1/2   small bottle maraschino cherries, drained well (optional)

Use these tips for easier preparation of this heavenly dish.

- The coconut can be grated fresh, grated frozen, or packaged shredded sweetened, according to your taste. But the packaged coconut will save time.

- Seedless oranges are a must. And the better the oranges, the better the ambrosia. Splurge and get juicy flavor-filled navel oranges if you can.

- Get juicy orange sections without any white membrane attached by dropping the whole orange into boiling water for 5 minutes before peeling.

Cool and creamy peach fluff

Nutritional facts per serving: 129 calories; 29.4g carbohydrates; 2.4mg cholesterol; 0.8g total fat; 2g fiber; 3g protein; 28.4mg sodium

Peel peaches and remove the pit.

Puree the flesh with sugar in a food processor or blender. Strain the puree if necessary to be smooth. Fold the softened frozen yogurt into the fruit. Spoon into four stemmed glasses or individual containers, cover with plastic wrap, and chill half an hour, but do not let melt completely.

3   ripe peaches

1/4 cup sugar

2/3 cup softened frozen yogurt

4-6 servings

Nutrition **Note**

Sweet and juicy peaches can help keep you regular, and they're much more delightful to put in your mouth than fiber tonics or laxatives. Peaches are more than 80 percent water and a fine source of dietary fiber. This makes them the perfect remedy for constipation. But they'll do more than just that. Adding fruits like peaches to your diet each day may help prevent future problems like hiatal hernia, diverticular disease, hemorrhoids, and even varicose veins. So treat yourself to a rosy peach or two whenever you can. Not only will you enjoy a delicious snack, but it may keep you feeling just peachy for a long time to come.

Fantastic orange flummery

Nutritional facts per serving: 133 calories; 20.2g carbohydrates; 159.4mg cholesterol; 3.8g total fat; 0.1g fiber; 4.9g protein; 47.7mg sodium

Place sugar and water in a heavy saucepan, and heat for a few minutes until the sugar has dissolved. Bring to a boil, and boil steadily until thick, about 10 minutes.

Meanwhile, beat the egg yolks with an electric mixer until they are thick and light. Continue beating while slowly pouring the hot syrup onto the eggs. Add the juice and peel, and beat just until incorporated.

Beat egg whites until stiff, and fold them into the yolk and syrup mixture. Pour into individual stemmed glasses or other containers, cover with plastic wrap, and chill at least 30 minutes or up to several days. If the containers are freezerproof, you may place them in the freezer to chill rapidly.

4-6 servings

1/3　cup sugar

1/3　cup water

3　eggs, separated

Juice and grated peel of 3 oranges

Flummeries are an old-time, fluffy concoction from England. They're delightfully safe to eat as long as you make sure the hot syrup heats the eggs to a minimum of 140 degrees.

Exquisite chocolate-dipped fruit

Nutritional facts per serving: 286 calories; 27.1g carbohydrates; 31.1mg cholesterol; 21.5g total fat; 3.6g fiber; 1.8g protein; 13.2mg sodium

---

Melt chocolate with butter either over low heat or in the microwave. Stir in the corn syrup.

Remove from heat and dip the fruit in the chocolate. Place on a piece of wax paper until set, and then remove to a serving dish. May be refrigerated, taking care to keep the layers separated with wax paper.

1/2	cup semisweet chocolate or white chocolate bits
1	tblsp butter
1	tblsp corn syrup
1 1/2	cups fresh or dried fruit

4-6 servings

You can try all sorts of interesting variations with chocolate-dipped fruits.

- Use dried apricots, pineapples, apples, or pears. A step-up in the dried category would be candied oranges and good quality candied ginger. For fresh fruit, use strawberries.

- Although the recipe calls for semisweet bits, white chocolate bits or a top quality chocolate bar can be fabulous.

- The corn syrup gives a bit of gloss, particularly if the fruits are to be refrigerated.

- And here's a bonus tip for melting chocolate in the microwave. Stop the microwave every 15 seconds to stir, and stop heating just before it's completely melted. Continue stirring until the remaining heat finishes melting the chocolate.

Summer-sweet blackberry cream pie

Nutritional facts per serving: 425 calories; 55.2g carbohydrates; 80.5mg cholesterol; 20.9g total fat; 4.3g fiber; 6g protein; 153.7mg sodium

Preheat oven to 400 degrees.

Mix together sugar, 1/3 cup flour, eggs, sour cream, and vanilla, and blend until smooth. Gently fold in blackberries. Spoon mixture into unbaked pie crust. Bake 30-35 minutes or until center is set.

Combine remaining 1/3 cup flour, brown sugar, pecans, and butter, and mix well. Sprinkle over hot pie. Return pie to oven for 10 minutes or until topping is golden brown.

Remove from oven and cool. Garnish with whipped cream and whole berries, if desired.

8 servings

3/4	cup sugar
2/3	cup flour, divided
2	large eggs, lightly beaten
1 1/3	cups low-fat sour cream
1	tsp vanilla
3	cups fresh blackberries
1	9" pie crust
1/3	cup firmly packed brown sugar
1/4	cup chopped toasted pecans
3	tblsp butter, softened
	Whipped cream (optional)
	Fresh whole berries (optional)

Nutrition **Note** Fruits like blackberries are full of high-powered antioxidants that may help protect you from such dangers as heart disease, cancer, and perhaps even aging. Another plus is they are loaded with fiber. Fiber is best obtained from foods rather than supplements because foods provide many different types of fiber as well as other protective substances. Feasting on blackberries is a delicious way to protect your body in many ways.

Holiday-style plum pie

Nutritional facts per serving: 299 calories; 44g carbohydrates; 7.8mg cholesterol; 13.4g total fat; 0.7g fiber; 1.6g protein; 205.3mg sodium

Preheat oven to 425 degrees.

Divide pie crust in half, and roll one half to line a 9" pie pan. Roll out the second half into an 11" round for the top, and keep chilled.

Mix together sliced plums, half the sugar, flour, cornstarch, cinnamon, and ginger, and taste. Add more sugar if needed.

Pour the fruit mixture into the pie crust. Top with the second crust, and crimp the edges to seal. Make 4 or 5 slits or decorative cutouts in the top of the pie to allow steam to escape. Dot crust with the softened butter, and sprinkle with 1 tablespoon sugar.

Place the pie on a cookie sheet, and bake for 15 minutes. Reduce heat to 375 degrees, and bake for 50 to 60 minutes longer, until the filling is hot and bubbly and the top crust is golden brown. If the top begins to brown too quickly, cover loosely with foil, removing it for the last 5 minutes of baking. Cool on a wire rack, and serve.

6 servings

	Pastry for 1 9" double-crust pie
6	cups sliced plums
1	cup sugar
1/2	cup all-purpose flour
1/4	cup cornstarch
1/2	tsp ground cinnamon
2	tsp chopped candied ginger
2	tblsp butter, softened

Why throw away the scoop that comes with your box of laundry detergent? Wash it out and use it to scoop your flour, sugar, or coffee.

Lazy-day apple cobbler

Nutritional facts per serving: 358 calories; 61.8g carbohydrates; 32.3mg cholesterol; 12.3g total fat; 3.2g fiber; 3.3g protein; 49mg sodium

Preheat oven to 375 degrees. Melt butter in oven in an 8" x 11" ovenproof serving dish.

Toss apples, raisins, and sugar in a bowl. Sift flour, baking powder, and salt together in a separate bowl. Stir in milk to make a batter. Pull the hot dish of melted butter out of the oven, and pour in the batter, which will bubble around the sides. Quickly spoon the apple mixture evenly over the batter. Return to the oven, and bake until the dough is brown and has risen up around the fruit, about 35 minutes. Serve with Delightful lowfat maple-yogurt sauce (see page 314).

6-8 servings

5	medium Golden Delicious apples, peeled, cored, and sliced into 1/2" pieces (about 3 cups)
1/2	cup raisins
1	cup granulated or packed brown sugar
1	stick butter
1	cup all-purpose flour
1 1/2	tsp baking powder
1/2	tsp salt
1	cup milk

Nutrition **Note**

Snack wisely each day, and you may help keep arthritis away. In countries where fast, processed foods have replaced fruits and vegetables, up to 70 percent of the population suffers from some form of arthritis. Nutrition experts tie this trend in part to boron, a trace mineral many plants absorb from the soil. Most people get 1 to 2 milligrams (mg) of boron daily, primarily from non-citrus fruits, leafy vegetables, and nuts. Experts believe, however, you need 3 to 10 mg a day to affect your risk of arthritis. To make your daily joint-saving quota of boron, pair an apple with other boron-rich foods like a few tablespoons of peanut butter and a large handful of raisins.

Homemade blueberry cobbler

Nutritional facts per serving: 215 calories; 39.6g carbohydrates; 0.6mg cholesterol; 5.9g total fat; 2.5g fiber; 2.6g protein; 84mg sodium

Preheat oven to 400 degrees.

In a medium saucepan, combine sugar, cornstarch, lemon rind, and cloves. Stir in blueberries and lemon juice. Heat, stirring constantly, until the mixture boils and thickens. Continue boiling and stirring for 1 minute. Pour the mixture into a greased baking dish, and set aside.

In a medium bowl, combine flour, sugar, baking powder, and salt. Add milk and oil, stirring until a soft dough forms. Drop by tablespoonfuls onto the blueberry mixture. Bake for about 30 minutes or until the topping is golden brown.

6 servings

4	cups fresh or frozen blueberries
1/2	cup sugar
2	tblsp cornstarch
1	tsp grated lemon rind
1	tsp ground cloves
1	tblsp lemon juice
1	cup all-purpose flour
1	tblsp sugar
1 1/2	tsp baking powder
1/4	tsp salt
1/2	cup low-fat milk
3	tblsp vegetable oil

Nutrition **Note** They may be tiny, but blueberries pack a big nutritional punch. Chock-full of fiber, calcium, iron, and disease-fighting antioxidants like vitamin C, this delicious fruit is ready to fight the battle against cancer, heart disease, and diabetes — in fact, blueberries may even help stabilize your blood sugar. And if you want to feel younger, pile on the blueberries. Exciting new research suggests blueberry extract may improve your memory, coordination, and performance on speed tests. Keep your mind sharp while you enjoy the summer-fresh taste of this sweet treat.

Blueberry tart in nutty oatmeal crust

Nutritional facts per serving: 395 calories; 54.8g carbohydrates; 38.9mg cholesterol; 19.1g total fat; 4.2g fiber; 5.7g protein; 54.2mg sodium

Preheat oven to 350 degrees.

Mix almonds, brown sugar, flour, oatmeal, and butter. Pat into the bottom of a 9" springform pan. Bake for 12 minutes, or until just golden. Set aside to cool.

Spread cream cheese over the crust. Pick out 2 cups of the biggest berries, and spread over the cream cheese. Mash the remaining berries. Add enough water to make 2 cups. Add honey. Stir enough of the liquid from the mixture into the cornstarch to dissolve it. Stir this back into the blueberry mixture. Cook over medium heat until the mixture comes to a boil and begins to thicken. Pour over the berries in the crust. Chill thoroughly. Serve with frozen yogurt, if desired.

8 servings

1/2	cup almonds, coarsely ground or finely chopped
1/2	cup brown sugar
1/4	cup all-purpose flour
1/2	cup oatmeal
6	tblsp butter, melted
4	ounces cream cheese, softened
2	pints blueberries, rinsed and drained
1/2	cup honey
2 1/2	tblsp cornstarch
	Nonfat frozen vanilla yogurt (optional)

To turn this into a reduced-fat treat, just substitute low-fat cream cheese for the full fat variety.

Almost-too-easy blueberry pie

Nutritional facts per serving: 301 calories; 43.1g carbohydrates; 0mg cholesterol; 13.7g total fat; 5.1g fiber; 5.1g protein; 153mg sodium

Preheat oven to 425 degrees. Line an 8" pie plate with 1 pie crust.

In a large bowl, mix blueberries, sugar, cornstarch, almonds, lemon peel, and vanilla. Stir well to combine. Pour into unbaked shell. Lightly wet dough on the rim of the dish. Fold the second pie crust dough in quarters, and move to the top of the fruit. Unfold the dough to extend to the dampened rim. Press down the two pieces of dough, and cut off the excess. Decorate if desired. Cut slits for ventilation, and bake until golden brown, 50 to 60 minutes.

2	pie crusts
2	12-ounce bags frozen unsweetened blueberries
1/2	cup sugar
2	tblsp cornstarch
1/2	cup sliced almonds
	Grated peel of 1 lemon
1	tsp vanilla extract
	Whipped cream (optional)

Let the pie cool completely before cutting to be sure it will retain its shape. Serve with whipped cream, if desired.

6 servings

Nutrition **Note**   You may be burning up calories with exercise and not even know it. Gardening, stacking firewood, shoveling snow, and scrubbing floors all count as exercise. And don't discount things you enjoy — like dancing. Not only does dancing qualify as exercise, but ballroom dancing is actually recognized as a sport by the International Olympic Committee.

Apricot-glazed pear tart

Nutritional facts per serving: 213 calories; 24.6g carbohydrates; 24.1mg cholesterol; 6.2g total fat; 18.1g fiber; 31.3g protein; 305mg sodium

Preheat oven to 375 degrees.

Roll dough 1/8" thick, and move to a cookie sheet. Cut a 10" circle or rectangle. Brush the outer 1/2" edge with water. From the scraps, cut a 1/2" strip of dough long enough to go around your tart. Press the strip of dough lightly on the moistened part to form a rim. Chill. Prebake 20 minutes with pie weights.

1	pie crust
3	Bosc pears, peeled, cored, and sliced
1/4	cup dark brown sugar (optional)
1-2	tblsp lemon juice
1/2	cup sugar-free apricot jam
	Vanilla yogurt (optional)

Nutrition Note

If you carry extra fat around your waist, you have a higher risk of heart disease than those who carry their extra weight in the hips and thighs. Ask your doctor about ways to lower your risk.

Slightly overlap the fruit on the pastry, starting from the outside rim — always with the rounded edges towards the outside rim — and spiraling to the center. Sprinkle with brown sugar to taste. Bake 20 to 30 minutes, or until the fruit is soft.

To make the glaze, mix lemon juice and jam, bring to a boil, and strain. Brush the hot glaze on the pears. Cool the tart on a wire rack. Serve warm or at room temperature with vanilla yogurt, if desired.

8 servings

Sugar and spice apple-pear tart

Nutritional facts per serving: 422 calories; 68.3g carbohydrates; 17.5mg cholesterol; 17.2g total fat; 2.5g fiber; 1.7g protein; 221.8mg sodium

Bake one pie crust according to manufacturer directions. Thaw and roll out the second crust. Cut pears or apples or leaves from it to decorate the top of the pie. Bake them on a baking sheet. Set aside.

Melt butter in a large frying pan. Add sugar and spices. Mix well. Add the lemon juice and zest, and mix well. Add pears and apples.

Cook the fruit over medium heat, stirring occasionally, until it is tender, but still has some body. If a lot of juice remains, remove fruit, and strain off the juice. Return juice to the frying pan, and simmer until it becomes thick and syrupy. Return fruit to the pan, mix it with the thickened juices, and scoop it into the pie shell. Decorate the top with the pastry cut-outs.

8 servings

4 1/2	tblsp butter
1 1/2	cups packed brown sugar
1/4	tsp mace
1/2	tsp ground ginger
	Juice and zest of 1 1/2 lemons
1	large Granny Smith apple with skin, sliced
2	ripe pears, peeled and sliced
2	deep dish frozen pie crusts

To get the most juice from a lemon, make sure it's at room temperature, then roll it against your kitchen countertop using the palm of your hand.

Pear and apple phyllo triangles

Nutritional facts per serving: 128 calories; 19.5g carbohydrates; 10.4mg cholesterol; 5.2g total fat; 2g fiber; 1.5g protein; 923mg sodium

Preheat oven to 400 degrees.

Melt butter in a large skillet. Add apples, and sauté over medium heat for 2 to 3 minutes. Add the pear, nutmeg, cinnamon, orange peel, and pecans. Stir. Add honey to taste, if needed.

Unroll the phyllo dough. Until you need it, keep dough covered with a slightly damp lightweight dish towel. Place the first sheet of phyllo on a work surface or baking sheet, and brush with a bit of the olive oil. Fold in half width-wise and brush again. Fold that half in half to make a 4-layer strip, about 4 1/2" x 14" in size.

2	tblsp butter
1	large or 2 small Granny Smith apples, peeled, seeded, and chopped
1	large pear, peeled, seeded, and chopped
1/8	tsp freshly grated nutmeg
1	tsp ground cinnamon
2-3	tsp finely chopped orange peel
1/2	cup chopped pecans
	Honey (optional)
6	14" x 18" sheets phyllo pastry
1/2	cup olive oil

Place a sixth of the filling at the bottom of the strip. Fold the dough strip like a flag, making a large triangle. Brush again with oil.

Repeat with the rest of the dough and filling. They can be refrigerated several hours at this point. Bake 10 to 15 minutes or until golden brown. Serve hot.

6 servings

Nutrition **Note**

Apples and pears are natural laxatives. Their fiber and an unusual balance of natural sugars may help return you to regularity.

Twice-as-good apple half-pie

Nutritional facts per serving: 391 calories; 49.1g carbohydrates; 15.5mg cholesterol; 21.1g total fat; 3.7g fiber; 3.2g protein; 304.6mg sodium

Preheat oven to 375 degrees. Line a baking sheet with aluminum foil, and spray with nonstick spray.

Unfold or roll out the pie crust on a floured board. In a large bowl, combine apple slices, cinnamon, nutmeg, butter, salt, flour, and sugar. Place the apple mixture on half of the pie crust, leaving a 1" border at the edges. Fold the other half of the pastry over the apples, seal the edges with water, and press together with the tines of a fork.

Transfer the half-pie to the prepared baking sheet. Bake 20 to 25 minutes until golden brown. Serve warm or at room temperature.

1	pie crust or pastry for a 9" single crust
3	medium Granny Smith apples, peeled and cut into 1/4" slices
1/2	tsp cinnamon
1/2	tsp freshly grated nutmeg
2	tblsp butter, melted
	Pinch salt
1	tblsp flour
1/4	cup sugar

4 servings

This recipe is a great throw-together that somehow seems more exciting than plain apple pie. Keep prepared pie crusts around to help out in a pinch, but if you have the time and energy, make your own. For a fabulously flaky pie crust every time, try this old-fashioned baker's secret. Add one teaspoon of vinegar to the cold water used to make the dough.

Raspberry-marbled cheese pie

Nutritional facts per serving: 435 calories; 64g carbohydrates; 23.6mg cholesterol; 15.9g total fat; 1.6g fiber; 10.3g protein; 438.6mg sodium

Puree the raspberries in a food processor or blender and set aside.

In a large mixer bowl or food processor, beat cream cheese until fluffy. Gradually beat in condensed milk until smooth. Stir in lemon juice and vanilla. Pour into prepared crust. Top with the raspberry puree. Swirl through the batter with a knife to create a marbled effect. Refrigerate at least 3 hours before serving.

6 servings

- 1/4 cup unsweetened raspberries, fresh or frozen
- 1 8-ounce package cream cheese, softened
- 1 14-ounce can fat-free sweetened condensed milk
- 1/3 cup lemon juice
- 1 tsp vanilla extract
- 1 8" chocolate cookie-crumb crust

Nutrition **Note**

According to a recent study, raspberries are one of the leading fruit sources of disease-repelling antioxidants. Only blueberries, blackberries, and cranberries have more. Raspberries also contain promising plant nutrients like cancer-fighting anthocyanins and ellagic acid. Just 10 of these juicy little berries can give you 1.2 grams of fiber, while 3 cups of sweetened raspberries could give you all the fiber you need for the day. That's a lot of fiber bounce per ounce. So instead of reaching for a fiber supplement or fiber drink mix, try this sweet treat with a cool, shimmering glass of water.

Nutrient	Benefits	Signs of deficiency	DRI Women Age 51+	DRI Men Age 51+	Foods high in nutrient	Content
Calcium	• builds bones and teeth • contracts muscles and nerves • sends nerve messages • controls blood pressure	• bone loss (osteoporosis)	1,200 mg	1,200 mg	• 1 c part-skim ricotta cheese • 8 ozs plain low-fat yogurt • 1 c skim milk • 1 c cooked spinach • 1 oz mozzarella	• 669 mg • 415 mg • 300 mg • 277 mg • 207 mg
Copper	• makes red blood cells • produces energy • fights free radicals	• weakness • pale skin • unhealed wounds	900 mcg	900 mcg	• 1 oz cashews • 1 baked potato, with skin	• 629 mcg • 616 mcg
Folate	• makes and repairs DNA • removes homocysteine from blood	• tiredness • depression • smooth and sore tongue • digestion problems • headaches	400 mcg	400 mcg	• 1 c cooked lentils • 1 c cooked okra • 1 c cooked spinach • 1 c cooked asparagus • 1 c kidney beans	• 358 mcg • 268 mcg • 262 mcg • 243 mcg • 230 mcg
Iron	• carries oxygen throughout body • produces energy	• weakness • pale skin • trouble concentrating	8 mg	8 mg	• 3 ozs canned clams • 1 c cooked lentils • 1 c cooked spinach	• 24 mg • 7 mg • 6 mg

Nutrient	Benefits	Signs of deficiency	DRI Women Age 51+	DRI Men Age 51+	Foods high in nutrient	Content
Magnesium	• builds bones and teeth • relaxes muscles • makes proteins • helps body use nutrients • steadies heart rhythm	• tiredness • loss of appetite • muscle cramps and twitches • convulsions • depression • confusion	320 mg	420 mg	• 1 c raw pearled barley • 1 c cooked lima beans • 1 c cooked okra • 3 ozs halibut • 1 oat bran muffin • 1 c canned pork and beans	• 158 mg • 101 mg • 94 mg • 91 mg • 89 mg • 86 mg
Manganese	• produces energy • builds bones and joints	unknown	2-11 mg	2-11 mg	• 1 c pineapple • 1 c cooked oat bran	• 3 mg • 2 mg
Phosphorus	• builds new cells • produces energy	• loss of appetite • tiredness • pain in bones	700 mg	700 mg	• 1 c ricotta cheese • 5 ozs salmon • 3 ozs canned sardines, in oil	• 450 mg • 428 mg • 417 mg
Potassium	• sends nerve messages • relaxes nerves • maintains chemical balances • steadies blood pressure	• dehydration • weakness • trouble concentrating	3,500 mg	3,500 mg	• 1 c canned white beans • 1 c dates • 1 c raisins • 1 c cooked squash • 1 c cooked sweet potato • 1 banana	• 1,189 mg • 1,161 mg • 1,089 mg • 896 mg • 796 mg • 467 mg

Nutrient	Benefits	Signs of deficiency	DRI Women Age 51+	DRI Men Age 51+	Foods high in nutrient	Content
Selenium	• makes thyroid hormones • fights free radicals • strengthens immune system	• muscle weakness and pain • cataracts • heart trouble	55 mcg	55 mcg	• 1 oz brazil nuts • 5 ozs halibut • 3 ozs canned tuna in water • 5 ozs salmon • 1 c roasted turkey • 1 c cooked couscous	• 543 mcg • 74 mcg • 68 mcg • 59 mcg • 52 mcg • 43 mcg
Sodium	• balances fluid levels • sends nerve messages	• muscle cramps • trouble concentrating • loss of appetite	500 mg	500 mg	• 1 tsp table salt • 1 c canned tomato sauce • 3 ozs lean ham • 10 pretzels • 1 c low-fat cottage cheese	•2,325 mg •1,482 mg •1,128 mg •1,029 mg • 918 mg
Vitamin A (Retinol, Retinoic acid)	• controls eyesight • builds new cells • protects skin and mucous membranes • fights infection and free radicals	• weak immune system • night blindness • diarrhea • dry skin and hair	800 RE or 4,000 IU	1,000 RE or 5,000 IU	• 1 c cooked carrots • 1 baked sweet potato • 1 raw carrot • 1 c red pepper • 1 c cantaloupe	•38,304 IU •31,860 IU •20,253 IU • 8,493 IU • 5,158 IU

Nutrient	Benefits	Signs of deficiency	DRI Women Age 51+	DRI Men Age 51+	Foods high in nutrient	Content
Vitamin B1 (Thiamin)	• produces energy • sends nerve messages • brings on healthy appetite	• swollen and puffy skin (edema) • tiredness • depression • trouble concentrating	1.1 mg	1.2 mg	• 3 ozs lean ham • 1 plain 4" bagel • 1 c cooked green peas • 3 ozs yellowfin tuna • 1 c cooked black beans • 1 c cooked rice • 1 c soy milk	• 0.8 mg • 0.4 mg • 0.4 mg • 0.4 mg • 0.4 mg • 0.4 mg • 0.4 mg
Vitamin B12 (Cobalamin)	• makes new cells (especially red blood cells) • protects nerves	• numbness in extremities • muscle weakness • weight loss • depression • smooth and sore tongue	2.4 mcg	2.4 mcg	• 3 ozs canned clams • 3 ozs king crab • 5 ozs salmon • 3 ozs canned sardines, in oil • 3 ozs canned tuna, in oil	• 84 mcg • 10 mcg • 9 mcg • 8 mcg • 2 mcg
Vitamin B2 (Riboflavin)	• produces energy • helps vision • builds new cells	• cracked lips • skin rash • trouble seeing in bright light	1.1 mg	1.3 mg	• 8 ozs plain skim-milk yogurt • 1 c cooked mushrooms • 1 c cooked spinach • 1 c lowfat cottage cheese	• 0.5 mg • 0.5 mg • 0.4 mg • 0.4 mg

Nutrient	Benefits	Signs of deficiency	DRI Women Age 51+	DRI Men Age 51+	Foods high in nutrient	Content
Vitamin B3 (Niacin)	• produces energy • builds DNA	• diarrhea • black and smooth tongue • trouble concentrating • skin rash	14 mg	16 mg	• 1 chicken breast • 5 ozs halibut • 3 ozs canned tuna, in water • 1 c cooked brown rice	• 12 mg • 11 mg • 11 mg • 3 mg
Vitamin B5 (Panto-thenic acid)	• produces energy	• nausea • insomnia • tiredness	5 mg	5 mg	• 1/4 c sunflower seeds • 1 c canned corn • 1 c cooked peas	• 2 mg • 1 mg • 1 mg
Vitamin B6 (Pyridoxine)	• makes red blood cells • builds proteins • regulates blood sugar • makes brain chemicals • protects immune system	• fatigue • poor moods • smooth and sore tongue • skin inflammation	1.5 mg	1.7 mg	• 3 ozs yellowfin tuna • 1 baked potato • 1 banana • 1 c roasted turkey • 1 c prune juice • 1 c cooked sweet potato • 1 oz pistachios	• 1 mg • 1 mg • 1 mg • 1 mg • 0.5 mg • 0.5 mg • 0.5 mg
Vitamin C (Ascorbic acid)	• makes collagen for skeleton and skin • fights free radicals • bolsters immune system • helps body absorb iron	• bleeding gums • weak bones and joints • blotchy skin • unhealed wounds	75 mg	90 mg	• 1 c red pepper • 1 c cooked broccoli • 1 c sliced strawberries • 1 c papaya • 1 kiwi • 1 orange	• 283 mg • 116 mg • 106 mg • 87 mg • 75 mg • 70 mg

Nutrient	Benefits	Signs of deficiency	DRI Women Age 51+	DRI Men Age 51+	Foods high in nutrient	Content
Vitamin D (Calciferol)	• builds bones • controls calcium and phosphorus levels in your body	• joint pain • bowing legs • muscle spasms	10 mcg or 400 IU (15 mcg if age 70+)	10 mcg or 400 IU (15 mcg if age 70+)	• 3.5 ozs salmon • 3.5 ozs mackerel • 1 c nonfat milk • 1 tbl margarine	• 360 IU • 345 IU • 98 IU • 60 IU
Vitamin E (Tocopherol)	• fights free radicals	• weakness • leg cramps • pale skin	15 mg or 22 IU	15 mg or 22 IU	• 1 oz almonds • 1 c cooked spinach • 1 tbl sunflower oil • 1 c cooked broccoli	• 7 mg • 7 mg • 6 mg • 2 mg
Vitamin K (Phylloquinone)	• forms blood clots • controls calcium levels	• excessive bleeding • unknown bruises	65 mcg	80 mcg	• 1 c cooked kale • 1 c cooked broccoli • 1 c romaine	• 1,000 mcg • 1,220 mcg • 157 mcg
Zinc	• produces energy • makes DNA • helps body use vitamin A • fights free radicals • heals wounds • boosts immune system	• diarrhea • infections • loss of appetite • weight loss • unhealed wounds	8 mg	11 mg	• 3 ozs fried oysters • 3 ozs king crab • 3 ozs cooked lean ground beef • 3 ozs cooked turkey • 1 c cooked lentils • 8 ozs plain yogurt	• 74 mg • 6 mg • 5 mg • 4 mg • 3 mg • 2 mg

*Nutritional information taken from USDA National Nutrient Database for Standard Reference, Release 15 and 16-1.

Nutrition index

A

Allergies
  buckwheat for 40
  mold and 100
  walnuts and 73
Alpha carotene, for lung cancer 258
Alzheimer's disease
  antioxidants for 96
  exercise and 295
  fish for 168
  folate for 97
  fruit for 30
  omega-3 fatty acids for 96
Amino acids
  for cholesterol 227
  for cold sores 226
  for hair and nails 225
Anesthetics, nightshade plants and
  320
Antacids, oysters and 19
Antioxidants
  for Alzheimer's disease 96
  for cancer 99
  for lowering cholesterol 335
  for osteoarthritis 98
  for sinusitis 160
  for skincare 165
  fruit for 323, 350, 356, 359, 366
  vegetables for 93, 126, 292
Arthritis. *See also* Rheumatoid
  arthritis
  boron for 358
  exercise and 60, 306
  fish for 168
  flaxseed for 37

  fruit for 72
  oysters and 19
  triggers of 20
  water for 25
Asthma, oysters and 19
Atherosclerosis
  fruit for 197
  tea for 24
  vegetables for 254

B

Bacteria, yogurt for 74
Bad breath, calcium for 6
Beta carotene 269
  fruit for 104
  parsely for 279
  vegetables for 79
Beta cryptoxanthin, for osteoarthritis
  98
Biotin, for diabetes 77
Blood clots
  calcium for 239
  garlic for 3
  vegetables for 231, 232, 235
  vitamin B for 232
  vitamin K for 262, 264
Blood pressure, high
  barley for 205
  calcium for 239, 254
  exercise and 282
  fish for 162
  flaxseed for 37
  folate for 97
  fruit for 104, 227, 311

Z

W